LIGHT
for our
PATH
2002

Bible readings with short notes

International
Bible Reading
Association

Cover photograph – Our thanks to Sister Paula Fairlie OSB for permission to use her work

Editor – Kate Hughes

Published by:
The International Bible Reading Association
1020 Bristol Road
Selly Oak
Birmingham B29 6LB
Great Britain

ISBN 0–7197–0992–X
ISSN 0140–8267

Typeset by Avonset, Bath BA1 3AU

Printed and bound in Great Britain by
Herald Forms Group

CONTENTS

Foreword

Dear Friends

Welcome to this year's *Light for our Path*. The readings in *Light for our Path* are grouped into thirteen themes, which are numbered and named in the Contents list on pages 3 and 4. Some of the themes concentrate on one book of the Bible, and the names of the books are also mentioned in the Contents list.

For many years, the themes and readings for *Light for our Path* and its companion volumes, *Words for Today* and *Sharing God's Word* (formerly *Preachers' Handbook*), were put together by Maureen Edwards. This was a huge task for one person, which Maureen did with great insight and inspiration. Now she has retired, and the work of finding themes and bringing together readings has been taken over by a small group. This year's books are our first effort, and I hope that you will find the themes and the selection of readings a source of new insights, new challenges and new thinking, as well as comfort and support.

Each year, we find new themes and new insights in the Bible text, and the writers from many countries and many churches bring new perspectives. The Bible is inexhaustible; truly it is God's word to us. May it speak to you through your use of these notes.

Kate

Kate Hughes (Editor)

Stop press

At the time of going to print, the National Christian Education Council (NCEC), the parent company of IBRA, is preparing to amalgamate with the Christian Education Movement (CEM). The new charity, which will be known as **Christian Education**, will continue to publish IBRA materials through its publishing company, Christian Education Publications. You will still be able to order your books through your usual supplier or direct from our office in Birmingham.

Reading LIGHT FOR OUR PATH

- Before reading, be quiet and remember that God is with you. Ask for his Holy Spirit to guide your reading.

- If you do not have a Bible with you, you can work solely from *Light for our Path* by referring to the short Bible passage printed in bold type. (Only the editions printed in English have this.)

- You can begin by reading just the short extract from the daily Bible passage which appears in the notes. Or you may prefer to read the full text of the daily passage from your Bible. The weekly notes use several different Bible translations, which are named at the beginning of the week. You may like to see how the extract in bold type compares with the same passage in your own Bible. And if your Bible mentions parallel passages in other places, comparing these passages can widen your thinking.

- At the beginning of each week's notes there is a text for the week, which can be used as a focus for worship or reflection throughout the week.

- When you finish each day's reading, spend a little time reflecting on it. What does it say to you about God? About yourself? About others? About the world in which we live? Has it changed your thinking? Does it suggest something that you should do? Then use the final prayer (marked with a cross), or any prayer of your own you need to make.

- At the end of each week's notes, there are questions and suggestions for group discussion or personal thought. These are only suggestions – your own reading and prayer may have drawn your attention to other aspects which you would like to explore further. The important thing is that you should let God speak to you through his Word, so that as you read steadily through the year you will be able to look back and see that you have got to know him better and have grown spiritually.

ABBREVIATIONS AND ACKNOWLEDGEMENTS

We are grateful for permission to quote from the following Bible versions:

Christian Community Bible (Catholic Pastoral Edition), published by Claretian Publications.

GNB   *Good News Bible*, 4th edition, published by The Bible Societies/HarperCollins, © American Bible Society, 1976.

JB   *The Jerusalem Bible*, Students' Paperback edition, published by Geoffrey Chapman, © Darton, Longman & Todd Ltd and Doubleday & Company, Inc., 1968.

NEB   *New English Bible*, © Oxford and Cambridge University Presses, 1970.

NIV   *The Holy Bible, New International Version*, Hodder & Stoughton, © International Bible Society, 1980.

NJB   *The New Jerusalem Bible*, published by Darton, Longman & Todd, © Darton, Longman & Todd Ltd and Doubleday & Company, Inc., 1985.

NKJV   *New King James Version*, © Thomas Nelson & Sons. Used by permission.

NRSV   *New Revised Standard Version Bible*, published by HarperCollins, © Division of Christian Education of the National Council of the Churches of Christ in the United States of America, 1989.

REB   *Revised English Bible*, © Oxford and Cambridge University Presses, 1989.

RSV   *The Holy Bible, Revised Standard Version*, published by Thomas Nelson & Sons, © Division of Christian Education of the National Council of the Churches of Christ in the United States of America, 1952.

IBRA INTERNATIONAL APPEAL

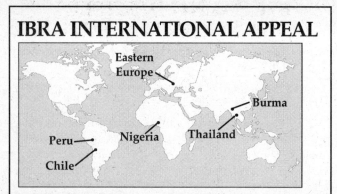

In five continents you will find Christians using IBRA material.

Some Christians will be using books and Bible reading cards translated into their local language, whilst others use English books. Some of the books are printed in the UK, but more and more countries are printing the books and cards themselves. The IBRA International Fund works through churches, Christian groups and Christian publishing houses overseas to make these publications available.

Each year we receive more requests for help from the IBRA International Fund, with greater emphasis on helping our overseas friends to produce their own version of IBRA material.

The only money we have to send is the money you give, so please help us again by giving generously.

Place your gift in the envelope provided and give it to your IBRA representative, or send it direct to:

The IBRA International Appeal

1020 Bristol Road, Selly Oak,
Birmingham B29 6LB, Great Britain

Thank you for your help.

BECOMING DISCIPLES: READINGS IN MATTHEW'S GOSPEL 1

God with us

Notes by Mike Pennington

based on the New Jerusalem Bible

Mike Pennington lives in the north-east of England. A retired Anglican priest, he helps regularly in a city church, works for church schools, and belongs to a specialist ministry team. He is married, with two children and two grandchildren. Before ordination he served as an electrical engineer in the Royal Navy, and he gives talks about ships to raise money for the lifeboat service.

We are very good at saying that God is everywhere, all the time, and sees and knows everything – that he is always with us. When we face the realities of life, things do not always seem so simple. This week's readings, based on Matthew's Gospel and related readings, examine a number of different ways of thinking about God's presence with us.

Text for the week: Psalm 80:7

Tuesday January 1   **Matthew 25:31–46**

NEW YEAR – NEW THINKING   Many will see this passage as a reminder to the Christian to look after people who are in distress. That is one level of understanding – but there is something deeper, expressed in Jesus' words:

> **'in so far as you did this to one of the least of these brothers of mine, you did it to me.'**   **(verse 40)**

In the face of the person in distress we see the face of Christ – God is with us. But we cannot stop even there. These words are not spoken as an example to guide us, but as a warning of judgement at the end of time.

> **'When the Son of man comes in his glory ... he will take his seat on his throne.'**   **(verse 31)**

And it is not just an individual who is being judged – it is all the nations. 'God with us' is not just a comforting thought – it makes huge demands on us as individuals, and as part of a larger community, such as a nation.

✝ *Lord of glory, guide our thoughts and deeds to see you in the face of others, and to play our part in making our society holy and compassionate.*

Wednesday January 2   **Matthew 1:1–7**

OUR ANCESTORS LIVE ON IN US

Roll of the genealogy of Jesus Christ, son of David, son of Abraham.   **(verse 1)**

You will not often hear these verses read in church. They do not seem to tell the story of Jesus' life and teaching. But in fact they set the life of Jesus very firmly in the history of his nation. The 'Roll of the genealogy of Jesus Christ' tells us, for example, why Jesus was born in Bethlehem – because he was 'of David's House and line', as St Luke tells us in his Gospel (*Luke 2:4*). This list puts Jesus in the line of Abraham, Isaac and Jacob – a great tradition of noble and holy ancestors. It shows us that this human line also had its bad moments – for example, in the description of Solomon, 'whose mother had been Uriah's wife' (see *2 Samuel 11*). We can rejoice in the past or regret it, but we cannot change it; God touched the lives of our ancestors – and this knowledge can give us a very strong sense of his continuing presence with us.

✝ *Heavenly Father, you have been with my family throughout the years. May I both know your presence with me in my own time, and teach those who follow me to seek your face in their own age.*

Thursday January 3   **Isaiah 7:10–14**

GOD'S SIGNS ARE ALWAYS IN THE WORLD

**Are you not satisfied
    with trying human patience
that you should try
    my God's patience too?**   **(verse 13)**

Centuries before the birth of Jesus, it seems that Isaiah was writing about him. King Ahaz was reluctant to seek a sign, although God asked him to do so. Compare God's response in verse 13 with what Jesus said when the Pharisees and Sadducees asked him for a sign from heaven (*Matthew 16:1–4*): 'It is an evil and unfaithful generation asking for a sign'. Sometimes the signs of God's concern and presence may seem strange and mysterious. They may be encouraging us to go in a different direction – his direction rather than our own. Even when we do not like what he seems to be saying, God is still with us.

† *O Lord our God, you know the secrets of our hearts and minds, and seek to keep us in your love. Open our eyes to the signs of your presence and your will, that we may follow the path of Jesus, who is the way, the truth and the life.*

Friday January 4   **Matthew 1:18–25**

GOD'S MESSAGES GUIDE US THROUGH HUMAN CONFUSION   Poor Joseph! He seems to have been a kindly man, confused by the facts of Mary's pregnancy. He makes the best judgement he can – and then finds everything upset by God's message to him, as 'the angel of the Lord appeared to him'. St Paul in 2 Corinthians 12 expresses so well the difficulties we all face – you, me, Joseph – as we try to balance our own understanding of eternal things with what we suddenly realise that God is telling us. In today's passage, Matthew links Joseph's story with what Isaiah wrote, and reminds us of the meaning of 'Immanuel' (or Emmanuel):

Now all this took place to fulfil what the Lord had spoken through the prophet:

> ***Look! the virgin is with child and will give birth to a son whom they will call Immanuel,***

a name which means 'God is with us'.   **(verses 22–23)**

† *Heavenly Father, we proclaim the angels of heaven to be your messengers. Give us clear spiritual vision and hearing, so that your will, which is announced to us amidst all the concerns and confusions of this world, may be made clear to us.*

Saturday January 5   **Psalm 80:1–7**

GOD IS WITH US – EVEN IN TIMES OF DESPERATION This psalm was written at a time of severe depression, when the people of Israel felt that God had abandoned them to their fate, as enemy nations triumphed over them. Yet despite all this, they knew with a deep faith that the only hope for the future was to trust in God.

Come to our help.
God, bring us back,
let your face shine on us and we shall be safe.

(verses 2c – 3)

It may seem unlikely, it may go against our natural feelings, we may feel threatened because our own resources are fragile and our own schemes for arranging our lives fail so utterly. But the fact remains that, if Almighty God really is as powerful, caring and loving as we say, we have to turn to him and rely on him. This is how trust must be measured. It is very easy to speak well of God when things are going smoothly. Faith lets us say, 'God is with us' even when the affairs of life are at their most devastating and difficult.

† *Into your hands, O Lord, I commend my soul and body. Let your tender power hold me and guide me through the difficult times of life. May I put my whole trust in you in all things, for you brought me into being, you save me from the forces of evil, and you hold me in the pathways of holiness.*

For group discussion and personal thought

● We have seen how the understanding that God is with us runs throughout the Bible. Can you remember any occasion when you were very conscious of God's presence? What made you so sure of his closeness? Do you feel that God was encouraging you to do something you already wanted to do, or persuading you not to do something? Was it God – or were you just having second thoughts?

BECOMING DISCIPLES: READINGS IN MATTHEW'S GOSPEL 2

Strangers

Notes by Mike Pennington

based on the New Jerusalem Bible

Meeting strangers can be confusing. If they come to our home, we may feel that they are trying to invade our territory, or to become our friends when we know nothing about them – do we like them, can we trust them? If we visit their land or home, we may feel uncertain about how we will be received. Yet meeting strangers can help us to see things in a new light – they ask questions which make us think in new ways about things we have always taken for granted. They broaden our minds by showing us new places and giving us new experiences. Being a disciple of Jesus means learning to live more fully in God's world. This week's readings give us examples – some good, some very difficult.

Text for the week: Exodus 3:12

Sunday January 6 (Epiphany)   **Matthew 2:1–12**

THE WORDS OF STRANGERS Mary and Joseph must have been completely astonished when the three wise men appeared in their doorway. They may have become used to unusual visitors like the shepherds in the stable – but kings? Magi? However we think of them, the gifts that they brought marked them out as very special strangers. Gold, frankincense and myrrh offered to a young child – this must have made many people think much more deeply about what had happened in Bethlehem. And many people would have known – you cannot keep such a visit quiet in a small village! But the wise men did not come simply to welcome another person into their fellowship of knowledge, wisdom and riches. They came because they recognised that here, in this small child in a small village in an ordinary home, was someone who was destined to turn the world upside down and change people's lives for ever.

They saw the child with his mother Mary, and falling to their knees they did him homage.   **(verse 11)**

13

The magi were foreign people from distant lands – people who would be regarded in the Holy Land as strangers. Yet God spoke to these strangers and, through what they did, those strangers spoke to others about God's interest in, and love for, all people.

† *Heavenly Father, we rejoice that you speak both to and through strangers. By the power of your Spirit, make us receptive to those whom we meet, willing to listen and eager to proclaim your glory. Through Christ our Lord. Amen*

Monday January 7   Matthew 2:13–15

STRANGERS IN A FOREIGN LAND   Very many people in our own time know what it means to be refugees, to be driven out of their own country by political pressure, national identity, or economic failure. How will they be received in the land where they finally try to settle? The Holy Family became refugees, not as one of many families, but as a result of Herod's fear and jealousy of one child – Jesus. We will never know how they were treated in Egypt. Did they disguise their true identity, in case Herod sent people to look for them? Were they able to tell their true story in the midst of strangers? Or did they have to keep it hidden until the call came to return home? Matthew sums up the experience of the Holy Family by taking us back into the Old Testament; he sees their journey as a fulfilment of the words of one of the prophets – Hosea – and quotes Hosea 11:1:

> **This was to fulfil what the Lord had spoken through the prophet:**
> *I called my son out of Egypt.*   **(verse 15)**

This gives a sense of God still being in charge of things, even when humans are doing their worst.

† *Heavenly Father, we pray for those who are forced from their homes and live in fear and anxiety. Give to their new neighbours a spirit of tolerance and compassion, and a willingness to absorb strangers into their community. So may the kingdoms of this world become like your Kingdom of Heaven, where divine love reigns supreme.*

Tuesday January 8   Matthew 2:16–18

I WAS ONLY OBEYING ORDERS   Herod's violence was a result of his jealousy and his anger at being outwitted by the wise men. Matthew suggests (2:3) that he had public opinion behind him. The soldiers banging on the doors of Bethlehem and the surrounding district would be strangers to the people of the villages – strangers bringing death, fear and heartbreak to family after family.

> A voice is heard ...
> lamenting and weeping bitterly ...
> weeping for her children,
> refusing to be comforted
> because they are no more. (verse 18)

Here people experience their worst anxieties about strangers. How did the soldiers feel about it? Compare what they did in Bethlehem with the model of behaviour for soldiers given by John the Baptist (*Luke 3:14*): 'No intimidation! No extortion! Be content with your pay!' Armies have always relied for their success on having totally obedient soldiers, who do exactly what they are told to do by higher authority. When that authority is wrong, or evil, how should soldiers behave? It is so much easier to do evil if you do not know the person you are hurting; being a stranger lets you hide from personal involvement. Today's reading reminds us that the experience of meeting a stranger can be rich – but it can also be terrifying and dehumanising.

† *Heavenly Father, we pray today for children who suffer at the hands of people whom they think they can trust; shield them from friends who turn out to be violent strangers, and from parents without love; by the power of your Holy Spirit protect the young and innocent, restrain the evildoers, and let goodness prevail in the world.*

Wednesday January 9   Matthew 2:19–23

WHEN DO FRIENDS BECOME STRANGERS? St Luke in his story of the birth of Jesus tells us (*Luke 2.4*) that Joseph originally came from Nazareth, so it was perhaps a natural place to return to when he came back from Egypt. Bethlehem was attractive, but how could he trust one of Herod's family who was now ruling in that area? Archelaus had succeeded his father Herod as ruler of Judaea, and Joseph was afraid to go there.

> Being warned in a dream he withdrew to the region of Galilee. There he settled in a town called Nazareth.
> (verses 22b – 23)

Would he still know many people in Nazareth? It was quite a long time since he had lived there; would they remember him? How would they receive him, after he had gone so far away because of Herod? Would people be anxious in case his past caught up with him and brought trouble to the area? In short, would his old friends still want to be friends with him, or would they treat him as a stranger? Such anxious thoughts must have been in the minds of Joseph and Mary as they made the long trip back from Egypt. Human relationships are never very easy to define. We all have areas about which we are cautious or secretive, as well as areas in which we are open and friendly. We deal differently with different people. Everyone is a mixture of stranger and friend, and all relationships change from day to day. But becoming a disciple of Jesus is different: in every respect he is open and friendly. We may find that difficult to live with, but, just as human relationships develop and we grow to trust someone we hardly knew a short time ago, so we find that we grow in our knowledge and appreciation of Jesus.

✝ *Lord Jesus, increase our understanding, so that when we trust you we may experience the peacefulness of your love surrounding us, the power of the Holy Spirit guiding us, and a vision of eternity that holds the Kingdom ever before our eyes.*

Thursday January 10　　　　　　　　　　　　　　　**Isaiah 60:1–7**

NO LONGER STRANGERS　　Isaiah addresses these words to the people of Israel at a time when they were probably unsure of themselves after a long time away from Jerusalem, in captivity in Babylon. Now he paints a picture of the holy city, splendid with the glory of the Lord and the riches of the land, a place where all people, and even camels, sheep and other animals, will gather together in unity.

> **The nations will come to your light**
> **and kings to your dawning brightness.**　　　　　　　**(verse 3)**

This is a vision which Christians understand as the Heavenly Jerusalem, described in Revelation 21:1–7 and 24–26. This is what St Paul describes, in rather less imaginative language (*Ephesians 1:9–10*), as the mystery of God's purpose – a great sense of people belonging together under the headship of Christ. There can then be no strangers, for all are one in him.

† *Lord, help us in our daily lives to build up your kingdom on earth, and as we make our pilgrimage through this world, hold ever before our eyes the vision of your glory, and the hope which you hold out for all humankind.*

Friday January 11   Exodus 3:1–12

THE STRANGER WHO IS OUR FRIEND   In the middle of an ordinary working day, a message came to Moses. Certainly he had gone to a particularly holy place – Horeb, the mountain of God. Even so, to see the blazing bush, and hear a voice addressing him must have been a rather disturbing event! Again we are told that it was the angel – the messenger – of the Lord that appeared to him. Moses covered his face, for he was afraid to look at God. In this foreign land, Moses had his divine friend; in the various stories about him we get the distinct impression that God was no stranger to him, and yet it was not the friendship of equals.

> **'I AM the God of your ancestors,' he said, 'the God of Abraham, the God of Isaac and the God of Jacob.' At this Moses covered his face, for he was afraid to look at God.**
> **(verse 6)**

So God's friend was commissioned to face cruelty and oppression. Moses was not at all enthusiastic – God was sending him into a very difficult situation. He felt quite unprepared, and he would effectively be a stranger without, he felt at first, any visible sign of authority. What would happen to him? Hundreds of years later, Jesus spoke about a life lived in the service and friendship of others: 'No one can have greater love than to lay down his life for his friends' (*John 15:13*). When the glory of God floods into our life, we may find it hard to realise that we are being called to work for him, not just enjoy things. There are plenty of strangers out there that need to have God as their friend.

† *Lord God of the Burning Bush, flood our lives with the power of your presence; send us out in the strength of that power to help those who are not strangers to you, but who do not yet know you as their friend, to become your disciples.*

Saturday January 12   Ephesians 3:1–12

HOW BIG IS THE BODY OF CHRIST?   To the Jews, the people who really were strangers were the Gentiles, or 'the nations' – those who were not Jews. Yet here is Paul, who saw himself as very much part of the Jewish race and establishment (*Philippians 3:3–5*), counting Gentiles as part of the body to which he also belonged.

> **This mystery ... was unknown to humanity in previous generations: that the gentiles now have the same inheritance and form the same Body and enjoy the same promise in Christ Jesus.** (verses 5–6)

Paul uses very specific words (*Ephesians 2:19*): 'you are no longer aliens or foreign visitors; you are fellow citizens with the holy people of God'. A disciple is someone who is changing his or her life and moving from being a complete stranger to the things of God, towards an ever deepening friendship with, and trust in, him. It is a mysterious process of learning in which we will all be involved until at least the day of our death.

† *Lord, not everyone takes the same path towards you. In spite of our differences, there is one Lord, one faith, one baptism and we have all been baptised into one body. Help me to realise that although others have found your love in different ways, this does not make them strangers to me. Together, may the variety of our experience help us to know more of the wonder of your love for all your people.*

For group discussion and personal thought

● We can never understand the complexity of God's love for us, for we can only express it in human terms. Among the people that you have dealings with day by day, who would you regard as strangers? What is stopping you from becoming more friendly with them? By enriching your relationship, could you show them something of your life as a disciple and your relationship with God?

BECOMING DISCIPLES: READINGS IN MATTHEW'S GOSPEL 3

Child of Abraham

Notes by Charles F Makonde

based on the Good News Bible

Charles F Makonde is a minister from the Methodist Church in Kenya, currently serving as a Mission Partner in the World Church in Britain Partnership. He is stationed in the Edinburgh and Forth Circuit of the Methodist Church in Britain, with pastoral responsibility for three congregations; he is also chaplain to the local Methodist sheltered housing.

The main theme that runs through the passages of scripture this week is becoming disciples in the Kingdom of God. John the Baptist announces that the kingdom of heaven is near. Jesus confirms that truth as he begins to preach. As we read this gospel and study together the passages of scripture, let us learn to live as disciples of the kingdom of God.

Text for the week: Isaiah 42:6

Sunday January 13   **Matthew 3:13–17**

A VOICE OF APPROVAL   Each individual has their own way of seeking approval for what they would like or choose to do. Jesus here receives approval for his decision to leave his home and his choice to go to the Jordan to be baptised by John the Baptist.

> **Then a voice said from heaven, 'This is my own dear Son, with whom I am pleased.'**   **(verse 17)**

The approval brings encouragement for what we have decided to choose to do. When we receive God's approval through prayer or in other ways, it brings glory and honour to God and adds to our joy.

† *Lord, help us to make the right decisions and choices.*

Monday January 14   **Matthew 3:1–6**

PREPARING THE WAY   This passage gives us an account of the preaching and baptism of John the Baptist. This God therefore raised up John the Baptist, who had a unique ministry and message which was a special preparation for the entrance of Jesus into this world. What was John's message?

> **'Turn away from your sins,' he said, 'because the Kingdom of heaven is near!' ... 'Prepare a road for the Lord; make a straight path for him to travel!'**   **(verses 2 and 3b)**

John fearlessly denounced evil and called people to change their way of life. He pointed people beyond himself. In our world today, people have to accept challenges and changes to life.

† *Lord of grace, help us to help others in our daily preparation for your coming in glory.*

Tuesday January 15   **Matthew 3:7–10**

ESCAPING FROM DANGER   One day in our small village in coastal Kenya, I was outside our small African house doing my homework before the sun set. One of our neighbours, a woman who lived in a makeshift hut on her farm, came running towards me calling my name and saying 'python' – a long snake was crawling towards me. She was warning me of the danger. Here, John also warns people of the danger that was coming:

> **'You snakes – who told you that you could escape from the punishment God is about to send? ... The axe is ready to cut down the trees at the roots; every tree that does not bear good fruit will be cut down and thrown in the fire.'**
> **(verses 7b and 10)**

To escape from danger demands a decision to act. That action is repentance. Repentance is indeed the very centre of our Christian faith. When we repent we turn away from sin and we turn towards God who gives us the life that we should live.

† *Lord, give us simplicity of heart to learn to confess our shortcomings to you in sincerity.*

SEPARATING WHEAT FROM CHAFF   When we attended a
Methodists for World Mission Conference at Swanwick in the
north of England, my wife Joyce demonstrated how, in our
local community in Kenya, women sift corn as a way of
separating the grain from the husks.

> 'He has his winnowing shovel with him to thresh out all
> the grain. He will gather his wheat into his barn, but he
> will burn the chaff in a fire that never goes out.'
>
> **(verse 12)**

The coming of Christ brings in the baptism of fire as
experienced in the Holy Spirit. It also brings in separation
between the righteous and the unrighteous. Though Christ has
the power to separate the clean from the unclean, he gives
people the opportunity to decide to choose. The Kingdom of
God is a matter of choice – a choice either to accept the kingdom
or to reject the kingdom.

† *Lord, making a choice is not easy. Help us to choose the right way*
of not being separated from you and your kingdom.

THE LORD CALLS AND EQUIPS Sunday's passage of
scripture showed us that Jesus was the Son of God with whom
God was well pleased. In today's passage, God calls Jesus as the
Servant whom he has chosen.

> The LORD says,
> 'Here is my servant, whom I strengthen –
> the one I have chosen, with whom I am pleased.
> I have filled him with my spirit,
> and he will bring justice to every nation.'   **(verse 1)**

Though a Son, yet he takes the form of a servant. The Father
shows all that confidence in him and stands by him and
strengthens him. He equips his servant by putting his Spirit in
him. We too need to be equipped for our duties in life. As
Christians, God equips us with his Spirit for his mission and for
service of the Church.

† *Lord, we thank you for your presence with us always.*

ACCEPTING CHANGE FOR BETTER Growing up in a village, I used to see my late grandfather stitch pieces of cloth to mend a hole in his shuka – the cloth sheet that he wore. He washed the new piece of cloth before mending the hole on his old shuka and told me that washing the new piece of cloth before putting it on as a patch did not shrink the old cloth so much.

> **'No one patches up an old coat with a piece of new cloth, for the new patch will shrink and make an even bigger hole in the coat. Nor does anyone pour new wine into used wineskins, for the skins will burst, the wine will pour out, and the skins will be ruined. Instead, new wine is poured into fresh wineskins, and both will keep in good condition.'** (verses 16–17)

Because Christ's disciples were new to the ministry, they were not able to bear severe religious exercises in the way that the disciples of John the Baptist and the Pharisees did. They could not fit into the old ways immediately, or they might get discouraged. At the same time, new ideas are essential. Some organisations see new ideas as a challenge to the establishment, and people reject them because 'they have never done things that way before'. In a changing society, people must be prepared to accept new ideas or new ways of doing things better.

✝ *Lord, help us in our lives to be examples to others of the life of discipleship to which you have called us.*

MIGHTY ACTS OF GOD Here the ministry of John has come to an end. He is in prison as a result of speaking too fearlessly and too directly to Herod Antipas for marrying his brother's wife. So John in prison sends his disciples to double-check whether this Jesus that he hears about really is the man for whom he prepared the way and to whom he pointed. And yes, he was! And the answer of Jesus to John's disciples confirms the words of the prophet Isaiah (*Isaiah 61:1–2*), quoted in Luke 4:18–19.

> **Jesus answered, 'Go back and tell John what you are hearing and seeing: the blind can see, the lame can walk, those who suffer from dreaded skin-diseases are made**

clean, the deaf hear, the dead are brought back to life, and the Good News is preached to the poor.' (verses 4–5)

God acts mightily in Jesus Christ. People often say, 'Do what I say and not what I do.' Jesus' reply challenges that. It is as if he is saying, 'See and learn from what I am doing. Look what I can do for you; see what I have done for others.' The powers of evil are being defeated not by irresistible power, but by unanswerable love. Christ continues to do great and mighty works. What he did in Galilee he can still do today.

† *Lord, work miracles in us, so that we can be a miracle to others.*

For group discussion and personal thought

- How can you respond fully to the responsibility and the joy of following Christ?
- What does the title 'servant' reveal about the one chosen, and how he will accomplish the tasks ahead of him?

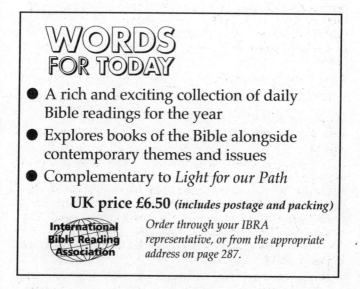

BECOMING DISCIPLES: READINGS IN MATTHEW'S GOSPEL 4
Testing

Notes by Alec Gilmore

based on the Revised English Bible

Alec Gilmore is a Baptist minister who was a pastor in England for 20 years. He then spent the next 20 years in Christian publishing, mainly for the benefit of the Third World and Eastern Europe, first as Editor of Lutterworth Press and then as Director of Feed the Minds. He lives in Sussex and is a freelance writer and lecturer. Recent books include *A Dictionary of the English Bible and its Origins* (Sheffield Academic Press), *Aid Matters* and *Preaching as Theatre* (SCM Press).

Readings this week focus on the marks of discipleship and our prayers are intended to help us to recognise them and cultivate them day by day. They are not a checklist or a means of evaluating our own commitment, but if you spot something you had not seen before, consider whether it might be worth giving more attention to this aspect of discipleship.

Text for the week: Matthew 4:19

Sunday January 20   **Matthew 4:12–17**

WHEN TO GIVE UP Many of the burdens of discipleship arise because of the notion that when something is tough we should never give up. Often that is sound advice. But not always. Discipleship is not necessarily about 'banging your head against a brick wall' or 'obstinacy to the point of persecution' on every detail of the faith. At the beginning of his ministry,

> **when he heard that John had been arrested, Jesus withdrew to Galilee; and leaving Nazareth he went and settled at Capernaum on the sea of Galilee, in the district of Zebulun and Naphtali.**   **(verses 12–13)**

There is wisdom in knowing when to 'withdraw'. Jesus was very good at it. Look up some of the other occasions when he did it (*Matthew 12:15, 14:13, 15:21*). In this case Capernaum, with its large Gentile population, needed him. Nazareth, for some reason, did not. Withdrawal may provide an opportunity to begin again in another place, or to make discoveries about ourselves or the world we live in. The wise disciple knows this and uses it to discover, believe and find faith in his own way. Sometimes it is only by giving up 'Nazareth' that we find our 'Capernaum'.

✝ *Father, when things seem not to be coming together, help me to sit back, wait for your time, and spot your leading.*

Monday January 21   Matthew 4:17–22

IDENTIFY YOUR NETS Forget the 'following' and the commitment and begin with the nets, the boat and the father. One step of discipleship, before 'following the new', is to abandon the familiar. We all have our nets and boats. Daily work, perhaps – earning a living, things we enjoy doing, long-established habits and attachments. And our home and family – the place where we feel comfortable and safe. Together they rule our daily life, mainly perhaps because we just take them for granted. Discipleship does not necessarily require us to give them up, though it might, and for these four disciples apparently it did.

> **Jesus said to them, 'Come with me ... (and) ... they left their nets ... and ... they left the boat and their father, and followed.**   **(parts of verses 19, 20 and 22)**

Even when we don't have to give everything up, discipleship always requires us to keep everything else in its place, and that place is always second to the claims of the kingdom. And if nets and boats do have to go, spare a thought for the father – symbol of other people who are left 'holding the baby', keeping things going, and possibly feeling abandoned and puzzled as to why all at once we seem to have changed.

✝ *Father, when I feel called to make a stand on any issue or suddenly to change my way of life, keep me sensitive to those around me and what it might mean for them.*

Tuesday January 22   Matthew 4:23–25

A SUCCESS STORY After Jesus withdrew,

> **he travelled throughout Galilee, teaching in their synagogues, proclaiming the good news of the kingdom,**

**and healing every kind of illness and infirmity among the
people ... Large crowds followed him.   (verses 23 and 25a)**

If teaching, preaching and healing are marks of discipleship,
what chance have most of us got? And widespread fame, with
large crowds following us, could be terrifying! But think of
teaching as helping someone to understand, to solve a problem
or to see things differently. Think of preaching as brightening
somebody's day with a bit of good news, or a more hopeful and
encouraging angle on life at a time when they are down. And
healing is helping someone to grow into wholeness – to be a bit
more honest with themselves, perhaps, and more ready to
acknowledge their weaknesses or to receive help from others.
Healing may even mean growing in their capacity to laugh at
themselves. Haven't we all done some of these things for
somebody at some time or other?

† *Father, instead of dwelling on extraordinary forms of discipleship
and feeling frustrated, help me to recognise the wonder of the
ordinary things I am already doing – and even to rejoice and give
thanks for success.*

Wednesday January 23   **Matthew 4:1–11**

ME FIRST!   Avoid trying to find three similar temptations in
your own life or in contemporary society. If you spot three
temptations that you have never had, or three that you have
successfully handled, this story will have nothing positive to
say to you, and even if you cannot spot similar temptations,
concentrating on them may still limit your area of search. Focus
instead on the link which underlies all temptation: the
temptation to self-interest. Me first!

> **'All these', (the devil) said, 'I will give you, if you will only
> fall down and do me homage.'**   **(verse 9)**

Underlying them all is the temptation to see everything from
my own point of view. Hunger, my basic needs. Sensation,
proving that I am right. Popularity, that people may like me.
'Doing homage to the devil' is evaluating everything in terms of
what it means for me and mine. It is playing your cards right!
And when the chips are down there is no cross, because what
matters is my personal survival. To think about this may make
us feel that we will never get there, but it does at least point us

in the right direction. That is growing in grace. It is moving towards wholeness and healing.

✝ *Father, help me to be alert to the times when I am guilty of 'me first', and give me grace to overcome this temptation.*

Thursday January 24   1 Corinthians 1:10–18

THE RIGHT CREDENTIALS   The church at Corinth was developing cliques. What was worse, they were lining up behind eminent names and using them to claim divine authority for their own position. Wave the right banners. Wear the right T-shirt. Join the right party. Claim the right credentials. Paul was horrified!

I appeal to you ... agree among yourselves, and avoid divisions ... What I mean is this: each of you is saying, 'I am for Paul,' or 'I am for Apollos'; 'I am for Cephas,' or 'I am for Christ.' Surely Christ has not been divided!
(part of verses 10, 12 and 13)

The offence was not their views or opinions, nor the credentials of the people they were following, but rather the underlying spirit of arrogance and judgement which led to ill-feeling and division. They were building up personal loyalties instead of loyalty to Christ, and destroying their relationships with one another. Much better, in Christ, to seek unity and a common understanding – not 'my truth over against your truth' but sharing in a common quest where we find ourselves both moving and perhaps even finishing up where we least expected to be.

✝ *Father, help me constantly to find Christ in my relationships with people and never allow any other loyalty to come between us.*

Friday January 25   Psalm 27

THE CONQUEST OF FEAR   A child psychiatrist, leading a training course for young parents, committed himself to the generalisation that children can come through most of the mistakes new parents make and survive unscathed, provided they have 'a general hunch', a general feeling, that all is well – that whatever happens they can sense overall care and love. Ancient Jews felt like that about the Temple. It was the place where you could always go and feel safe, and this psalm seems to be the expression of a man seeking that 'hunch'. Verses 1–6 express his confidence and find their climax when he says,

> **One thing I ask of the LORD ...**
> **that I may dwell in the house of the LORD**
> **all the days of my life,**
> **to gaze on the beauty of the LORD**
> **and to seek him in his temple.** (verse 4)

The rest of the psalm is a prayer for someone to listen (*verses 7–8*), to care (*verses 9 -10*), to guide (*verse 11*) and to deliver (*verse 12*), followed by a brief cry of confidence (*verse 13*). But we do not need all those things all the time, so focus on the one you need most right now. And note that the love of God in all its fullness does not mean that we do not still need his gifts of strength, courage and patience (*verse 14*).

✝ *Father, keep alive in me that hunch that, with you, all is well.*

Saturday January 26 Isaiah 9:1–7

SPOTTING THE LIGHT   In the days of Isaiah, Zebulun and Naphtali were regarded as the outlying parts of the empire – the back of beyond! – and Isaiah sees a ray of hope even for them. In the time of Jesus, their descendants (mostly Gentiles who lived in Capernaum) often felt the same. That is why Jesus, when he came, seemed to be fulfilling an ancient prophecy (compare *Matthew 4:16*):

> **The people that walked in darkness**
> **have seen a great light;**
> **on those who lived in a land as dark as death**
> **a light has dawned.** (verse 2)

Even those on the edge of society can now find hope (*verses 2–3*), rejoice in the overthrow of their oppressors (*verses 4–5*) and see the dawn of a new age (*verses 6–7*). But not everybody saw that this was happening and some refused to see even when it was pointed out to them. Too threatening! It would upset all the things that were familiar to them and that they had learned to love. Discipleship is the capacity to see the light, to find hope in situations of despair (*verses 3–5*), to experience authority and strength and enjoy peace in the most unlikely places.

✝ *In times of darkness, help me to recognise the light shining.*

For group discussion and personal thought

- Beginning with the prayers at the end of each day's notes, make your own list of the marks of discipleship (List A) and reflect on them. Then list them in the order of importance you think they should have in your life (List B). After a month, return to List A and (without looking at List B) put these marks of discipleship in the order of importance which they actually have in your life. Then compare the two lists.

- Each day we have tried to focus on one mark of discipleship and to be positive. We have not tried to state the whole truth about it. Often you may have found yourself wanting to say, 'Yes, but...' See how many 'Yes, buts' you can find and use them to sharpen your understanding of what is being said.

- Recall some event in the last few days where you have been guilty of 'me first'. Check yourself when the same temptation comes again in the next few days.

- Reflect on occasions when you have seen the light shining in the darkness. See if you can spot it in one or two dark places over the next few days.

BECOMING DISCIPLES: READINGS IN MATTHEW'S GOSPEL 5
New teaching

Notes by Peter Tongeman

based on the New International Version

Peter Tongeman is a retired Baptist minister in England who has worked in town and country churches, national youth leadership, and as an Area Superintendent. He was President of the Baptist Union of Great Britain for a year and is now a freelance writer and poet.

Living in a relationship of love and trust with God cannot be confined to private devotion or public worship. It finds expression in the way we relate to people around us, in the way we think about them, treat them, behave towards them. When asked what was the most important commandment, Jesus replied by quoting two: 'Love God ... and love your neighbour'. God-love leads on to neighbour-love. Neighbour-love finds its source and inspiration in God-love. This week we explore how being a disciple of Jesus affects the way we live. Eugene Peterson, author of *The Message*, translates Matthew 5:48 as 'You are Kingdom subjects. Now live like it. Live out your God-centred identity. Live generously and graciously towards others – the way God lives towards you.'

Text for the week: Micah 6:8

Sunday January 27   **Matthew 5:1–12**

A TEST OF CHARACTER   To follow Jesus is to adopt a lifestyle that is different. Things that previously seemed desirable, like money, possessions and status, are of secondary importance. It is character and outlook that make a person happy in God's kingdom. The 'beatitudes' or happy sayings of Jesus describe an ideal character seen from eight different angles, like the facets of a diamond. Jesus alone fully displayed these qualities; we strive to reach them as our goal. A special kind of happiness accompanies each one.

'Blessed are the merciful,
   for they will be shown mercy.
Blessed are the pure in heart,
   for they will see God.
Blessed are the peacemakers,
   for they will be called sons of God.' (verses 7–9)

When we care for others, we find ourselves cared for too. When our desire to please God is 'pure', that is sincere, unmixed with other motives, the result is a closer relationship with our Lord. When we devote energy to making peace with others we discover peace in ourselves, the inner peace of belonging to God's family. Other 'happy sayings' speak of spiritual riches, comfort, satisfaction as the reward of Christian character.

† *Father, let me grow more like Jesus so that my life displays some of the beauty of his character.*

Monday January 28   **Matthew 5:13–16**

AN INFLUENCE FOR GOOD   Jesus here explains the impact he expects his disciples to make on the lives of other people.

'You are the salt of the earth ... you are the light of the world ... let your light shine before men, that they may see your good deeds and praise your Father in heaven.'
(parts of verses 13, 14 and 16)

We are to be like salt. Salt rubbed into a wound protects it from infection. Salt mixed with meat and certain vegetables preserves them against decay. The purpose of being 'salt' in society is to help stop the process of degeneration brought about by sin in the form of selfishness, greed, jealousy, injustice, false dealing. Jesus calls us to fight the causes of decay by bringing an opposite influence – unselfishness, generosity, kindness, truthfulness, fair dealing. Furthermore, we are to help preserve all kinds of goodness by displaying it in Christian character and action. In the same way, we are called to be like light because goodness, kindness, Christlike actions pierce the darkness of sin and evil. They make life brighter and happier for everyone. As this light spreads, so God's kingdom comes.

† *Lord, make me like salt, a purifying influence to bring out the God-flavours of life. Make me such a light that dark shadows of sin may be lifted and the brightness of your glory revealed.*

THOUGHT UNDER CONTROL

'You have heard that it was said to the people long ago, "Do not murder, and anyone who murders will be subject to judgement." But I tell you that anyone who is angry with his brother will be subject to judgement.'   **(verses 21–22a)**

Someone once said, 'The thought is father of the deed'. It is in the mind that battles are fought and won. If we fail to control our thoughts, we will soon lose control of our actions. For this reason, Jesus pointed out the need to deal with hidden anger and resentment while it is in the mind. Uncontrolled, it leads inevitably to violence. Cain allowed resentment against his brother to fester until he could control it no longer and killed Abel (*Genesis 4:1–12*). Similarly, if lustful thoughts are allowed complete freedom, they lead to sinful action (*verse 28*). Anger, lust and unjust criticism damage good relationships. It is by self-control that broken friendships are restored. It is by plain and considerate speaking about others that relationships are strengthened.

✝ *O Lord, you know my thoughts. Forgive me when they lead to actions that hurt others. Help me to control the way I think so that my actions reflect the thoughts of a true disciple.*

WEAKNESS IS NO BAR TO ACHIEVEMENT   It is widely assumed that you have to be strong, dominant or wealthy to achieve anything in life. It is not so in God's kingdom.

But God chose the foolish things of the world to shame the wise; God chose the weak things of the world to shame the strong. He chose the lowly things of this world and the despised things – and the things that are not – to nullify the things that are, so that no one may boast before him.   **(verses 27–29)**

Long ago, John Bunyan was dismissed by many people as an ignorant seller of pots and pans. But he wrote the book called *Pilgrim's Progress*, a parable of our journey from earth to heaven. It has been translated into countless languages and is still today a devotional guide for Christians around the world. Mother Teresa was a frail Catholic nun living among the poor of Calcutta. But her influence in caring for the sick and dying has challenged and inspired people everywhere. When you are touched by the Spirit of Jesus, trying to live as his disciple, there is no limit to what may be accomplished for good.

✝ *Take me as I am, O Lord, even when I feel weak and inadequate, and let my life be an influence for good wherever I go.*

Thursday January 31   Micah 6:1–8

JUSTICE AND COMPASSION God's prophet Micah challenged the people of his day. They thought that if they made large offerings and generous sacrifices to God, he would be pleased with them. By no means, said Micah. If they then exploited other people, treating them badly and following a self-important lifestyle, their offerings would count for nothing. Worship of a holy God requires a holy life.

> He has showed you, O man, what is good.
>   And what does the LORD require of you?
> To act justly and to love mercy
>   and to walk humbly with your God.   (verse 8)

Here are principles of living for all who belong to God's kingdom. To treat others fairly and to resist injustice in all its forms. To show compassion where there is suffering, to treat others with kindness, to share what we have, to learn to live unselfishly. To live in humble dependence on God's gracious provision in the knowledge that without him we can do nothing.

✝ *God of justice, help me to treat others fairly. God of compassion, let my sympathy for those who suffer lead me to stretch out a helping hand. God almighty, grant that I may live each day grateful for your loving provision.*

Friday February 1   Psalm 15:1–5

FREE FROM CORRUPTION Because God is holy, we are meant to pursue holiness of life. 'Be holy because I, the Lord your God, am holy' (*Leviticus 19:2*). Treating other people without consideration or care is not consistent with holy living. When we are in a truly right relationship with God, it is natural to desire warm and wholesome relationships with those we meet in the course of a day's work. We should avoid words and actions that damage human relationships.

> LORD, who may dwell in your sanctuary?
>   Who may live on your holy hill?
> He whose walk is blameless
>   and who does what is righteous,
> who speaks the truth from his heart ...

who does his neighbour no wrong ...
    but honours those who fear the LORD.   **(verses 1–4)**

Holiness and corruption cannot live together. The psalmist makes clear that holiness consists of integrity of character, doing and speaking what is true and fair to others, keeping promises, never exploiting or diminishing other people. None of us can be entirely 'blameless' (*verse 2*) because we are sinners. But we are to strive for holiness of life in the strength God gives us.

✝ *Lord, I want to be holy. Show me where I am failing. Help me to be a better person. Help me to deal with others as kindly as you deal with me.*

Saturday February 2   **Matthew 28:18–20**

TEACHING OTHERS

'Therefore go and make disciples of all nations, baptising them in the name of the Father and of the Son and of the Holy Spirit, and teaching them to obey everything I have commanded you. And surely I will be with you always.'
    (verses 19–20)

In his great commission, Jesus tells us we are to replicate ourselves. We, in whose lives the flame of Christian discipleship has already been lit, are expected to pass on the flame to others so that they can become disciples too. Those who receive the truth of Jesus' kingdom are to mark the beginning of their spiritual journey by being baptised. Subsequent progress depends on each one of us following Jesus' footsteps and acting in obedience to his teaching. The path of discipleship will not be easy. The evil one is likely to be active (*1 Peter 5:8–9*). But we are not alone. We have not been left to struggle by ourselves. We have Jesus' promise to be with us to the end.

✝ *'Grant, Lord, such harmony of words and deeds, my teaching and my lifestyle shall agree. Bid falsehood and pretence depart that I, in Christ, may be what I profess to be.' (Peter Tongeman, from* A Pastor's Prayer)

For group discussion and personal thought

● Does my lifestyle embody love for people, especially those who are poor or disadvantaged?
● Draw up a statement of Christian living which begins: 'This is how true disciples of Jesus should behave . . .'

BECOMING DISCIPLES: READINGS IN MATTHEW'S GOSPEL 6

Integrity

Notes by Emmanuel Asante

based on the New International Version

Emmanuel Asante is the President of Trinity Theological Seminary, Accra, where the mainstream Protestant Churches train their ministers. He is an ordained minister of the Methodist Church in Ghana.

No careful reader of the Gospel of Matthew can overlook the pastoral interest of its author. Matthew's Gospel includes blocks of teaching by Jesus which show a very real concern for instruction in the Christian community. These blocks of teaching have been written in a way that enables young converts to grasp and memorise them. They have also been presented as a teaching manual for pastors and teachers. The objective is to make disciples by teaching them to observe all that Jesus taught his followers. This week's readings are intended to bring to the attention of Christians what it means to be disciples of Jesus.

Text for the week: Matthew 6:33

Sunday February 3   **Matthew 6:24–34**

SERVING ONE MASTER True discipleship demands commitment to one master. Anything that has control over a person's life has become its master. The first commandment calls for singleness of commitment to God: 'You shall have no other gods before me' (*Exodus 20:3*). We commit ourselves to other gods, or masters, when we allow ourselves to be controlled by powers other than God. When we organise our lives around material concerns, as though they are ends in themselves, we submit to the lordship of materialism (mammon). Many who claim to be serving God have allowed themselves to be controlled by material concerns which have stifled their commitment to the lordship of God.

> **No one can serve two masters. Either he will hate the one and love the other, or he will be devoted to the one and despise the other. You cannot serve both God and Money. (verse 24)**

True disciples of the Lord serve him with singleness of heart, mind and purpose. They know that anything or anyone that competes with God in his lordship over their lives is an idol. We do not always recognise the masters we serve; a football team, a soap opera, success, money, our children, house, car, business – anything, even if it is good in itself, can become an idol if it replaces God at the centre of our lives: 'You cannot serve both God and Money.'

† *Lord, help us to serve you with singleness of heart and to get rid of the many masters who compete with you for control of our lives.*

Monday February 4 — Matthew 6:1–4

DO NOT SEEK PEOPLE'S PRAISE One of the puzzling statements in the Bible can be found in 1 Corinthians 13:3: 'If I give all I possess to the poor and surrender my body to the flames, but have not love, I gain nothing.' The question is, how can I give all I possess to the poor and submit myself to martyrdom for the sake of the gospel without love? The motive or impelling power behind an act defines the value of that act. An act can be either self-centred or other-centred. A self-centred act draws attention to myself and exploits situations to enhance my self. Self-centred people love to be praised by others and feel sad when their good deeds are not acknowledged by people. Other-centred acts aim at the good of the other. Here righteous deeds are done for the sake of righteousness, not for reward. People who are motivated by other-centredness are motivated by love, they derive fulfilment from doing righteous deeds. God will reward such people.

> **Be careful not to do your 'acts of righteousness' before men, to be seen by them. If you do, you will have no reward from your Father in heaven.** (verse 1)

Be motivated by other-centredness in your acts of righteousness and you will be rewarded by God.

† *Father God, give us right motives in all we do, help us to feel fulfilled even when our good deeds are not acknowledged by people. Help us to know that what other people do not see, you see and that you will reward us at the right time. Amen*

Tuesday February 5 — Matthew 6:5 -15

PRAYER The centrality of prayer in the life of the Christian disciple cannot be overstated. Prayer is the Christian's lifeline, the Christian's breath. All the saints before us have been men and women of prayer. James Montgomery said that 'We perish if we cease from prayer.'

Prayer is the Christian's expression of his or her dependence upon God. In prayer, Christians say to God, 'Apart from you there is nothing we can do'. In prayer, Christians acknowledge God's greatness, dependability and providence. Prayer is not a public show. In prayer we commune with God, without whom we are nothing.

'When you pray, go into your room, close the door and pray to your Father, who is unseen. Then your Father, who sees what is done in secret, will reward you.' (verse 6)

In prayer we seek communion with God, not the acknowledgement of other people. If our motive in praying, whether in public or in private, is to be acknowledged by others, we have missed the point. Prayer is no prayer if it is not motivated by a desire to commune with God as an end in itself.

† *Lord, teach us how to pray aright,*
With reverence and with fear,
Though dust and ashes in Thy sight,
We may, we must draw near.

(Montgomery, Methodist Hymn Book *539)*

Wednesday February 6   Matthew 6:16–18

FASTING   One of the neglected Christian disciplines is fasting. Abstaining from all or some kinds of food at a given period and humbling oneself before God in prayer with a contrite heart is a very important spiritual discipline that every Christian should cultivate. Among the Jews, fasting was a regular discipline. The Jews put ashes on their heads when fasting to indicate repentance of sin. Putting oil on the head and washing the face were reserved for joyous occasions. Like almsgiving and prayer, fasting is not intended to impress others by your religiosity. Fasting is directed to God. It is an act by which Christians acknowledge their failures and plead for God's mercy and forgiveness.

When you fast, do not look sombre as the hypocrites do, for they disfigure their faces to show men they are fasting ... But when you fast, put oil on your head and wash your face, so that it will not be obvious to men that you are fasting. (parts of verses 16–18)

Fasting and prayer are the contrite sinner's private pleadings for God's mercy and forgiveness. Fasting ceases to be fasting when it is motivated by self-centredness.

† *Dear Lord, deliver us from the desire to be recognised by other people in our acts of righteousness. In all our acts of righteousness may we seek your honour and approval.*

TREASURES IN HEAVEN Many people behave as if their lives consist in the possession of an abundance of earthly goods. In fact, however, we have no permanent earthly treasures. The things we see, smell and feel around us are all transient. Things which were very valuable to us when we were children are no longer valuable. They have outgrown their usefulness and value. A time comes when we have no need of the things we cherished before. Worldly possessions are subject to rust, decay, destruction and theft. The permanent derives from doing the will of God. Heavenly treasures are spiritual treasures which cannot be measured in earthly terms.

> **Do not store up for yourselves treasures on earth, where moth and rust destroy ... But store up for yourselves treasures in heaven, where moth and rust do not destroy.**
> **(part of verses 19 and 20)**

The heavenly treasures accrue to us as we commit our lives to the Lord and seek his glory and honour in all we say and do. Invest in heavenly treasures.

✝ *Lord, help us to set our minds on things above and to invest in those spiritual treasures that are permanent, rust-free, indestructible and cannot be taken away from us.*

HAPPINESS IS REVERING THE LORD Many have sought happiness in material possessions, success, popularity, education, titles and acquaintances. All or some of them may bring us transient happiness. But they cannot give us access to lasting happiness, which is only for those who revere the Lord and do his will.

> **Blessed is the man who fears the LORD,**
> **who finds great delight in his commands. (part of verse 1)**

The godly person, that is, the one who reveres God and seeks his honour and glory in all he or she does, enjoys God's permanent blessings. 'Blessed is the man who does not walk in the counsel of the wicked or stand in the way of sinners, or sit in the seat of mockers. But his delight is in the law of the Lord and on his law he meditates day and night. He is like a tree planted by streams of water' (*Psalm 1:1–3a*)

✝ *Lord, grant us the grace to delight to do your will, to honour and revere you. For our happiness lies in doing these things.*

ACCEPTABLE RELIGION   The people of Israel felt that simply by abstaining from food, lying on sackcloth, putting ashes on their heads and praying, God would answer their prayer. Humbling yourself before God through the religious acts of fasting and prayer is vain, unless you also turn away from your wicked actions and do things which promote harmonious living in community. When we go through such spiritual exercises as fasting and prayer and do not turn from our wicked ways; when, in spite of our fasting and praying, we oppress the poor and turn deaf ears and blind eyes to the people we can help; when we amass wealth by impoverishing others; then, although we may fast and pray, we put on only the outward form of godliness and deny its power.

> Is not this the kind of fasting I have chosen:
> to loose the chains of injustice
>   and untie the cords of the yoke,
> to set the oppressed free
>   and break every yoke?
> Is it not to share your food with the hungry
>   and to provide the poor wanderer with shelter?

(verses 6–7a)

Our godliness must not be limited to external spiritual acts such as fasting, prayer, worship, preaching, daily devotional life and so on. 'Religion that God our Father accepts as pure and faultless is this: to look after orphans and widows in their distress and to keep oneself from being polluted by the world' (*James 1:27*).

† *Lord, help us not only to fast and pray and cultivate an other-worldly spirituality, but to have a spirituality with a keen sense of justice that turns away from sin and wickedness and seeks to address the unjust situations around us.*

For group discussion and personal thought

● In what sense is it true to say that our godliness must not be limited to external spiritual acts such as fasting, prayer and daily devotional life?
● Reflect on the following statements:
    Faith that does not materialise in righteous living is dead.
    The true disciple seeks the master's praise, and not the praise of humans.

BECOMING DISCIPLES: READINGS IN MATTHEW'S GOSPEL 7

Clear choice

Notes by Philip Wadham

based on the New Revised Standard Version

The Revd Philip Wadham is a member of the staff of the national office of the Anglican Church of Canada. He is the Partnership Co-ordinator for the Latin America/Caribbean programme. He has worked in South and Central America and continues to travel regularly in the region.

During my visits to Latin America and the Caribbean I meet a variety of people, some of whom are very poor. In different ways they are all trying to build a better future for themselves and their communities. Central to their hopes is their faith in a God who loves them and who is with them in this task. As the following brief stories show, despite setbacks and disappointments God's work advances through faith in action.

Text for the week: Deuteronomy 30:19b

Sunday February 10   **Matthew 7:21–29**

THE RAINS FELL, THE FLOODS CAME   Honduras, Central America. In October 1998 heavy rain from Hurricane Mitch fell on this small country. Thousands of people died in the floods that followed. Tens of thousands of lives were changed for ever as homes and complete villages were washed away. Seeing the devastation, people and governments around the world offered their assistance.

> **'Not everyone who says to me, "Lord, Lord" will enter the kingdom of heaven, but only the one who does the will of my Father in heaven.'**   **(verse 21)**

In our information age the Episcopal (Anglican) Church of Honduras was immediately in e-mail contact with partner churches overseas. As the story was told, offers of help poured in and a plan was put in place to receive the promised gifts, using them for rebuilding not only fallen buildings but also broken lives. Four years later, there are few signs now of the physical damage caused by 'Mitch', though for many families the emotional scars remain. A consistent sentiment among those who witnessed the Church's good news (gospel) in action is thankfulness. Actions always speak louder than words and there is harsh judgement in this reading on those whose words of concern are not made real through their actions. (See also *Matthew 25:31–46*.)

† *Loving God, through our Lord Jesus Christ we see your love in action. Work through us to follow his example.*

Monday February 11   Matthew 7:1–5

WITH THE JUDGEMENT YOU MAKE YOU WILL BE JUDGED Guyana, north-east South America. In the jungle interior of this tropical 'Land of Many Rivers', John, the new missionary priest, asks himself a question. 'Should I work to teach my brand of Christianity to the Amerindian people here (as other groups are doing) or begin by learning about local customs, practices and beliefs?' John chose to do the latter, believing that not to do so would be a great offence against the people, their history and their worship.

'How can you say to your neighbour, "Let me take the speck out of your eye," while the log is in your own eye?' (verse 4)

This pattern of respect for a people's tradition guided John's pastoral ministry in Guyana over the next 40 years. He listened for God speaking to him from within the local culture. He argued that 'In God's world God, already present, invites us to discover him in the people, in their traditions and in their worship.' It was a new understanding of missionary work when John arrived in Guyana and, four years after his death, it is still new for some Christians and rejected by others. But we who are often quick to judge those different from ourselves might do better to look at our own lives. We may discover that a log in our eye is blinding us to God who is already at work.

† *'Open my eyes that I may see, glimpses of truth you have for me, ... Spirit divine.' (lines from a popular hymn)*

Tuesday February 12   Matthew 7:6

PEARLS In El Salvador, Central America, many people were hearing the gospel (good news) with joy. After so many years of pain it was good news that an Archbishop spoke out against those 'who oppress the poor and crush the needy' (*Amos 4*) and called for a fairer sharing of land and wealth. But there were others who were offended by this gospel. To those who have much, sharing is seldom good news (see *Matthew 10:17–21*). Because he worked for an end to killings and for a more just society, in March 1980 Archbishop Oscar Romero was murdered.

'Do not give what is holy to dogs; and do not throw your pearls before swine, or they will trample them under foot and turn and maul you.' (verse 6)

The holiness of his gospel offended the powerful people who murdered him, people deliberately deaf to good news. Twenty-four years later, although pastor Antonio gives thanks that the brutality of earlier days has passed, he talks about the poverty and deprivation in his neighbourhood that continue to oppress his people. 'But,' he adds with enthusiasm, 'for the past five years our church has been able to provide schooling and we now have 70 students. Next year we will be adding an extra classroom and another teacher. We have to charge a fee, but it is small and most parents can afford it. They understand that they are helping to build a better future for their children.'

✝ *God, you look for justice in your world. Strengthen us as we work here to build a fairer community.*

Wednesday February 13   **Matthew 7:7–12**

DO TO OTHERS   In Olinda, an industrial city in north-east Brazil, the parish priest was shocked by what she saw: families working and living on the garbage dump; small children collecting discarded cardboard, tins, bottles for resale; mothers sorting though rotting food in the search for something that the family might eat; shacks of wood and tin and plastic that were their homes.

'Is there anyone among you who, if your child asks for bread, will give a stone? Or if the child asks for a fish, will give a snake?' (verses 9 -10)

Simea prepared Sunday's sermon. In it she described what she had seen and told the congregation, 'This is wrong.' In the months that followed, Simea, members of her church and people who lived on the garbage dump met with some influential people in the city. From their small resources they started a fund to provide some help and wrote to friends in Brazil and overseas for support. Their work was grounded in prayer, but was also a prayer in itself. The results were promising: some land made available for housing; the start of 'Living Waters' community centre, which is a clinic, a church and a school; modest homes for 35 families. A drop of water in an ocean of need? Yes, but also a sign of God's kingdom.

† *Loving God, when we see your children in pain, work through us to bring some relief and healing.*

Thursday February 14   **Matthew 7:13–14**

THE GATE THAT LEADS TO LIFE 'It wasn't easy during the first years of the revolution. Many Cuban pastors had left our Caribbean island for Florida in the United States. Our government was suspicious of Christians and we were discriminated against, so our churches had few members.' This is Hector talking. He is describing what life was like between 1965 and 1985 for him, a Christian leader in Cuba. 'With life so difficult, how was it that you stayed in Cuba?' I asked. 'Two reasons,' Hector replied. 'First, this is my country. Second, I supported our government that was working to build a fairer society. This is central to my Christianity.'

> **'Enter through the narrow gate; for the gate is wide and the road is easy that leads to destruction, and there are many who take it.'**   **(verse 13)**

Hector's wide gate could have been to join those who left Cuba. His easy road would have been to hide his Christianity and thus escape discrimination. But both actions would have destroyed him. Instead he remained committed to expressing his faith, both in his worship on Sundays and in working to build a fairer society. Those years were not easy for Hector or for his family. But for all of them there is the deep satisfaction that, despite the difficulties it caused, they remained faithful to God.

† *Ever-present God, you call us to be faithful. Give us the courage to follow your way, especially when it is difficult.*

Friday February 15   **Matthew 7:15–20**

KNOW THEM BY THEIR FRUIT In his tiny home in a poor district of San Pedro, a city in the Caribbean nation of the

Dominican Republic, Miguel sat confused. Since his motorcycle accident, walking was difficult but a small loan from Sister Jean had helped him start a pizza bakery. Business was good and he was quickly repaying the loan. His confusion came from a neighbour's comment about the Sisters and 'their type of religion'. Quoting the Bible, his neighbour warned him, 'Beware of false prophets'. It didn't help that his neighbour seemed to have a verse for every occasion. What should he do? He was, after all, friends with his neighbour.

> **'A good tree cannot bear bad fruit, nor can a bad tree bear good fruit.'**   **(verse 18)**

Miguel thought long and hard. He had first met the Sisters before his accident. His wife had helped at the nursery school the Sisters had started. When she was pregnant with their child, their 'Good Shepherd' clinic had provided inexpensive care for her. Miguel searched in his head for a verse but he knew so few. Instead he thought of his bakery. He said to his neighbour, 'People buy my pizzas because I use good ingredients and bake them well. They know that I can be trusted. It's the same with the Sisters. I trust them.'

✝ *Faithful God, work through our lives to bear good fruit, and may we always appreciate the good fruit that others bear.*

Saturday February 16   Deuteronomy 30:15–20

CHOOSE LIFE   Poor people in rural Peru, South America, are drawn to Lima, the capital, in search of a better life. Lima is already large and overcrowded, so many begin by occupying vacant land outside the city. At first they are ejected from this land, but their persistence often succeeds and they are allowed to stay. Thus they overcome the first obstacle in their new life.

> **I call heaven and earth to witness against you today that I have set before you life and death, blessings and curses. Choose life so that you and your descendants may live.**
> **(verse 19)**

From their Christian tradition many look for a place of worship when they arrive. A variety of churches respond to this and in these 'new districts' simple worship centres spring up. Community meetings often take place in these churches, nursery schools are begun and elementary education follows. These people, like those of Israel in our reading, have journeyed to a new land and are making choices about how they will live.

Being poor, their choice is limited but together they work for a better future. It is very far from 'heaven' and they will continue to struggle, but thanks be to God for people working together to build a more hopeful future. Pray to God that they will succeed.

† *We pray for all people who are seeking a more hopeful future, that the God of hope will guide their lives and they may find fulfilment.*

For group discussion and personal thought

- Jesus said, 'I came that they may have life, and have it abundantly' (*John 10:10*). Imagine yourself in any one of the stories above. What would 'abundant life' be for you?
- John, a missionary priest in Guyana (Monday) said, 'In God's world he invites us to discover him in the people, in their traditions and in their worship.' Is this right? Can you think of local examples?
- From Wednesday's reflection, 'Their work was grounded in prayer, but was also a prayer in itself.' How is work also prayer?

LENTEN ENCOUNTER 1
In sin and in forgiveness

Notes by Carol Mouat

based on the New Jerusalem Bible

Carol Mouat is a Roman Catholic Dominican Sister who was involved in Theological Education by Extension in South Africa throughout the 1990s. Currently she is on the staff at Hawkstone International Pastoral Centre in Shropshire, England.

The meditations this week are based on a simple theme: In the beginning it was good, and then it got worse! Jesus looks for those who have hidden themselves. He seeks out the lost. The mission of Jesus is to save sinners on behalf of the compassionate Father who forgives and heals the repentant sinner.

Text for the week: Psalm 32:1

Sunday February 17   **Psalm 32**

LIBERATION FROM SIN The book of Psalms is Israel's hymnbook. The tradition of attributing many of the psalms to King David links this psalm to his penitence after his adultery with Bathsheba and his murder of her husband Uriah. But the psalm also shows how the people of Israel experienced conversion when they admitted their sin and asked forgiveness from God.

> **I made my sin known to you, did not conceal my guilt.**
> **I said, 'I shall confess my offence to Yahweh.'**
> **And you, for your part, took away my guilt, forgave my sin.**
> **(verse 5)**

Most of us do not commit serious sins like murder; however, none of us can pride ourselves on being sinless. How often do we gossip and denigrate others? Are we perhaps in the habit of discriminating against people because of their class, colour, age or sex? What about jealousy, gluttony and, above all, the failure to love? This Psalm cries out for reconciliation and a return to Yahweh's faithful love.

† *Lord my God, let my heart always recognise my sinfulness and seek forgiveness in you.*

Monday February 18   Genesis 2:15–17; 3:1–7

GOD OR SELF   This meditation is about the choice between self or God. As we enter into the story of Adam, Eve and the Serpent we are confronted with our own situation. The norms and values of this world often contradict God's values. What seems pleasurable can appear to be 'all good', whereas sacrifice, in any form, can appear to many people as bad, or simply a waste of time! This story illustrates how the symbol of evil, expressed in the form of a serpent, entices the woman to disobey God's command:

> **The woman ... took some of its fruit and ate it. She also gave some to her husband who was with her, and he ate it. Then the eyes of both of them were opened.**
>
> **(chapter 3, parts of verses 6 and 7)**

What follows is feelings of shame and guilt – feelings that usually accompany a sinful act.

† *O God, give me the courage to recognise and resist evil temptations. Help me to choose good and avoid all evil.*

Tuesday February 19   Romans 5:12–19

THE DISTINCTION BETWEEN OBEDIENCE AND DISOBEDIENCE   Adam sinned and as a result the reality of darkness, conflict and pain spread throughout humankind. Through one act of disobedience to God, sin entered into the world. St Paul tells us that through the Father's act in sending his Son Jesus into the world he reversed the situation. Paul very cleverly makes a parallel between Adam and Jesus Christ. The sin of Adam brought about death, pain and destruction. The single act of love by God the Father brought about *new life* for all people.

> **One man's offence brought condemnation on all humanity; and one man's good act has brought justification and life to all humanity.**   **(verse 18)**

† *O God, give me the grace to ask for forgiveness from people against whom I have sinned.*

Wednesday February 20   **Genesis 4:3–16**

LOVE AND FORGIVENESS   The story of Cain and Abel fills us with repulsion, but how often is this same act re-enacted in society today? Families are full of favouritism and jealousies and we read about similar happenings in our daily newspapers. For example, a member of a family receives an inheritance and others are ignored. People will sometimes go to great lengths to destroy one another because of jealousy. We read that

> **Yahweh looked with favour on Abel and his offering. But he did not look with favour on Cain and his offering, and Cain was very angry and downcast.   (verses 4b – 5)**

How do I feel when someone is favoured and I am overlooked? Do I get jealous and angry? How do I act towards this person? Do I rejoice and praise God for him or her?

✝ *Help me, Lord, not to fret and get depressed when people prefer others to me. Help me to rejoice in my gifts and not be envious of others.*

Thursday February 21   **Genesis 9:8–17**

COVENANT   The biblical account of the flood suggests that God destroyed a corrupt and evil society. The Old Testament story clearly points out that God punishes evil and rewards good. Noah lived in a society where most people openly boasted of their immoral deeds. Noah and his family lived a life of piety and seemed to be unaccepted by other people. God blessed Noah and his family and made a covenant with them:

> **'I am now establishing my covenant with you and with your descendants to come, and with every living creature that was with you.'   (parts of verses 9 and 10)**

It was a covenant of life, not of death. The command was to be fruitful and to fill the earth. The world will never perish again by water. God's covenant is binding and lasting. God makes a covenant with you and me and establishes a relationship which is binding. I, therefore, have a responsibility to put God first in my life. I have a responsibility to live a good, holy and moral life.

✝ *Help me, Lord, to spend quality time with you daily and keep my commitment to you.*

SALVATION HAS COME TO THIS HOUSE As chief tax collector, Zacchaeus seems to have exploited others for his own purposes. He was probably regarded as a traitor and hated by his fellow Jews. Jesus singled him out and accepted his invitation to a meal in his house. Jesus recognised him for who he was, a person in his own right, and Zacchaeus responded to Jesus:

> **'If I have cheated anybody, I will pay him back four times the amount.'**   **(verse 8b)**

He not only repents of his bad behaviour but is ready to pay back those whom he has cheated. Society had rejected him because of his bad behaviour, and now Jesus is accepting him – 'today salvation has come to this house' (*verse 9*). The unconditional love of Jesus reaches out to the sinner who is ready to be healed and forgiven. Where am I in this story? Do I see myself as Zacchaeus, or as one of the self-righteous Jews?

† *Loving Father, I pray that I will never exploit others.*

MERCY AND COMPASSION In this parable of the lost sheep Luke highlights God's mercy and compassion. God is depicted as the shepherd who searches for the one that is lost.

> **'Rejoice with me, I have found my sheep that was lost.'**
> **(verse 6b)**

Jesus challenges the Pharisees and the scribes to change their way of relating to sinners. He wants everyone to share the joy of the repentant sinner.

† *Lord, I ask for a deepening awareness of my sinfulness and the courage to return to you when I am lost. I also pray that I never judge others.*

For group discussion and personal thought

● How do you respond to change in your life?
● What can you do to help sinners repent?

LENTEN ENCOUNTER 2
In danger and in safety

Notes by Norman Kayumba

based on the New International Version

Bishop Norman Kayumba is from Rwanda, a small country in Central Africa that knew a terrible genocide in 1994. Norman was the bishop of a young diocese in southern Rwanda and witnessed the ordeal of his people. He served five more years before resigning from the position and is at present serving a small urban church in Coventry, England, as a team vicar. He is also involved in the work of the International Reconciliation Centre based in Coventry Cathedral.

When things go wonderfully well in our lives, we are in danger of taking our situation for granted. We forget our creator and the wise prayer of the psalmist often used in funerals: 'Teach us to number our days aright, that we may gain a heart of wisdom' (*Psalm 90:12*). People who have not experienced 'the days of darkness' still need to know that only God is unchanging. Good times always come to an end (*Ecclesiastes 11:8 and chapter12*). Trusting in God's love and accepting his will, in good days as well as bad: that is our only security. God always rescues our souls and he can also rescue our bodies from terrifying earthly situations. Our faith inspires us to trust him and to accept with happy gratitude whatever answer he gives to our cries.

Text for the week: Daniel 3:15b-18

Sunday February 24   **Psalm 121**

SING YOUR CONFIDENCE IN GOD   This psalm, known as one of the songs of the ascents, was sung at times of pilgrimage and celebrations in Jerusalem. The dialogue at the beginning may have been exchanged between the priest and the assembly in a liturgy:

> **[Priest] I lift up my eyes to the hills –**
> **where does my help come from?**
> **[People] My help comes from the LORD,**
> **the Maker of heaven and earth.**   (verses 1–2)

This psalm tells us about the character of the God of Israel: the maker of the universe who neither slumbers nor sleeps, who protects day and night, everywhere and for ever. Singing songs to accompany dancing or work, reciting poetry, telling stories and meditation – these have given strength to people of all times and helped to communicate culture, history and deep convictions from generation to generation. Even today music, dance, film and television influence the beliefs and the behaviour of our societies, especially in cities. The good values as well as the vices of our society, the sense of emptiness, the violence and the unlawfulness are all communicated. Faith is not an idle sleeping thought; it is a lived conviction of God, his work and his character. Faith cannot survive the increasing poison of our time unless it stands firm as a constant reaffirmation, through songs, stories, meditation and daily living, of our determination to please God. To succeed, we need to encourage one another every day. 'Speak to one anot er with psalms, hymns and spiritual songs. Sing ... giving thanks to God the Father for everything, in the name of the Lord 'esus Christ' (*Ephesians 5:19–20*).

† *Thank you, Lord, for all the ways we have to affirm our faith in you.*

Monday February 25   Genesis 12:1–4a

LEAVE YOUR PRESENT SECURITY FOR GOD'S SAKE
Some dangers can be foreseen, but God asks Abram to go and meet the danger, the insecurity and the terrifying surprises of an unknown land. He is called by God and has a choice to make. Abram knew what a dear situation he was leaving: his family, his friends, his status and material security. He knew, better than we do, the dangers of exile. There were no international treaties and conventions to give dignity and rights to emigrants. The strongest fighter won, and Abram and his people would be a tempting prey for whichever enemy met them first. He knew this, but there was a call from God and he made a choice, probably frightened of his vulnerability; but he chose to trust God.

So Abram left, as the LORD had told him.   **(verse 4a)**

The Bible doesn't tell us any details of the circumstances of God's call to Abram. It may have taken time for Abram to realise that it was God who was calling. However desperate or unwanted your situation may be today, it could make a great difference if you ask God to open your eyes to his purpose in allowing you to be there. What is God's call where you are today?

✝ *Open my eyes, Lord, that I may see your purpose in bringing me to where I am today.*

Tuesday February 26   **1 Kings 19:1–18**

GOD SURPRISES HIS SERVANT   Elijah finds himself in a desert of depression, in extreme sorrow and fear. Even God's servant can experience terrible suffering, death, or life-threatening dangers. The only difference is that they don't lose faith in God; he is with them even through death. Peace, wealth, health, friendship, family life, honours, social justice, dignity, human rights and a sense of belonging all come to an end. And when we see that end coming to us, we shall fear the worst and feel discouragement and a sense of loss – unless we trust in God. Our merciful God sent an angel with water and bread to the discouraged Elijah. Like a caring mother God's messenger insisted that the prophet ate. Then he could look up at God, hear his gentle whisper and face his question:

'What are you doing here, Elijah?'   **(verses 9 and 13)**

Which could mean: are you where you are supposed to be? Where I want you? Elijah was sent back the way he had come with new strength, without fear and with a mission.

✝ *Lord, you promised to be with us always, to the very end of the age. Please show me the way back to your mission and end my loss of direction. Amen*

Wednesday February 27   **Exodus 14:15–29**

WHEN A TERRIFIED LEADER NEEDS FAITH   All leaders need support and encouragement, especially when those they lead respond with anger and rebellion. Earlier in this chapter, the people's complaints had exhausted Moses. Threatened with genocide, they blamed him more than ever for the whole impractical plan for freedom. Moses reminded them (*verses 13–14*) of God's promise to fight for them, and then turned to God himself. Time was running out and Moses was running out of ideas. But there is no need to shout at our gracious God: he has a plan and only needs a listening servant.

Then the LORD said to Moses, 'Why are you crying out to

me? Tell the Israelites to move on. Raise your staff and stretch out your hand over the sea to divide the water.'

(verses 15–16a)

He has given Moses' staff the power to divide the sea and his angel will take care of the Egyptians behind them as soon as he is not needed to lead them. At the last minute, the time of God, Israel is saved. Praise God.

† *Lord, teach me to recognise your plans, so that I can serve you better.*

Thursday February 28   **Psalm 107:23–32**

CRIES HEARD, GRATITUDE DESERVED In the midst of suffering, it is easy just to cry for help and to be concerned with our own needs or pain. If our cry is extended to others, we may limit this to our own family, our own group of people. Often, these cries for help are not even addressed to God; rather, we attack him, asking what we have done to deserve this suffering. We do not think of the goodness of God, his blessings and patience in the past. Yet these thoughts could have strengthened us and honoured God. In exile, the Jews learnt some hard lessons. They included these lessons in their songs of gratitude to God, so that people would not forget when God had been angry with them and had to discipline them. This psalm was probably written after the exile in Babylon, to be sung in celebrations in Jerusalem.

> **Then they cried out to the LORD in their trouble,**
>   **and he brought them out of their distress ...**
> **Let them give thanks to the LORD for his unfailing love**
>   **and his wonderful deeds for men.**   **(verses 28 and 31)**

Singing joyful songs of praise and gratitude to God pleases him and is a powerful weapon against discouragement and all the devil's efforts to depress us and make us lose faith in God.

† *Lord, help me to use the spiritual weapon of joyful songs of praise and gratitude to you.*

Friday March 1   **Daniel 3:16–29**

THE GOD WE SERVE IS ABLE TO SAVE US Daniel and his friends were taken to Babylon when Jerusalem was destroyed in 586 BC and trained to serve the king. But their Jewish faith and culture confronted Babylonian idolatry and the customs of the court. They had no privacy, so their lifestyle could not be hidden. This situation put them in permanent danger and their success led to jealousy. But they lived faithful to the God of Israel and trusted him for better and for worse. He in return blessed them and wrapped them in supernatural protection. In real danger of execution, they dared to tell the king:

'the God we serve is able to save us from [the blazing furnace], and he will rescue us from your hand, O king. But even if he does not ... we will not serve your gods or worship the image of gold you have set up.'

(part of verses 17 and 18)

These four young men, living far from their home, remind me of the millions of refugees and displaced people today and those in the slums and poor areas of our huge cities, who are faced with a dangerous and misleading lifestyle in society and the rapid spread of the selfish individualism of Western culture. Those who live in such a stressful and alien environment, without proper care, identity or dignity, need to learn from Daniel and his friends that with God they can turn their history in the right direction – if they choose to entrust their lives to him and say, 'Come what may I will live for God'.

✝ *Help me to know without any doubt that you can rescue me from danger.*

Saturday March 2   **2 Corinthians 12:7b-10.**

I KNOW WHOM I HAVE BELIEVED AND HE IS ABLE   We trust God because of what he is and what his power can do. We do not believe in him in order to be spared suffering and hardship in our lives on earth. We trust him to direct our lives for his glory, for the service of others, or for our own education. In any case we invite him to come with us through whatever he allows. Because we do not know all that God has planned for us, we resist whatever seems to come from the devil; we pray for healing, success and wellbeing, and for God's wisdom to resist offers of power and wealth that might compromise our faith.

There was given me a thorn in my flesh, a messenger of Satan, to torment me. Three times I pleaded with the Lord to take it away from me.   **(verses 7b – 8)**

We will never know for sure the nature of Paul's torment. Some people think that he may have had an illness like a stomach problem, or poor sight, so that he always needed Luke the doctor with him. Whatever it was, notice God's clear answer to Paul:

'My grace is sufficient for you, for my power is made perfect in weakness.' **(verse 9)**

Paul's prayers could bring the dead back to life, but here God's answer is that, by his grace, Paul must learn to live with 'the devil's thorn' and endure that 'devil's messenger'. Paul learns that suffering for Christ brings us in touch with God's special grace and power.

✝ *O Lord, transform all my suffering through your presence and your grace.*

For group discussion and personal thought ·

● What is your experience of God in both danger and safety?
● If you are a person who gets very anxious and worried, what small steps can you take to increase your ability to co-operate with God in difficult situations?

LENTEN ENCOUNTER 3
In doubt and in faith

Notes by Maureen Edwards

based on the New Revised Standard Version

Maureen Edwards, a former editor of *Words For Today*, IBRA's other book of daily Bible readings, served for seven years as a mission partner with the Methodist Church in Kenya, and since then her work has involved getting to know people from many other parts of the world.

The Bible is full of stories of people like ourselves whose faith is tested in times of suffering and in facing new challenges. They struggled with doubt and even expressed anger in their prayers to God. This is a natural response. Faith that has not gone through this process is hardly faith at all. Christ's faith was also tested, especially in Gethsemane. He walks with us not only when life is good but through the storm. He knows what we are going through. We can hold on to that conviction even in the darkest moments.

Text for the week: Mark 9:24b

Sunday March 3   **Psalm 95:7b – 11**

FAITH IS TESTED   The Psalmist makes an appeal to each generation:

> O that today you would listen to his voice!
>   Do not harden your hearts, as at Meribah,
>   as on the day at Massah in the wilderness,
> when your ancestors tested me,
>   and put me to the proof,
> though they had seen my work.   (verses 7b – 9)

Massah (meaning 'test') and *Meribah* (meaning 'quarrel') are the names Moses gave to the place in the desert where he struck the rock and gave the people water (*Exodus 17:1–7*). The Psalmist speaks here of people who turned away from God completely. He does not mean that we cannot cry out to God in times of confusion, pain and loneliness. Jesus did so on the cross (*Mark 15:34*). God hears such cries and shares our suffering, for God is closer to us than we are to ourselves. To turn from such a God would be sheer stubbornness. We would only end up feeling more alienated and lost.

† *Loving God, when we are depressed and lonely lead us gently to those places where the water of life springs up to renew and strengthen us.*

Monday March 4   Exodus 17:1–7

FAITH IN ACTION   The people Moses led on that difficult journey from slavery to freedom experienced times of real drought. No wonder they complained, and Moses had to use his knowledge of the desert to find a way to quench their thirst.

> So Moses cried out to the LORD, 'What shall I do with this people? They are almost ready to stone me.' The LORD said to Moses, '... Take in your hand the staff with which you struck the Nile, and go. I will be standing there in front of you on the rock at Horeb. Strike the rock, and water will come out of it, so that the people may drink.' Moses did so, in the sight of the elders of Israel.   (verses 4–6)

A few years ago, on a visit to the Church of South India, I was taken early on a Sunday morning to a village near Secunderabad. Over a hundred people joined in worship outside the evangelist's house. They were waiting eagerly to drink from the Word of God. Then I saw the rising sun shining on the water pots of some Muslim and Hindu women coming to draw water from a pump nearby. The pump had been installed by Christian Aid to bring clean water to that village. That morning, both spiritual and physical thirst was quenched. The two cannot be separated: the 'water of life' inspires and sends us out to combat famine and drought.

† *Loving God, renew us as we seek the water of life, so that we may not fail to relieve the physical thirst of those who struggle to survive in desert places.*

Tuesday March 5   Romans 5:1–11

FAITH AND ENDURANCE   Paul is very aware of the uncertain, changing world in which we live. He knows from his own experience that life is full of suffering and testing, but he also knows that the death of Christ makes a difference to the way we cope with it. Through his death we experience the deepest love – that 'while we still were sinners Christ died for us' *(verse 8)*.

> Therefore ... we have peace with God through our Lord Jesus Christ, through whom we have obtained access to this grace

in which we stand; and we boast in our hope of sharing the glory of God. And not only that, but we also boast in our sufferings, knowing that suffering produces endurance, and endurance produces character, and character produces hope, and hope does not disappoint us.

(verses 1–5a)

Some years ago, I was talking to a group of ministers in Sri Lanka who were risking their lives to take parcels of food and clothing to refugees in the north. Their faith was strong and nothing would stop them. One of them said, 'Our leaders and our ordinary members have to act in situations like this. We decide to put our foot forward, and we find a power greater than ourselves giving us strength to go on.'

† *Loving God, we praise you that we are reconciled to you through your Son, Jesus Christ. May no hard experience or testing time take away our hope, or prevent us from acting in his name.*

Wednesday March 6   Psalm 40:11–17

FAITH AND LOSS The writer of this psalm has experienced persecution and suffering. He talks of people who tried to 'snatch away his life', but he writes,

But may all who seek you
    rejoice and be glad in you;
may those who love your salvation
    say continually, 'Great is the LORD!'
As for me, I am poor and needy,
    but the LORD takes thought for me.
You are my help and my deliverer;
    do not delay, O my God.

(verses 16–17)

A former colleague recently visited Sierra Leone to encourage the Church in its efforts to recover after many years of civil war. Some people had lost their home and possessions more than once, but their faith was remarkable. She went into schools where the teachers had not been paid for months. They accepted this because they cared so much about the welfare of children who had experienced great trauma and loss. School provided stability and occupied their minds; it was part of the healing process. 'What a humbling experience this was,' she said. 'They appeared to have nothing, yet they had riches beyond imagination.'

† *Loving God, your name is Emmanuel, 'God with us'. You share the pain of conflict and suffering. We pray with Christians in Sierra Leone for political stability and lasting peace.*

Thursday March 7   **Mark 9:14–29**

FAITH AND DOUBT   Faith does not come easy, as the man in
today's reading discovered. He had a long story to tell about
coping with his child's epileptic fits. No one had ever been able to
help, and Jesus' disciples, who had a growing reputation for
miracles, could not help either. And so he brought his child to
Jesus, but there was a big 'if' in his voice:

> **'If you are able to do anything, have pity on us and help us.'**
> **Jesus said to him, 'If you are able! – All things can be done**
> **for the one who believes.' Immediately the father of the child**
> **cried out, 'I believe; help my unbelief!'... He rebuked the**
> **unclean spirit, saying to it, 'You spirit that keeps this boy**
> **from speaking and hearing, I command you, come out of**
> **him, and never enter him again!' ... He said to them, 'This**
> **kind can come out only through prayer.'**
> **(verses 22b – 24, 25b, 29)**

We may never be able to perform a healing miracle like this, but we
can learn much from the man's honesty about his doubts. Many
Christians like to be seen to have a strong faith, and do not want to
admit their doubts before others. Yet only when we face our doubts
can we ask for help, like the man did in his very direct prayer, 'I
believe; help my unbelief!' Prayer begins by recognising our own
emptiness. Only then can we begin to grow in faith (*verse 29*).

✝ *Loving God, we come to you with empty hands, aware of our inability*
to perform the simplest tasks you ask us to do. Fill us with your
compassion, so that we can care for those who need our help, and give
us strength and hope to carry out your will.

Friday March 8   **Matthew 14:22–33**

FAITH IN THE STORM   The disciples had spent the day
fishing, but towards evening a sudden, violent storm arose on the
lake. In spite of their considerable experience, they became very
fearful, and then they saw Jesus walking towards them on the
water.

> **Peter answered him, 'Lord, if it is you, command me to come**
> **to you on the water.' He said, 'Come.' So Peter got out of the**
> **boat, started walking on the water, and came toward Jesus.**
> **But when he noticed the strong wind, he became frightened,**
> **and beginning to sink, he cried out, 'Lord, save me!' Jesus**
> **immediately reached out his hand and caught him, saying to**
> **him, 'You of little faith, why did you doubt?' When they got**
> **into the boat, the wind ceased.**   **(verses 28–32)**

I remember a church leader in the Caribbean telling me that his church was like 'a ship on troubled water'. Perhaps Matthew had the first-century Christian community, with its many challenges in a changing world, in his mind when he wrote this story. Perhaps Matthew is saying to us, 'We're in this storm together, and we have faith because we know that Jesus is walking through the storm with us. He knows what it is to be blown in two or three different directions at once. He comes into the heart of all that we're facing, and his presence makes all the difference.'

† *Living Christ, you know the power of the storm, especially when we appear to be sinking. Give us courage to pause and listen to your voice and to know its calm.*

Saturday March 9   Luke 7:1–10

LEARNING FROM THE FAITH OF OTHERS A Roman centurion asked Jesus to heal his servant. He believed that just as his words carried authority and his soldiers usually obeyed, so Jesus' words had power to heal.

> **When Jesus heard this he was amazed at him, and turning to the crowd that followed him, he said, 'I tell you, not even in Israel have I found such faith.'** (verse 9)

Sometimes our faith too is challenged by people of other religions. For example, a friend told me how sometimes, when she phones Muslim or Hindu neighbours, they say, 'Sorry, we're at prayer. Can we talk later, please?' That never happens, she said, when she rings a Christian friend! She went on to tell me how much she has learnt from Hindus and Muslims through the depth of their faith and their love of God.

† *Loving God, open our minds to discover more of the many ways you have revealed yourself to people of other cultures.*

For group discussion and personal thought

● Reflect on some of the bad experiences you have faced. What feelings and questions did you have and how did you resolve them? What have you learnt from the struggle that could help you in the future?
● When have you been aware of God speaking to you through the insights and expressions of faith of people outside the Church? How have you responded?

LENTEN ENCOUNTER 4
In darkness and in light

Notes by Paul Duffett

based on the New International Version

Paul Duffett was ordained in 1959 and worked in the Diocese of Zululand for sixteen years. Returning to England, he was rector of two Hampshire villages and then spent almost eleven years as rector of Papworth and chaplain to a major organ transplant hospital. He retired in 1998 and now lives near Cambridge.

I have only once been asked if I was saved. I was in a Church of Scotland hostel, where people could eat and relax, while I was in Germany doing National Service as a soldier. I answered that I had asked Jesus as Lord and Saviour into my life and made a commitment to follow him. Whatever salvation means, it includes an encounter with God and the discovery that he is with us in sin and forgiveness, danger and safety, doubt and faith, and darkness and light. He does the 'saving'.

Text for the week: John 3:17

Sunday March 10   **Psalm 23**

LOVE FROM CRADLE TO GRAVE If and when David wrote this psalm he was meditating on the nature of the eternal God. When Jesus said, 'I am the good shepherd' (*John 10:11*) he was expressing his role as the image of God in the flesh. In some churches, today is celebrated as Mothering Sunday – a day to think about and thank mothers for their unique role. God is mother and father of us all. Think how parents act like shepherds: looking after their children, guiding them, planning ahead for them, being there for them, providing home, food, education and so on. The NIV gives an alternative translation for verse 4:

> **Even though I walk**
> > **through the darkest valley,**
> **I will fear no evil,**
> > **for you are with me.**   **(verse 4)**

Thirty years ago, a girl at a boarding school was in my confirmation class. I spoke about God's total love. At the next class I asked if anyone had felt different. She said, 'Yes, there is a corridor at school I wouldn't walk through when it was dark; and I thought – but I can if God is with me!' St Peter in his first epistle asks ministers in the Church to be 'shepherds of God's flock'. We can all do our bit of shepherding.

† *For your name's sake, O God, lead us in right paths and let your mercy follow us, to dwell with you always.*

Monday March 11   **Psalm 139:7–18**

GOD'S FAMILY PLANNING   My parents may have given birth to me, or I may have come out of a test tube; whatever happened, one thing is sure: God thought about me long before anyone else did! God is omniscient – that is, he knows everything. The picture language of our psalm may sound strange to us: 'woven together in the depths of the earth' (*verse 15*); but the meaning is clear: 'I am fearfully and wonderfully made' (*verse 14*). Just think for a moment of the mystery of the brain, the depths of consciousness, and the intricacies of personality. God knows me more deeply than I know myself. Another sure thing is that God made me with a gap. A gap which can be filled only by himself.

> **Where can I go from your Spirit?**
> > **Where can I flee from your presence?**
> **If I go up to the heavens, you are there;**
> > **if I make my bed in the depths, you are there.**
> > > > > > > **(verses 7–8)**

It is then that we can praise God for his precious thoughts – the vast sum of them which outnumbers the grains of sand; and thank him that he loves us just as we are and for our sake. He is the only one we can go to with everything that we are and do and still be loved unconditionally.

† *Dear God, you created us and know us, abiding with us through light and darkness; give us grace to live out this truth today and always.*

Tuesday March 12   **Ephesians 5:8–14**

SHINE, JESUS, SHINE   The other day our home was broken into. Under the cover of darkness someone wearing gloves and commando shoes did a deed of darkness, robbing us of precious property and a sense of security. Now we shall have a bright light outside the back door to expose a would-be intruder. Fred Lemon broke into houses for nearly twenty years – sometimes into the same house twice in one night. When he was put in prison for twelve years, Christ appeared to him in his cell. Now he tours prisons telling what a difference Jesus has made to his life.

You were once darkness, but now you are light in the Lord. Live as children of light. (verse 8)

Of course, the darkness hangs about! Temptation and sin don't go away, but there is always that desire to be good and do good and to 'find out what pleases the Lord' (*verse 10*). And above all, Christ shines on us, in us and out from us; and who knows what doers of dark deeds will be changed as a result?

† *Now to him who is able to do immeasurably more than all we ask or imagine, according to his power that is at work within us, to him be glory in the church and in Christ Jesus throughout all generations, for ever. (Ephesians 3:20–21)*

Wednesday March 13 Micah 7:1–9

WHEN THINGS FALL APART Disaster and destruction and death bring terrible distress, but perhaps even worse is the disintegration of a nation. It has happened too often, either as a result of a totalitarian dictatorship or the misuse of freedom to feed sinful appetites. Jesus took up this theme in his teaching about his return in glory (for example, *Mark 13*) and St Paul pursues it in his teaching about the last days (for example, *2 Timothy 3*). Sadly, however, these things are happening somewhere in the world all the time. What is the Christian to do?

The day of your watchmen has come. (part of verse 4)

This phrase reminds me of chapter 3 of Ezekiel, where he is commanded to warn the wicked. I know a priest who baptised the baby of a computer whiz-kid who had bought the biggest house in the village. Soon after, this man closed the footpath across his land that had been used by the congregation of the local church since 1400. My friend went to him and warned him about his action. The man took my friend to court about it and lost, and a year later he went bankrupt and had to sell his big house. God is not mocked.

But as for me, I watch in hope for the LORD,
   I wait for God my Saviour;
     my God will hear me.   **(verse 7)**

† *We pray for all who are persecuted for the cause of right. Be their light in darkness until your justice is done.*

Thursday March 14   **Isaiah 45:1–7**

THE GOD OF SURPRISES   Suddenly, things turn around – the Berlin Wall collapses, for example. Isaiah encourages his fellow Jews by telling them that Cyrus, an unbelieving ruler of the Medes and Persians, will conquer Babylon where they are exiled and enslaved, set them free and allow them to return to Jerusalem and rebuild the temple. God is free to choose whom he will use for what he wills.

   'I am the Lord, and there is no other.
  I form the light and create darkness,
    I bring prosperity and create disaster;
    I, the LORD, do all these things.'   **(verses 6c – 7)**

We might find this hard; does God send earthquakes and floods which kill thousands of people? Sometimes, of course, these are the result of human error or sin (global warming, for instance), but not always. It seems that God does not interfere in the way that this fragile world behaves. He allows things to happen. At the same time, whatever happens, God is there to bless and use it for our spiritual growth. St Francis' habit once caught on fire and he forbade his brothers to put it out and stop 'Brother Fire' doing his work!

† *Give us grace, Lord, in good or bad times to thank and praise you.*

Friday March 15   **Luke 1:67–79**

THE SUN WHICH NEVER GOES DOWN   I have a friend who saw the sun rise and go down again during her husband's sermon! The date was 15 December in the north of Sweden, when the daylight is very, very short. Of course, in June it is the other way round, and it is hard to sleep with the sun shining brightly at midnight! John the Baptist's father prophesied about a redeemer and saviour who was about to come, and the role that John would have as his herald. Living after the Christ event, we can see a different meaning in his words, but perhaps, under the influence of the Holy Spirit, some of what he said surprised Zechariah himself.

> 'To give [God's] people the knowledge of salvation
>   through the forgiveness of their sins,
> because of the tender mercy of our God,
>   by which the rising sun will come to us from heaven.'
>   (verses 77–78)

That sun has never set. Forgive the pun, but it is the risen *Son* of God who now saves us from sin and death by his grace freely lavished on us. We are guided in peace to peace. He lived and died for that. Alleluia!

† *Come, visit us, O God, so that in your strength we may rise each day to rejoice in the resurrection of your Son, our Saviour.*

Saturday March 16   John 3:16–21

LIFE-GIVING LOVE   This passage is part of the teaching Jesus gave to Nicodemus, the Jewish teacher who came to see him secretly at night. Was he being asked to come out into the light and follow Jesus?

> 'Whoever lives by the truth comes into the light, so that it may be seen plainly that what he has done has been done through God.'   (verse 21)

Here it is, then: the great exchange. In love, God has given his life through his Son, on behalf of the whole world, to transform it into a place where people live in mutual love. So we respond to this love by giving ourselves to God. Then God's love, and the service which is its result, go out through us. This love and life never end because they come from the eternal one. We live in him and he in us. This means the life of a disciple in prayer and God-centred behaviour. Let's do it today.

† *Your love, Lord, cost you all your life. Grant me grace today to offer mine in your service.*

For group discussion and personal thought

- God wants to 'save' the world. How are we involved with him in this?
- How do we understand God's love for the dark side of our nature?
- Does God punish? If so, how?

LENTEN ENCOUNTER 5
In death and in life

Notes by David Huggett

based on the Good News Bible

David Huggett is a Baptist minister living in Somerset, England. Now retired, he continues to be involved in adult Christian education.

Many people live as if this life is all there is. All their money, all their energies are poured into making the best of it. For some that means simply a struggle to survive. For others it is a constant effort to reach ever higher standards of living. Either way, death is the end. The Bible takes a different view. It never underestimates the importance of this life, but its emphasis on an eternal dimension, even in the Old Testament, sheds a different light on both life and death.

Text for the week: Lamentations 3:21–23

Sunday March 17   **Psalm 130**

HONEST BEFORE GOD   Life can be a miserable business if, like the Psalmist, we are in the depths of despair. The feeling of devastation is even worse when God appears to be absent, or at least remains silent. Add to that a sense of guilt because we imagine (and sometimes our fellow believers encourage this belief) that somehow being a follower of Jesus must mean always being happy, and we can very easily end up in what St John of the Cross described as 'the dark night of the soul'. There is, however, a cure for this condition:

> **I wait eagerly for the LORD's help,
> and in his word I trust.**   **(verse 5)**

Waiting in such circumstances is never easy and so we can make the mistake of thinking that the cure for such despair is to throw ourselves into busy activity. Or if that doesn't work, we try to put on a mask of false happiness. The Psalmist was not afraid to face life as it really is at times. Reality and honesty demand that we acknowledge things as they are and accept that the only way of transforming them is to wait on God.

† *Father, in your mercy draw near to all those who are in the depths of despair today. Whatever the cause of their suffering, help them to face it bravely and to trust you for deliverance.*

Monday March 18   **Ezekiel 37:1–14**

DRY BONES CAN LIVE   Life can be tough for communities as well as for individuals. Ezekiel wrote for a people in exile in Babylon, hundreds of miles from home. Their beloved city of Jerusalem was in ruins and its population scattered. Many of their friends and relatives were dead. As far as they were concerned, their existence was pointless. In effect the nation was dead, like a valley of bones bleached white in the harsh sun. Could that attitude of waiting and hoping, spoken of by the Psalmist in yesterday's reading (she or he may well have been one of these exiles), be applied to the community? The job of a prophet is to interpret God's words and ways to his people, and Ezekiel knew that God had not forgotten Israel but was at work on their behalf.

> **'I will put my breath in them, bring them back to life, and let them live in their own land. Then they will know that I am the LORD.'**   **(part of verse 14)**

Israel's political and religious awakening eventually came, although it was partial and incomplete. Ezekiel's vision needs to be seen in the perspective of the life that Jesus came to bring (*John 5:21* and *10:10*).

† *Thank you, Lord, for the life you give us. Help me and all your people today to live it to the full whatever good or bad experiences we may have.*

Tuesday March 19   **Lamentations 3:19–33**

THE BLESSING OF A GOOD MEMORY   My memory often lets me down. Vital pieces of information – somebody's birthday, an important appointment – all go missing from time to time. That is bad enough. Far worse, it happens in my walk with God. Faced with one of life's unpleasant experiences I can very easily forget all his goodness to me over the years. When that happens I am likely to fall into the trap of depression or feel sorry for myself. The author of today's reading may have reacted in this way to the exile. Far from home, the temptation to grow bitter must have been strong. Instead,

Hope returns when I remember this one thing:
The LORD's unfailing love and mercy still continue,
  Fresh as the morning, as sure as the sunrise.

(verses 21–23)

These words have been described as the 'theological high point' of the book. They are more than that. They provide us with a simple, yet profound, principle by which to live our lives when we are faced with difficulty, suffering, or even death itself.

† *Lord, we pray for those today who can see no way out of their problems and no escape from their sufferings. Jog their memories so that they think of all your goodness to them every day.*

Wednesday March 20   Romans 8:6–11

LIFE IN CHRIST A crucial aspect of the preaching of the early Christians was the resurrection of Jesus Christ. It was this which led to early persecution, as Peter and John found when they were thrown into prison for preaching about it (*Acts 4:2–3*). Paul, too, fell foul of the authorities for the same reason (*Acts 24:21*). Such a hostile reaction is understandable, for a dead saviour is no threat to anyone. A living Christ, on the other hand, and one who has conquered even death itself, cannot be ignored. And that same power that raised Jesus from the dead has been passed on to his followers.

If the Spirit of God, who raised Jesus from death, lives in you, then he who raised Christ from death will also give life to your mortal bodies by the presence of his Spirit in you.

(verse 11)

We have already seen this week that God's people are not immune from the limitations and normal experiences of our humanity. In Jesus, however, that humanity is transformed – another dimension has been added (*verse 9*). Sin, suffering and death do not have the last word. That belongs to the resurrection life of Christ within us.

† *Lord, you who have caused the bright dawn of salvation to rise on all those who live in the dark shadow of death, guide our steps into the path of peace (compare Luke 1:78–79).*

Thursday March 21   Psalm 116

DELIVERED FOR A PURPOSE It is a sobering thought that at the time when Jesus died in his early thirties the average life expectancy of a male in Palestine is thought to have been only 25 to 30 years. Probably it was about the same when the Psalmist wrote. Life was short, and whoever the author was, he (or perhaps she) knew what it was like to stare death in the face (*verse 3*). But it was natural both to praise God for deliverance and also to share that joy with the rest of God's people. Those who have had similar life-threatening experiences – perhaps an accident that was almost fatal, or a serious illness like cancer – know the deep sense of wonder and thanksgiving that comes with deliverance. Life takes on a new significance. Every day is precious. But most important of all is when that experience of deliverance leads to a richer and deeper relationship with God himself, so that we can say with the Psalmist,

> **The LORD saved me from death ...**
> **And so I walk in the presence of the LORD**
> **in the world of the living.   (part of verses 8 and 9)**

✝ *O God, who delights to bring us deliverance, grant us the grace to match the praise of our mouths with the quality of our lives.*

Friday March 22   **Luke 8:40–42, 49–56**

ONLY BELIEVE Death is always a tragedy, but there is something particularly poignant about the death of a child. It must have seemed as if this nameless twelve-year-old had everything to live for. The daughter of an important and influential man, she could look forward to a 'good' marriage, for at twelve she was of marriageable age according to the customs of the time. But death respects no one. Age, influence, wealth do not make us immune to tragedy. Although people welcomed the miracle for its own sake and for the blessing it brought, Luke clearly saw a deeper meaning in the event. Jesus foreshadows his own resurrection and the life it brings when he says to the girl, 'Get up' (*verse 54*), a word that is used for the resurrection. There is further significance in his statement,

> **'Don't be afraid; only believe, and she will be well.'**
> **(part of verse 50)**

Although the word 'well' includes the idea of physical healing, it also means 'saved'. In Mark's account, Jairus uses the same word when he asks that his daughter might 'be saved, and live'.

✝ *Loving and powerful Father, we remember before you today all those anxious about the safety or health of their children. Be especially near those who mourn the loss of a child.*

LOVE IS STRONGER THAN DEATH   Death is sometimes seen in the Bible in terms of separation. So physical death is the separation of body and soul, while spiritual death is seen as the separation of the individual from God. These verses remind us that the opposite is also true: life can be thought of in terms of being joined together. In the beginning, when God created the first human beings, he 'breathed life-giving breath [spirit] into his nostrils and the man began to live' (*Genesis 2:7*). And here we finish our week by thinking about life and death together with the amazing fact that spiritual life means actually being united with God.

There is nothing in all creation that will ever be able to separate us from the love of God which is ours through Christ Jesus our Lord.   **(part of verse 39)**

The basis of it all is God's love for us. Unlike our love, which is deeply flawed, getting bigger and smaller according to our varying moods, God's love is unchanging and all-powerful. As we approach Holy Week we are reminded of the scale of that love, which brought us life and will eternally maintain that life in us.

✝ *Lord, these are words to take our breath away. As we meditate upon them may they rekindle our love for you.*

___

For group discussion and personal thought

● What do you think Jesus meant when he said that he had come to give us 'life in all its fullness' (*John 10:10*)? How would you try to explain it to a Christian who is passing through a particularly difficult time in his or her life?

● In what ways could your church community help people, particularly the elderly, to prepare for death?

___

LENTEN ENCOUNTER 6
In rejection and in recognition

Notes by Meeli Tankler

based on the New International Version

Meeli Tankler lives in Pärnu, Estonia, where her husband is pastor of a Methodist Church. She is a psychologist and teaches part-time in the Theological Seminary of the Estonian Methodist Church. She is active in women's work both internationally and nationally, and is a local preacher, Sunday School teacher and Bible Study leader in her local congregation. She is also the mother of three children.

The contrasting events and moods during Passion Week may frighten and confuse us. Some people sincerely believe that it is easier to grow in faith while they are under pressure. For others, trials and tribulations raise numerous questions about God's presence, omnipotence and goodness, and they almost lose their faith. But even when things go well for us and our faith is strong and recognised, we may face all kinds of temptations and problems which are not easy to overcome. The good news is that we have a wonderful God who is always there for us, in rejection and in recognition.

Text for the week: Psalm 118:27

Palm Sunday March 24   **Psalm 118:1–2, 19–29**

THE GATE OF THE LORD   Thank God for festive days! Our hearts are lifted up and we feel as if the whole world is filled with gladness and happiness. We wish it could last for ever. But usually it will not. As the crowds are rejoicing and praising our Lord Jesus at Jerusalem's gate, he is thoughtfully looking up to his Father. He can see the whole picture, not simply this single day filled with celebration and jubilation. On his way towards the cross and resurrection, this day is only one among all kinds of days. And his obedience to the Father does not depend on people's moods or deeds around him.

> **Open for me the gates of righteousness;**
> **I will enter and give thanks to the LORD.**

This is the gate of the LORD
through which the righteous may enter.

(verses 19–20)

However great the joyful recognition, it may end very quickly and unexpectedly. The good news is that the gate of the Lord is open even when all the celebration is over and things may have taken a bad turn. Enter this gate with Jesus – go in obedience to God, and he will be there for you every day.

† *Lord Jesus, help me to turn my eyes upon you, whatever the circumstances of my life.*

Monday March 25

Isaiah 50:7–10

WALKING IN THE DARK   Human beings seem to have a natural fear of darkness. The reason for this may be the fact that God created light and separated it from darkness as one of the very first acts of the whole creation (*Genesis 1:3*). All plants, living creatures and human beings are created into a world full of light. So we have never been meant to live in darkness, although we sometimes experience it very dramatically at some periods of our lives. However, there is a difference between the darkness without God and the darkness with God. Even if there is no visible sign of the light, those who know God can still be sure about his presence.

Let him who walks in the dark,
who has no light,
trust in the name of the LORD
and rely on his God.

(verse 10)

We are invited to walk further and to put our trust in our Lord who is always near us. As we are assured twice in this short passage: 'The Sovereign Lord helps me!' (*verses 7 and 9*). Even when the darkness is still dark around me, my God is near!

† *Dear God, thank you for the wonderful gift of your presence. Help me to believe in your presence even when I see nothing around me but darkness.*

Tuesday March 26

Luke 17:11–19

RISE AND GO   Jesus says the word 'Go!' twice in today's passage. But what a difference between the two occasions. Firstly, there are ten outcasts, ten hopeless human beings begging for pity – and Jesus compassionately tells them to *go* and show themselves to the priests (*verse 14*). They obey him and their obedience is greatly rewarded:

72

As they went, they were cleansed. (verse 14)

So the journey to the priests has turned into celebration of health and comeback into society! What a wonderful day! Let's make a party, let's invite our friends and relatives, let's make great plans for the future! The whole richness of life will be open before us again. There is only one person in all this excitement who wonders how it actually happened. Where is the source of this miraculous healing? This man seems to know the Living God as the ultimate source of life and health. He is sincerely willing and ready to express his gratitude, so he goes back to Jesus. This Samaritan, whose name we do not know, challenges us today to remember God even in the middle of the greatest excitement. Is there anything more Jesus wants to tell him? Yes, there is – this second 'Go!'

'Rise and go; your faith has made you well.' (verse 19)

Have you gone back to Jesus after miracles and great changes in your life, to hear this second 'Go!', this quiet blessing which really marks the new quality of your life?

† *Lord, help me to see your healing and life-giving hand in all good things that happen to me.*

Wednesday March 27 Isaiah 5:1 -7

PROTECTION GUARANTEED FOREVER? What are vineyards for? Usually they are expected to bear some fruit, and the owner judges whether the vineyard is good or bad according to the quality of the grapes. There is a great amount of work put into a vineyard before there is any harvest at all. When the harvest is not good, the owner is not simply disappointed – he also feels deceived; he has wasted his time and energy.

> What more could have been done for my vineyard
>   than I have done for it?
> When I looked for good grapes,
>   why did it yield only bad?
> Now I will tell you
>   what I am going to do to my vineyard:
> I will take away its hedge,
>   and it will be destroyed;
> I will break down its wall,
>   and it will be trampled. (verses 4–5)

As we grow in God's vineyard, we are supposed to bear some fruit. Our God is merciful, but he can still withdraw his protection from us when we consciously fail. He has given us excellent conditions to grow and be fruitful – but we have to do our part. These excellent conditions, as well as the protection, could be taken from us one day, and then we shall find ourselves in the wasteland.

✝ *Dear God, help me to grow in faith in your protected and cultivated vineyard, and bear good fruit. Keep me always inside your walls, in the garden of your delight.*

Thursday March 28   Psalm 80:8–19

THE ROOT YOUR RIGHT HAND HAS PLANTED There it is – yet another vineyard story. This time the vineyard has already been destroyed and damaged, and the vine ravaged, cut down and burned with fire. But the writer of the psalm still firmly believes that restoration and revival are possible, and he begs for it. Nothing is impossible for Almighty God.

> **Return to us, O God Almighty!**
> **Look down from heaven and see!**
> **Watch over this vine,**
> **the root your right hand has planted,**
> **the son you have raised up for yourself.**   (verses 14–15)

Some people lose their faith just at the moment they need it most. In the most desperate situations, when God may be their only hope, they quit praying and believing in him. There was a newspaper article recently about a young man who was diagnosed as HIV positive. His reaction was: 'I used to go to church now and then but now it would not make any sense. I cannot believe in God any more.' Today's passage encourages us to believe in God even more when we are in desperate situations. There is still hope and we are not forsaken even if it seems so. For God has planted a root in you and me, and God is still here and willing to restore it.

✝ *Restore us, O Lord God Almighty; make your face shine upon us, that we may be saved (verse 19).*

Good Friday March 29   Matthew 21:33–46

HARVEST TIME PROBLEMS Sometimes it is very hard for us to accept that all the harvest in our life finally belongs to the Lord. We are only tenants of his vineyard. The problem is that we easily tend to forget his part – all the preparations he has made, all the protection he has given – and congratulate only ourselves on good results. But it is not only a memory problem. We may find it difficult to accept his ownership even when we are reminded of it like the wicked tenants in this parable. In today's passage we are given a serious warning:

> **Therefore I tell you that the kingdom of God will be taken away from you and given to a people who will produce its fruit.** (verse 43)

May this word help us to remember that our God is the Lord of all the harvest, and yet he gives us this unique opportunity to be his co-workers in producing the fruit of the kingdom.

† *Lord, help me to be a responsible tenant of your vineyard. Let me always remember that all the harvest belongs to you.*

Saturday March 30   **Luke 23:39–48**

JESUS, REMEMBER ME   During this week we have looked into many different situations. But here is one of the most dramatic. As we think of our Lord hanging on the cross between two criminals, he does not look very majestic to us. We may feel compassion – but are we able to sense his majesty and really worship him as our king in this pitiful situation? When James and John asked for high places in the heavenly kingdom (*Mark 10:37*), there seemed to be a much more realistic hope that this kingdom would come. The criminal in this story, however, does not seem to have any doubt about Jesus' position. His plea is very simple indeed:

> **'Jesus, remember me when you come into your kingdom.'** (verse 42)

Being able to see Jesus' glory in moments like this requires great faith. Can you worship him as your king in the midst of despair, darkness, hopelessness and even while facing death? Perhaps you should pray today like the desperate father described in Mark's Gospel:

† *'I do believe; help me overcome my unbelief!' (Mark 9:24)*

For group discussion and personal thought

- Think about some occasions when your faith was challenged. What helped you to persevere?
- Do you have any favourite promises in the Bible that strengthen your faith in critical situations?
- Think about some moments in your life when you have experienced God's presence very clearly.

EASTER PEOPLE, EASTER PLACES 1

Easter people 1: women

Notes by Jember Teferra

based on the Good News Bible

Jember Teferra is an Ethiopian who has been working with the urban poor in the slums of Addis Ababa for the past 20 years. Since childhood she has responded to the Lord's call to alleviate poverty. The philosophy that Jember and her team promote in their work is known as the Integrated Holistic Approach.

Even though the theme of this week is 'Easter people, Easter places', the selected portions of the Bible do not affirm the generally held views about women. All over today's world women are fighting for equality; but in a great many parts of the world women are still disadvantaged and marginalised. Culture and religion have been used as justification for such treatment, but this week's texts do not reflect this view of women. While most atheists, both men and women, believe that the Bible is responsible for these so-called cultural or religious norms, these passages challenge their misconceptions. They show our Lord Jesus giving women the same importance as the rest of his followers, and show women taking the lead in the events of the crucifixion and resurrection.

Text for the week: Mark 16:1–2

Easter Sunday March 31   **Mark 16:1–8**

HE IS RISEN!   Our Lord and Saviour is a risen God; even death could not hold him. In my church, the Ethiopian Orthodox Church, Easter is a very important day. It is celebrated in much the same festive spirit as the West celebrates Christmas. Following the long fast of Lent, the whole of Holy Week, known as 'Hemamat' (the pain, agony and suffering of our Lord), is carefully observed and Good Friday is a full day of family worship (even children attend, carried on their mothers' backs!). The Easter 'fever' begins soon after the serious service ends at 3 p.m. on Good Friday. Suddenly the weeping and sorrow of crucifixion turn into joy. From inside the church the drumming and the noises of joy outside are almost a contradiction. The packed church echoes the joy Then the priest announces: 'Jesus has liberated the sinners in hell, no one is now condemned in hell – hell is empty!' The midnight service which follows used to be my favourite service as a child; at 2 or 3 o'clock in the morning, the head priest announces:

'He is not here – he has been raised!'   (verse 6)

and the whole congregation claps for joy, crying, '*El, El, El...*'. What a privilege for the two Marys to be the bearers of such unique and special news! Their heavy burden for their Lord's death is 'rolled away': he is alive, he lives!

† *Lord Jesus, thank you that you are eternal, you are alive and we have that faith and confidence that you are everlasting. Thank you for who you are.*

Monday April 1   **John 20:1–18**

THE DARING WOMEN The role played by Mary Magdalene is worth focusing on, especially because, although Jesus revealed himself to Mary, he did not then allow her to touch him.

'Do not hold on to me,' Jesus told her, 'because I have not yet gone back up to the Father. But go to my brothers and tell them that I am returning to him who is my Father and their Father, my God and their God.'   (verse 17)

Some Christians interpret this to mean that women are not worthy to serve as leaders, because they are not 'clean' or are inadequate in some other way. But women, such as Mary the mother of Jesus, Mary Magdalene and others, were right there for Jesus until he was taken down from the cross and buried; then they returned to care for his body on the third day – only to be surprised by his resurrection. 'Don't hold on to me' until Jesus had gone back to the Father applied equally to his male disciples: it was not one rule for men and another for women. Mary Magdalene did not doubt who Jesus was; she was daring, persistent and trusting, but she needed to be told that the relationship between Jesus and his disciples had changed. It was only doubting Thomas, and those who did not remember the scriptures, who needed to be invited to prove the reality of the resurrection by touching him.

† *Thank you, Lord, that in your sight no one is greater or lesser – all are equal.*

Tuesday April 2   **Luke 13:10–17**

JESUS THE HEALER   In the ministry that my team and I
promote, one of the key words in our philosophy is 'the bottom
up approach' (as against 'the top down'). The 'felt need' of
individuals and ultimately the expressed wish of the whole
community dictate our plans and actions. I learnt this from our
Lord's model of ministry. People who needed him had a way of
finding him amongst the crowd; when necessary they even
broke through the ceiling! Rather than impose his will, he
addressed requests, as he does here with the deformed disabled
woman who has been possessed by an evil spirit for 18 years.
He recognised her need, her faith and her confidence in him
when he was teaching in the synagogue and, in spite of the
usual criticism from the officials of the synagogue, he healed
her. She got herself there, looking for his help.

> **'Woman, you are free from your illness!' He placed his
> hands on her, and at once she straightened herself up and
> praised God.**   **(verses 12b – 13)**

Jesus heals all kinds of people, regardless of race, age, gender,
or social status. His healing is also holistic – physical, spiritual
and psychological.

† *Jesus, the equaliser, thank you that you are concerned about the
needs of all human beings, however marginalised, outcast or
forgotten. You address our needs as we pray to you; give us
praying hearts and discipline to express our needs in faith.*

Wednesday April 3   **John 19:25–30**

JESUS, THE CARING SON   It is commonly accepted that – at
least in theory – the peoples of developing countries, such as
Africans, Asians and South Americans, emphasise the
importance and value of caring for their families and extended
families. It therefore grieves me very much to see such a culture
and tradition slowly dying. I can see what has caused this in the
slums where I work: economic factors which make everyone
live 'from day to day' and 'from hand to mouth'; young people
abandoning their families and moving away, so that no one is
left to care for parents and grandparents. But today's reading is
different. There is the Lord Jesus nailed to the cross and at the
height of his suffering he looks out for John, the disciple he
loved, and asks him to look after his mother. In all the turmoil
he calls out to her:

'He is your son'

and says to John:

'She is your mother.' From that time the disciple took her to live in his home. (part of verses 26 and 27)

Tradition tells us that Mary lived and died in John's home. In his last moments, Jesus gives us a great lesson: he cared so much for his biological mother that he made sure she was cared for beyond his earthly existence. Christians should note that caring for our families is a Christlike obligation.

† *Lord Jesus, as well as spiritual instruction, you gave us all the practical teaching that we need. Help us to continue learning everything from you.*

Thursday April 4   **John 11:17–27**

ASK IN FAITH

'I am the resurrection and the life. Whoever believes in me will live, even though he dies; and whoever lives and believes in me will never die. Do you believe this?' (verses 25–26)

I love this verse so much that I have had it inscribed, in my native language, on my father's tomb. Jesus speaks beyond the immediate reaction to Lazarus's death and his sisters' grief and regret that Jesus was not there when their brother died. He still challenges their faith, by pointing out that whatever we ask, it has to be asked for in faith. In order to discover how we can help our poor community in Addis Ababa, we go from door to door asking them to tell us what they need. The fatalism of extreme poverty makes them distrust those people who can help them, and sometimes they show this by asking for irrelevant things. They are protecting themselves by not building up expectations that will not be met. Isn't this the way we treat our Lord? Our lack of trust must hurt him, but if we really want something from him our greatest need is for faith and trust, that he will supply our needs both here on earth and beyond earthly life. He has assured us that 'whoever lives and believes in me will never die'.

† *Whatever we need, whether it is resurrection, healing, forgiveness or anything else for our spiritual enrichment and growth, we need faith; like Peter, we plead: Lord, increase our faith.*

Friday April 5   **John 11:28–44**

THE SYMPATHISER AND EMPATHISER When I was a political prisoner between 1976 and 1981, as well as suffering as a prisoner I also experienced some misfortunes. One of these was a bereavement: my eldest sister died after being terminally ill for a couple of years. The radical Marxist prisoners always watched to see how we Christians handled our misfortunes. I took my bereavement very badly and my fellow-Christians could not handle my grief. They wanted me to show a brave front and I didn't. I did not perform my routine tasks or lead our devotions for some 10 days, and I think there were some negative comments. So one day, when they pleaded with me to lead the evening devotion, I simply got up and prayed: 'Lord, why did you do this to me, have I not suffered enough?' then I broke down again and wept. I have wept many times since for my loved ones when they die, but...

Jesus wept.   **(verse 35)**

As I discussed with my fellow-prisoners, our Lord is not stony-hearted – he sympathises and empathises. We do not question his authority to take life, but he shared in the mourning for his friend Lazarus and comforted Mary and Martha – then prayed for Lazarus to be raised from the dead.

✝ *You are the Lord of the impossible. You are great, supreme and the authority above all powers on earth or in heaven, but we thank you for your human aspects of sympathy and empathy. It is comforting to know that you understand what it means to agonise in mourning and bereavement.*

Saturday April 6   **Acts 9:36–43**

THE UNENDING MINISTRY Today's reading is about another woman who met the needs of widows, orphans and the disadvantaged – and was restored to life by a miracle. To me, this miracle has two lessons for us. One is that it helped many Jews and Gentiles to realise that our Lord's ministry had not come to an end. Peter and all the followers of Jesus were given a variety of gifts to continue extending God's kingdom on earth.

The news about this spread all over Joppa, and many people believed in the Lord.   **(verse 42)**

The other lesson that we can learn from Peter's miracle is about something which troubles many people: the death of a good person. Why does God allow people who do so much good, like

Tabitha/Dorcas, to die before their time? Another example in the New Testament is the murder of John the Baptist. One possible answer is that God allows people to die when their ministry is finished. John had completed his task of preparing for the coming of Jesus. Dorcas, on the other hand, still had a ministry to fulfil, and therefore Peter's miracle shows that God wanted her ministry to continue.

✝ *Thank you for all miracles, recorded and unrecorded. Help us to accept in faith when you allow lives to be extended or curtailed, because you know best.*

For group discussion and personal thought

● This week we have looked at three stories of resurrection: those of our Lord, Lazarus and Dorcas. What is particularly important about each of them, and why do you think the resurrections of Lazarus and Dorcas were recorded in the New Testament?

● What issues around the place of women and their ministry in society and in the Church have been raised for you by this week's readings?

EASTER PEOPLE, EASTER PLACES 2

Easter people 2: men

Notes by Iain Roy

based on the Good News Bible

Iain Roy is a retired minister of the Church of Scotland, active in the work of the Church through preaching and writing.

What the men who are now the subject of our study have in common is that Christ called each of them into his service and changed their lives. What makes their stories interesting is that, like ourselves, they were each called in a different way.

Text for the week: Luke 19:10

Sunday April 7   John 20:24–31

A MAN LIKE US Poor Thomas! Give a man a name and it sticks to him – 'Doubting Thomas'. Yet, of all the disciples of Jesus, Thomas is perhaps the one with whom we today have most in common. For we live in an age of scepticism.

> **Thomas said to them, 'Unless I see the scars of the nails in his hands and put my finger on those scars and my hand in his side, I will not believe.'** (verse 25)

What the story of Thomas shows us is that questioning faith is not the same as rejecting faith. Thomas asked questions to get at the truth of things, and the result was a life fully committed to the risen Christ. We must never be afraid to ask God questions, but neither must we be afraid to accept, like Thomas, the implications for our lives of the answers God gives to us.

† *Lord, our lives are full of questions which are still unanswered. Answer them, we pray, by your loving presence and spirit, and help us to trust you even when we are in the dark and have no answer.*

Monday April 8   John 21:15–19

A MAN ASHAMED It is no accident that Peter is depicted in John's Gospel as being asked the same question three times.

> Jesus said to Simon Peter, 'Simon son of John, do you love me more than these others do?' 'Yes, Lord,' he answered, 'you know that I love you.' (verse 15)

There are echoes here of that painful time in Peter's life when he was also questioned three times and by his answers betrayed Jesus (*John 18:15–18*, and *25–27*). In Peter's replies to Jesus' questioning we can detect feelings of guilt, the same guilt we often have ourselves when our witness does not correspond to our protestations of faith. But Peter was not rejected by Christ, nor are we. Like him we have a place in the risen Christ's purposes, but we have to have the humility to recognise it and fulfil it.

† *Lord Jesus, forgive us all that impairs our Christian witness and grant us again a sure place in your love and purposes.*

Tuesday April 9   John 21:20–25

A MAN WITH A MEMORY It is frightening to think that the words and deeds of Jesus might have gone unrecorded. Thus any man who can be spoken of in the following glowing terms is himself worthy of remembrance.

> He is the disciple who spoke of these things, the one who also wrote them down; and we know that what he said is true. (verse 24)

But not even this man, John, could record all that Jesus said and did, nor all that the risen Lord has done in the lives of men, women and children throughout the ages ever since. The story of the Gospel is always a story still being written. It is a story with no end in sight except the ending that will come for us and all humankind in God's love. We are very dependent for our faith on the evidence of those unseen witnesses, including this disciple. Others may be equally dependent on our witness in ages still to come.

† *Father, help us to be as faithful as John in our witness to what we know of your love and forgiveness in our lives, so that others may see in us and through us the greatness of your love.*

Wednesday April 10   Acts 6:8–15; 7:55–8:1

The saintliness of Stephen is perhaps seen best in the similarity between the words he uses to forgive those who put him to death and Jesus' words of forgiveness for his killers on the cross (*Luke 23:34*).

> [Stephen] knelt down and cried out in a loud voice, 'Lord! Do not remember this sin against them!' He said this and died. **(chapter 7, verse 60)**

It is a rare gift to be able to forgive others so deeply and so generously. Such deep forgiveness may even have begun the radical change in Saul's life which transformed him from Saul, the persecutor of the Church, to Paul, the great apostle of the Christian faith. We underestimate the power of forgiveness in human affairs. We turn too easily to revenge and retribution, despite the fundamental fact on which the Christian faith is based: Christ's forgiveness on the cross. His forgiveness remains the most powerful catalyst for change in both our own lives and the life of the world.

✝ *Lord, forgive us so that we may be better able to forgive others, and save us from the corrupting influence of the unforgiving spirit.*

Thursday April 11   Acts 9:1–19

A GENEROUS MAN What a good thing for both Paul and the Christian Church that there was a man called Ananias, a man willing to believe the best of someone who has done the worst, a man willing to offer the hand of friendship to one who was an enemy!

> Ananias ... entered the house where Saul was, and placed his hands on him. 'Brother Saul', he said, 'the Lord has sent me – Jesus himself, who appeared to you on the road as you were coming here. He sent me so that you might see again and be filled with the Holy Spirit.' **(verse 17)**

So many situations in our world today cry out for men and women with the same constructive, forgiving approach to people and situations. If Paul became a giant of the Christian faith, he owed it to Christ's forgiveness of him through his humble servant Ananias. It is a contribution each of us can make to the lives of others – to be as willing to forgive them as Christ is willing to forgive us.

✝ *Grant us, O Lord, the generous spirit that can see beyond the wrong that others have done to the good that they might do when forgiven by you.*

Friday April 12   Luke 19:1–10

THE MAN WHO GREW At the beginning of this story Zacchaeus is a small man: at the end of this story he has visibly grown, in spiritual stature if not in physical size. The measure of his growth is his new-found generosity.

> Zacchaeus stood up and said to the Lord, 'Listen, sir! I will give half my belongings to the poor, and if I have cheated

anyone, I will pay back four times as much.' Jesus said to him, 'Salvation has come to this house today.'   (verse 8 9a)

What brought about this radical change was the generous spirit of Christ himself. He made time for Zacchaeus just as he makes time for us. He saw in this little man what he sees also in us – the possibility for development and growth. It is a contradiction in Christian terms to say that others cannot change or even to say that we cannot change our own ways. The Gospel's fundamental truth is that by his death and resurrection Christ has the power to change us all.

† *Holy Spirit, enter into our lives and change us from what we are to what we can become through your love and your forgiveness.*

Saturday April 13   Mark 7:31–37

A MAN DEMENTED   The ability to communicate with others is one of the most essential human skills. Here Jesus was confronted with a man who, until he intervened, could not hear and could hardly speak.

Then Jesus looked up to heaven, gave a deep groan, and said to the man, *'Ephphatha'*, which means, 'Open up!' At once the man was able to hear, his speech impediment was removed, and he began to talk without any trouble.   (verses 34–35)

This is a miracle, to be able to remove another human being from his or her isolation in society. It is a miracle that we ourselves can sometimes bring about through giving friendship to others, spending time with others, giving them company, offering them comfort and serving them. One of the great gifts the Church itself has to offer to others is its fellowship. That is why we must be vigilant that our congregations never become clubs or cliques turned in upon themselves.

† *Help us to prize our friends and to cultivate the gift of friendliness, and make our churches open, friendly and welcoming.*

For group discussion and personal thought

● Look back on your life so far and try to identify and meditate upon the key moments in your personal growth in faith.
● Identify those who have played the role of Ananias in your life and faith, giving you support and encouragement, and let these thoughts guide your prayers of thanksgiving.
● Discuss the fellowship of your congregation: how open is it, and how could it be made more welcoming to others?

EASTER PEOPLE, EASTER PLACES 3

Easter people 3: church communities

Notes by John Holder

based on the Revised English Bible

John Holder was born in Barbados and for several years was deputy principal of Codrington College, the Anglican theological college for the province of the West Indies. He is now the Anglican Bishop of Barbados, and is married with one son.

This week we reflect on the importance of having strong Christian communities that work and witness for Jesus our Lord. We use St Paul's writings as our guide. He does not present to us faceless, neutral communities, but always identifies the people who are doing that extra bit to strengthen the Christian community to which they belong. The communities are thus given an individual touch. We are reminded that individuals should never become faceless members of the community. The emphasis must be on the person whom God is using rather than on the structure that facilitates the person's work and witness

---

Text for the week: 1 Thessalonians 1:3

Sunday April 14   **1 Corinthians 16:15–24**

A CHURCH'S COMMUNITY IS ITS PEOPLE Today's reading reminds us of the important fact that the Christian faith is about people. Paul identifies some members of the Christian community in Corinth who are playing significant roles in strengthening the church, and urges the congregation

> **to accept the leadership of people like them, of anyone who labours hard at our common task.   (verse 16)**

Paul acknowledges the need for good leadership if the local church is to thrive and grow. He himself had probably worked to develop the leadership skills in the family of Stephanas. It is through the leaders in particular that the Holy Spirit works in the community. And although, traditionally, Christians are encouraged to look forward to a 'reward in heaven', Paul believes that the good work of Stephanas, Fortunatus and Achaicus deserves recognition now. We need to be affirmed by our own communities.

✝ *We thank you, O God, for the wonderful experiences of community we have within your Church. Help us to be ever mindful of our responsibility to strengthen the work and witness of your Church. Amen*

Monday April 15   **Romans 16:1–16**

STRENGTH IN COMMITMENT   Once more, Paul identifies a number of people who are making significant contributions to the life of the church in Rome. Leaders such as Prisca and Aquila, who risked their necks to save Paul's life (*verse 4*), have been touched by the Easter experience in a special way. Paul's commendation of Phoebe tells the congregation what their attitude should be:

> **Give her, in the fellowship of the Lord, a welcome worthy of God's people, and support her in any business in which she may need your help, for she has herself been a good friend to many, including myself.**   **(verse 2)**

Paul, as always, brings Christianity down to earth: it is about being there for others and taking risks to defend those who suffer. Our modern world often emphasises the individual rather than the community; but Christians are called to live out the conviction of Jesus and the early Christians that we are called to 'bear each other's burdens'. Here is a model of human relationships that is as relevant today as it was in first-century Rome. Paul's list of the members of the Roman community sounds like a roll of honour. We need to honour and support our leaders, but all the members of the community have their contribution to make and deserve our solidarity and support.

✝ *God, you are a God who works through us to strengthen community and encourage solidarity. Give us the grace we need to strengthen your Church so that it may be a wholesome model for a divided world. Amen*

Tuesday April 16   **Ephesians 1:11–16**
THE TRUE SOURCE OF COMMUNITY STRENGTH
Today our focus shifts to what we have inherited as Christians.

Through Jesus our Lord, God has richly endowed us. Paul spells out our great spiritual resources and assets, the endowments that are present within the Christian community at Ephesus and to which every Christian there has access:

> **you were stamped with the seal of the promised Holy Spirit; and that Spirit is a pledge of the inheritance which will be ours when God has redeemed what is his own, to his glory and praise.** (verses 13b – 14)

Paul reminds us that the Christian community is God's and he is at work to ensure that it is strengthened and survives. We need to balance what Paul said about the contribution of the Christians at Corinth and Rome with his conviction here that it is all God's Church and he is working through us. However much we achieve as a Church, we must never lose sight of the fact that it is only through the grace of God that we can achieve anything. This will keep us sober and humble, a reminder that there is no room for 'blowing our own trumpet' when it comes to our Christian work and witness. We can only do it through the grace of God, which is available to every member of the community.

✝ *Give us, O Lord, the grace to acknowledge you as the source of all our strength. Help us to keep Jesus our Lord as the focal point of all our efforts as Christians. Amen*

Wednesday April 17   **1 Thessalonians 1:1–10**

BUILDING BLOCKS FOR A STRONG COMMUNITY
Here, Paul identifies some important elements that are essential for strong Christian community life, including

> **your faith [that] has shown itself in action, your love in labour, and your hope of our Lord Jesus Christ in perseverance.** (verse 3)

Action, hard work and perseverance: these are the required ingredients of good Christian work and witness. They move us from what we believe to what we do, and help us to understand the Christian faith, which must be reflected in action. The link between faith and action becomes the link between love and labour. Action strengthens rather than weakens community bonds. There will be times when we are severely tested. This is the time for hope and perseverance, and for community solidarity, especially in times of suffering (*verse 6*). Paul gives the Thessalonians a very good report card. But this achievement was the result of hard work and, according to verse 9, involved a radical turn by the Thessalonians – a turn away from idols to the Christian faith. This was no doubt partly the result of dedicated hard work by Paul, but the result is a Christian community of which he can be proud.

✝ *Help us, O God, to treasure and strengthen those great virtues that support our Christian community.*

Thursday April 18   **Colossians 4:7–18**

THE PERSONAL TOUCH   None of us likes to be lost in the crowd, especially when we have done things that deserve special praise. St Paul was surely aware of this, because he was careful to mention people who deserve special praise:

Greetings from Epaphras, servant of Christ, who is one of yourselves ... I can vouch for him, that he works tirelessly for you and the people at Laodicea and Hierapolis.

(verses 12a and 13)

The message is that the Christian community at Colossae consists of a number of people who have made significant contributions to building up the community. But however successful the community, people must never be swamped and lost in the crowd. Paul knows all the people by name; they are not simply faceless members of the Colossian church. He is on first-name terms even with women such as Nympha (*verse 15*), a small point of great importance in a world dominated by men. Women then, like women now, contributed significantly to the strength of the Christian community. Both individuals and the community are important.

✝ *Give us, O Lord, the vision and the strength to build a strong Christian community spirit without ever losing sight of those who work to make the community strong.*

Friday, April 19   **Revelation 2:1–7**

A CHRISTIAN COMMUNITY UNDER SEVERE STRESS
Revelation is like a commentary on the first major crisis that the Church had to face . It was a crisis brought on by the refusal of Christians in one part of the Roman Empire to worship the Roman emperor as God. Those who refused were punished, often by death. The church at Ephesus was caught up in this crisis and the writer of Revelation reminds them of their

Christian commitment and encourages them to hold on. But, under stress, the community seems to be falling apart.

The love you felt at first you have now lost. Think from what a height you have fallen; repent, and do as once you did. (verses 4b – 5)

The writer of Revelation warns them of the urgent need to turn around, or face dire consequences. This passage brings home forcefully to us what can happen to our Christian convictions if we are placed under severe stress, like the people of Ephesus. But we also need to ask ourselves how well our convictions stand up even when we are not under stress. We may not have to choose between our Christian convictions and life. But each day we have to make choices between what is Christian and what is unchristian. The writer of Revelation was convinced that nothing in this life – not even the threat of death – should lead us to fall short of our high Christian calling. We all need to heed his warning and stay away from the slippery road of compromise.

† *Give us grace, O Lord, to stand firm in the faith, even when under severe pressure to compromise our Christian convictions. Amen*

Saturday April 20   **Revelation 3:7–13**

WITNESS UNDER STRESS   Like the Christians at Ephesus, the Christians at Philadelphia were suffering under Roman persecution and trying desperately to keep the faith. They are commended for trying:

I know your strength is small, yet you have observed my command and have not disowned my name. (verse 8b)

They are not given 100 per cent for achievement, but at least they are praised for trying. Hardly any of us will reach 100 per cent, but we must try to do the best we can and guard against compromising our faith. The witness of the church at Ephesus teaches us that we *can* stand firm in the faith, in spite of any pressure that may be brought to bear upon us, and continue to proclaim Jesus as Lord, in word and deed. And always there is hope: the pain and loss and compromise of the present do not spell the end. They are simply experiences on the way to a glorious future. The message here is one that all Christians need to embrace. The present unpleasant experiences that we may have to endure are not to be treated as the final experience on the Christian journey to God.

✝ *Help us, O Lord, to continue to do the little things for you when we are unable to do greater things.*

For group discussion and personal thought

● How, if at all, do you recognise the people in your congregation who make an outstanding contribution to the Christian community? Should they be publicly recognised?
● What are the dangers of focusing only on the 'big achievers' in a congregation? How can you support those who do the 'little things'?
● What is there in your congregation that weakens Christian community? How can you strengthen community?

EASTER PEOPLE, EASTER PLACES 4
Easter places 1

Notes by Ngozi Okeke

based on the Living Bible and the New King James Version

Ngozi Okeke is theologically trained, and has been actively involved in Christian work for over thirty years. After twenty years in England, she and her husband now live in Nigeria where her husband is Bishop on the Niger. She is currently coming to grips with the challenge of running the women's work in the diocese. She is married with four children.

This week, we shall follow the disciples from despair following the crucifixion to the joy of the resurrection, ascension and the coming of the Holy Spirit. However, the fledgling Church was soon scattered through persecution, and one of their prominent leaders was murdered by the 'state'. Our Christian lives are much the same as theirs. Bad times follow good times and we often wonder where God is in all of it. I hope that this week's readings will help us find some answers to these questions.

Text for the week: Acts 2:44–45

Sunday April 21   **John 19:38–42**

THE COURAGE OF CONVICTION   When, a few years ago, the world woke up to the death of Diana Princess of Wales, the grief was palpable. People wept openly, brought floral tributes and signed books of condolence. Everyone wanted to identify with her because she was famous and much loved. It was different for the friends and family of Jesus. He was rejected, convicted, tortured and crucified. His closest friends deserted him. However,

> **Joseph of Arimathea ... a secret disciple ... boldly asked Pilate for permission to take Jesus' body down ... Nicodemus ... came too, bringing a hundred pounds of embalming ointment.**   **(verses 38–39 LB)**

It is one thing to jump on the bandwagon of the rich and famous at the height of their popularity. It is altogether different to identify with a discredited, rejected, dead leader. It required courage and conviction to swim against the tide of popular opinion, but Joseph and Nicodemus were prepared to stand up and be counted when it mattered. As our society becomes more liberal, are we as Christians prepared to have the courage of our convictions and stand up for Christ when it is unpopular and politically incorrect to do so?

† *Thank you, Lord, for those disciples who stood up for you when it mattered. Help us to be like them.*

Monday April 22   **John 21:1–14**

WHAT A CATCH!   After the excitement of the resurrection and the appearances of Jesus, things went a bit quiet. The disciples were at a loose end, not knowing how to move forward.

> **Simon Peter [therefore] said to them, 'I am going fishing'. They said to him, 'We are going with you also'. They went out ... and that night they caught nothing.   (verse 3, NKJV)**

The disciples' solution to lack of direction was to return to familiar territory, their comfort zone. However, they had to learn that whatever their anxieties for the future, going back to the old ways was not an option. By providing breakfast, the most important meal of the day, Jesus was trying to reassure the disciples and to teach them – and us – two lessons. First, though they were expert fishermen, they failed to catch any fish until Jesus turned up, emphasising that we must never depend on our skills and abilities to meet our needs, nor can we serve God in our own strength. Secondly, however uncertain the future may be, returning to the old ways can never be an option. We must look to God for direction.

† *Dear Lord, when the future seems so uncertain, help us to trust that you will always care for us.*

Tuesday April 23   **Matthew 28:1–10**

FEAR NOT   It has been said that this command appears 366 times in the whole Bible – one for every day of the year! The disciples had much to be afraid of, that week after the first Good Friday. Their Lord and Master, who had demonstrated power in a way they had not previously seen or experienced, lay buried in a borrowed tomb. The women, faithful to the end, were on their way to the tomb. Though afraid, their love was stronger and they were determined to perform the final burial rites. An angel had arrived there before them, and waited to greet them.

> 'Do not be afraid,' [he said], 'for I know that you seek Jesus who was crucified. He is not here; for He is risen, as He said.' (verses 5–6, NKJV)

The angel's message, 'Fear not', is typical of how God deals with us when events invade the safety of our world. Just as he sent the angel ahead of the women to provide help and comfort, he reassures us with the presence of his Holy Spirit. However, like the women, we must love him with a love that is stronger than our fears.

† *Dear Lord, thank you for the gift of your Spirit as our companion and helper, especially in times of crisis.*

Wednesday April 24 — John 14:1–14

THE FATHER, JESUS AND US When a new baby is born, we expect it to have a bit of each parent's features, and usually we are not disappointed. However, Jesus did better than take on some features of his Father; he was the exact representation (*Hebrews 1:3*). When Philip asked to be shown the Father, Jesus responded:

> 'He who has seen Me has seen the Father, so how can you say, "Show us the Father?" ... Believe Me that I am in the Father and the Father in Me.' (verses 9 and 11, NKJV)

Jesus expresses his Father so perfectly that to know him is to know the Father. Anyone who wonders what God is like only has to look at Jesus to find out. In the same way, Jesus has passed the torch to us. He told us that we are the salt of the earth and the light of the world (*Matthew 5:13–16*). He expects us to represent him in such a way that people will be drawn to God through our example. The question is, 'How well are we, his Church, living up to that expectation?'

† *Lord, forgive us for all the times when we have not been good ambassadors for you.*

Thursday April 25 — Matthew 28:16–17

TO HEAR AND OBEY The angel's message to the women on Easter morning was to go and tell the disciples to meet with

Jesus in Galilee, yet there is no evidence that they actually made that journey as instructed. But a few weeks later,

> **The eleven disciples went away into Galilee, to the mountain which Jesus had appointed for them. When they saw Him, they worshipped Him; but some doubted.**
> **(verses 16–17, NKJV)**

We learn three things from these verses. First, when the Lord gives instructions, he expects obedience. Only when they made the trip did the disciples get their commission. Secondly, our proper attitude to the risen Lord should be worship. We live with the tension of balancing our need for personal intimacy with the Lord with a proper sense of awe for who he is. Thirdly, some people in our church communities may be doubters. We need to support and encourage them into genuine faith. For the disciples, Galilee was the appointed place. Our Galilee may not be a place. It could be a situation or an event where the Lord chooses to meet with us. We must respond in obedience and worship so that his will for our lives can be made clear.

† *Father, please teach us to hear and obey your voice in our lives and situations.*

Friday April 26   Acts 2:42–47

NEW LIFE, RADICAL LIFESTYLE   What is radical Christian living? A servant doing his master's will can never consider himself radical. And Christians are called to do the will of our Father in heaven. Before Jesus died, he instructed his disciples to make sure that love and unity characterised them as his followers. The early Christians decided to do just that. After Peter's incredible sermon had yielded such a rich harvest,

> **[They] were together, and had all things in common, and sold their possessions and goods and divided them among all, as anyone had need.**   **(verses 44–45, NKJV)**

The early Christians recognised each other as part of God's family and shared their resources. In our modern society, with its emphasis on the individual, it is a great temptation for the materially comfortable to keep their wealth to themselves and enjoy their little paradise. But Christians have a responsibility to help one another. This produces a healthy Christian community which will attract others. If your local church community decides to live like the early Church, the world will probably condemn you as fanatics and even segments of the

Church will call you extremist. But will God consider you normal? Think about it!

† *Father, help us to show by the way we live that we truly belong to your family.*

Saturday April 27   Acts 12:1–17

WHY, GOD?

> **Now about that time, Herod the King ... killed James the brother of John ... He put [Peter] in prison ... intending to bring him before the people after the Passover ... but constant prayer was offered to God for him by the church.**
> **(parts of verses 1–5, NKJV)**

In our hurry to get to the happy ending, we tend to overlook a very important fact. James, the brother of John and one of the original twelve disciples, was killed by the same King Herod who put Peter in prison. We can assume that the Church prayed fervently for his safety too; so why did God allow him to be murdered but miraculously delivered Peter? We do not know. Life is full of such difficult questions and we live constantly with the tension between faith and uncertainty. We believe and pray with the conviction that nothing is impossible with God, yet sometimes we do not get what we ask. It is important to note that God loved both James and Peter, yet he allowed James to die. We may not always understand what God is doing, but we can trust that he loves us and will always do the best by us.

† *Thank you, God, that however bad our situation, we can count on your love.*

For group discussion and personal thought

● How often do you stand up for what you believe, especially when it means going against the tide of public opinion?
● How radical is your church's witness in your community?

EASTER PEOPLE, EASTER PLACES 5

Easter places 2

Notes by Miriam Lopes

based on the Revised Standard Version

Miriam Lopes is a minister of the Portuguese Methodist Church, in charge of the missionary area of Lisbon, with two congregations of mainly African members. She is married, with two children.

The holy place of Jerusalem lies devastated for rejecting Jesus as God's Messiah. This perception of the situation of the early Church is the starting point of a journey through the texts this week, along a new holy way towards a future and truly faithful Zion. Without a geographical holy place, we have to walk into the unknown, with only the guidance of his voice and the power of his presence with us in danger or despair, to find ourselves, after all, as holy temples where he is received to dwell as Lord.

Text for the week: Psalm 31:1–5, 15–16

Sunday April 28   Luke 19:37–44

LOST HOLINESS   Jesus entered Jerusalem and was acclaimed as Messiah by his disciples, in order to fulfil the expected moment of Israel's hope. But all these expectations were met with hostility and murder. Jerusalem did not recognise him. It seemed as if rejection of the Holy One who had made Jerusalem a holy place lost the city its holiness and brought it devastation.

> **And some of the Pharisees in the multitude said to him, 'Teacher, rebuke your disciples.' ... And when he drew near and saw the city he wept over it, saying ... 'For the days shall come upon you, when your enemies will cast up a bank about you and surround you ... and dash you to the ground ... because you did not know the time of your visitation.'**
> **(verses 39, 41 and parts of 43 and 44)**

This disappointing vision is still before us. More than its past, what makes a place holy is its openness to the coming at any time of an unexpected challenge from God. The special meaning of places does not depend on their beauty but on how they receive those who come to them. When we think that our capital city, our town, our own home is more important than people, it ceases to be a place where God dwells and it becomes desolate.

✝ *Oh Lord, help us to rebuild our communities in our home, town and country, broken by fear or possessive ambition; may we feel again your holy presence among us.*

Monday April 29 Isaiah 35:1–10

A JOURNEY FOUND HOLY   Now, after Jerusalem's disaster, there is no established holy centre. We lose the safety of a house and set out on a wandering journey. God is working to bring his believers to the new promised land; after the devastation of the beautiful city, he creates new beauty in the wilderness.

> **The wilderness and the dry land shall be glad...**
> **And a highway shall be there,**
>   **and it shall be called the Holy Way...**
> **And the ransomed of the LORD shall return,**
>   **and come to Zion with singing...**
>   **and sorrow and sighing shall flee away.**
> **(parts of verses 1, 8 and 10)**

When, in spite of all our efforts and trust, everything falls down, life becomes meaningless. Then, suddenly, we are in a new start, struggling for vital things like survival, direction and human support. Turning to God, we realise that he is leading and strengthening us for a better destiny. What seemed to be emptiness may be the only way to discover a different life created by God's love.

✝ *God, our Lord, how hard it is for us to lose our trust in the things, people and situations that we love so much, and find ourselves alone, like abandoned orphans. Your love is like coming home. May all who feel empty after the loss of life's securities be filled with your fatherly love and your help for the orphans and the homeless.*

Tuesday April 30 Song of Songs 2:3–13

AWAKENING TO LIFE   The voice of the Lord speaks over sterile chaos and flood to produce light and life. 'Mary!' calls the risen Christ, awaking her from the devastation of death. The beloved voice awakens us to the strongest human emotion: passionate love.

> **Sustain me with raisins,**
>   **refresh me with apples;**
>   **for I am sick with love...**

The voice of my beloved! ...
My beloved speaks and says to me:
'Arise, my love, my fair one,
     and come away;
for lo, the winter is past,
     the rain is over and gone.
The flowers appear.   (verses 5, part of 8, 10, 11 and 12a)

What makes a voice special? The voice of someone who loves us more than we love ourselves strikes us like an electric current. Jerusalem did not recognise the voice of Jesus, but we, who love him, will always recognise that sound. His passionate love for us enriches us and plants in us a desire for the future life which is already growing within us, like a child in the womb. The Holy One is embracing us from the future: a new sense of life growing in our hope and desire.

† *Suddenly everything turns colourful and bright, as we carry the sun under the heavy overcoat of our daily life. You, Jesus Christ, are the lover who never lets us down, and who has saved us from death by calling our name. Blessed be your voice in those who hear you.*

Wednesday May 1   Psalm 31:1–5, 15–16

POWER SURROUNDING US   It is a terrifying experience to discover that there is no refuge in anything else, not even in ourselves: everything fails. But whether we face destruction or death, the worst we can suffer will only bring us closer to God.

In thee, O LORD, do I seek refuge;
let me never be put to shame;
in thy righteousness deliver me! ...
Yea, thou art my rock and my fortress;
     for thy name's sake lead me and guide me,
take me out of the net which is hidden for me,
     for thou art my refuge.
Into thy hand I commit my spirit;
     thou hast redeemed me, O LORD, faithful God.
                                                      (verses 1, 3–5)

At the bottom of emptiness, after all the terror, we find the hand of God waiting, sustaining and leading us in a secure way while we cross the most deadly places. To fall into his hand is to feel the incredible power of his life around us and to know that nothing can ever destroy us. His own life in us and our togetherness with him will grow for ever.

† *As a father takes his sleeping child to bed, so your reliable and powerful hands will take our sleeping souls to heaven when we die. Forgive us for only believing in you when everything else fails, including ourselves. Help us to be aware of your holy saving love and power always.*

Thursday May 2   **Haggai 1:13–2:9**

A NEW FOUNDATION STONE   After being purified by the experience of death and freed from false securities by the touch of God's hand, we gain a new life and vitality. What remains, the essential person, can now be planted by God in new soil to produce a beautiful tree/temple (*Psalm 92:13*).

> **'I am with you, says the LORD.' And the LORD stirred up the spirit of Zerubbabel the son of Shealtiel, governor of Judah ... and all the remnant of the people; and they came and worked on the house of the LORD of hosts, their God ... 'The latter splendour of this house shall be greater than the former ... and in this place I will give prosperity, says the LORD of hosts.'**
> **(parts of chapter 1, verses 13, 14, and chapter 2, verse 9)**

The word of God becomes incarnate anew in people's history. This happened to exiled Israel, when they chose to forget the devastated temple of Jerusalem. Now, those who kept their faith in God and put themselves in his hand became part of a new, flourishing building rooted in God's word.

† *Praise be to you, God Almighty, who keeps your promise, even though we often think that the end has come and we will die under the fallen stones of the past. In unity with your living Word, a new dwelling place springs up before our eyes to proclaim your glory for ever.*

Friday May 3   **1 Corinthians 3:10–17**

HOLY TEMPLES: BUILDING AND BEING BUILT
Enthusiasm, care, sensibility, vision, effort and risk are some of the good materials used in spiritual building. In the end, the efforts of each worker will be tested by fire and made visible.

> **Like a skilled master builder I laid a foundation, and another man is building upon it. Let each man take care how he builds upon it. For no other foundation can anyone lay than that which is laid, which is Jesus Christ ... You are God's temple and ... God's Spirit dwells in you.   (verses 10b, 11, 16)**

The holy temple combines all the stones, and each of us is also ourselves a holy temple of the Spirit. Our part in the universal building will reflect the brightness of our dedication and the way in which we have welcomed the Spirit to dwell in us. Christ must be at the heart of both sorts of sacred temple: the building in which we are stones, and the building which is within us, influencing our words and our listening, our love, our community and our compassion for those in need.

† *Give us faith, O Lord, when we see our spiritual communities decaying or threatened by conflicts after all the love and hard work that has gone into them. Help us to think of the other side of this tangled embroidery: your side.*

Saturday May 4   Revelation 21:1–14

A NEW BLOSSOM Those who have crossed darkness and deadly waters without forgetting that the Spirit of God is always around and inside them, have been seeds of light and hope which are now blossoming, in the birth of a new creation.

Then I saw a new heaven and a new earth; for the first heaven and the first earth had passed away, and the sea was no more. And I saw the holy city, new Jerusalem, coming down out of heaven from God, prepared as a bride adorned for her husband ... 'Behold, the dwelling of God is with men ... he will wipe away every tear from their eyes, and death shall be no more.'   **(verses 1–2, 3b and 4a)**

Christ will never seem distant or absent, for he is living inside and among us. The new holy temple/multitude of temples shines with his presence. God's version will be: 'He came to his own home and his own people received him with joy'. Nothing can break our happiness. Everything is new.

† *Forgive us, O merciful Father, that in hard times we lack faith in your love, which always brings us closer to you; that in times of despair we forget that the true holy place is wherever you are recognised and received, whether this is in our hearts or in a new place ahead. Come, Holy One, and give us your peace.*

For group discussion and personal thought

- What would life be like without God forgiving, accepting and caring for us?
- What can we do for others to share what God has done for us?

BREAKING THE MOULD 1
Breaking traditions

Notes by Chris Duffett

based on the New International Version

Chris Duffett is an evangelist based at Hoole Baptist Church in Chester. He works for The Light Project, a charity with the vision to share the light of the gospel with all people through the body of Christ, and has a particular concern to share the gospel with young people and the homeless. He also teaches others to share their faith in relevant ways within their communities.

Imagine if we didn't have any traditions. Our cultures would all be much the same, without any distinctive characteristics. Life would be very dull. Our families and our faith communities are shaped by our customs and traditions. We create our own identity as we learn and hold on to what has been passed down to us from our ancestors and our brothers and sisters. An example of this is the custom of 'breaking bread' which was started by Jesus and has been passed down to us across the ages and takes a central place in most of our church services today. Not all traditions are good, and this week's readings challenge us to break free from traditions that can thwart God's plans and purposes for reaching out to all people.

Text for the week: Acts 10:13–15

Sunday May 5   Acts 10:9–44

GOD DOES NOT SHOW FAVOURITISM   Today's story introduces the truth that Jesus, the Messiah for Israel, was also the saviour for the Gentiles. Without Peter's experience, many of us would not be reading this today! A vision and a strong command by God – 'Do not call anything impure that God has made clean' (*verse 15*) – brought Peter to the point where he could break free from the ancient traditions he had grown up with. In the midst of a people that, only a few days before, Peter had considered unclean, he declared:

'**God has shown me that I should not call any man impure or unclean ... I now realise how true it is that God does not** show **favouritism but accepts men from every nation who fear him and do what is right.'**   (verses 28b and 34–35)

Are you able to echo Peter's conviction of God's love for all people? Even as Christians we may have prejudices against people from other nations and tribes. Jesus wants us to treat all people with equality, just as his love extends to all people regardless of their social position, background or traditions. Let God show you today how much he loves all people.

† *Heavenly Father, you have great love,*
Heavenly Father, you have abundant grace,
Heavenly Father, you have given your own Son,
Heavenly Father, help me not to be selfish in sharing you,
Heavenly Father, help me to bring your love to all.

Monday May 6   Mark 3:23–27

BLESS YOU!   When Christians work and worship together as God commands, they are blessed (*Psalm 133*). In my home town of Chester, church leaders from different denominations meet together for prayer and support. We can feel the blessing when we meet, as God seems to show his approval of us! Throughout the world there are stories of whole cities coming to Christ through churches coming together, laying aside their differences and seeking first the Kingdom of God. Jesus teaches that,

'If a kingdom is divided against itself, that kingdom cannot stand. If a house is divided against itself, that house cannot stand.'   (verses 24–25)

To work and build with other Christians may mean breaking out of our treasured traditions and customs. Do they speak in tongues – or not? Is the Bible central to their life – or not? Are you willing to lay aside differences and work together with your brothers and sisters who love Jesus? Only the cross can help us break free from traditions that hinder us from working with others, because there we recognise that we are all sinners saved by grace.

† *Abba, Father, you love your children, every single one of them!*
Abba, Father, help me to work and worship together with those who are different to me, to your praise and glory. Amen

Tuesday May 7   Mark 1:40–44

COMPASSION FATIGUE   Every day on television and in the newspapers, we are bombarded with images of people in need:

starving people or children living on the streets of our large cities. If we are honest, our empathy for these people in distress can be shallow. We can become too used to seeing their sad faces. Many of us suffer from what sociologists call 'compassion fatigue'. In my work amongst people who are poor and living on the streets, I constantly have to ask the compassionate Jesus to give me fresh supplies of his love and care for the broken and downtrodden.

A man with leprosy came to him and begged him on his knees, 'If you are willing, you can make me clean.' Filled with compassion, Jesus reached out his hand and touched the man. 'I am willing,' he said. 'Be clean!' Immediately the leprosy left him and he was cured. (verses 40–42)

I have never read a story about Jesus in which he says, 'I am not willing, go away.' Jesus is always ready, because he is filled with compassion. If you feel empty of compassion, try this simple way of renewing your compassion and love for people. Find a place where there are lots of people, perhaps a train station or a market. Stand out of the way and simply watch the people around you. Why do some people look sad, or lonely, or frightened? As you watch, God will fill you with his compassion for the lost, the compassion of the Father in the story of the Prodigal Son, or the shepherd who searches for the lost sheep.

✝ *Jesus, help me to be like you.*
Jesus, I praise you for the compassion you showed to all people.
Jesus, help me always to be willing to show your compassion to others.

Wednesday May 8   **1 Peter 3:13–22**

QUESTIONS, QUESTIONS! 'Why don't you worry about money?' 'Why do you give to the poor?' 'Why do you love one another?' 'Why do you care for the sick and lonely?' As Christians these are the kind of questions that people should ask us. Do people ask you questions about how you live your life? Peter seems to suggest that being a Christian will provoke regular questions:

Always be prepared to give an answer to everyone who asks you to give the reason for the hope that you have. But do this with gentleness and respect. (part of verse 15)

Peter's suggestion of preparing ourselves for questions will result in people asking us yet more questions. Take time to prepare yourself for giving an answer to everyone who asks you about your faith – perhaps by reading the Bible, praying more, and reading about the Christian faith. If we do these things, we shall become more like Jesus and thus provoke more questions! An ever-increasing circle of questions! Simply telling people about our faith is a tradition that needs to be broken; we need both to tell and to let others ask questions.

✝ *Father, may I be a person who provokes questions through what I say, what I do and who I am in you. Today, may I meet people who will ask me about you. In Jesus' name, Amen*

Thursday May 9, Ascension Day   Acts 1.1–11

STOP STARING AT THE SKY! Being one of the first disciples of Jesus must have been emotionally exhausting. First, you witnessed the cruel death of the man who taught, nurtured, loved and befriended you. Then, three days later, you were filled with joy and excitement because Jesus lived once more. And then, just as you are getting used to having Jesus around once more, he ascends to heaven and leaves you to fend for yourself amongst the people who killed him. But Jesus' last promise to his disciples was that they would not be alone, they would have another helper (*verse 8*); then he left them:

> **They were looking intently up into the sky as he was going, when suddenly two men dressed in white stood beside them. 'Men of Galilee,' they said, 'why do you stand here looking into the sky? This same Jesus, who has been taken from you into heaven, will come back in the same way you have seen him go into heaven.' (verses 10–11)**

Jesus is indeed enthroned in heaven, and he will come back from heaven soon; but like the disciples, we need to stop staring into the sky and make sure that our focus is also on the 'earth'. The angels are almost saying, 'Stop being so heavenly minded that you are no earthly use!' Stop focusing on where Jesus has gone and get on with the job! The disciples were promised a great gift of power; so are we, and through the power of the Spirit we shall be equipped to be witnesses who will change the world as we wait for Jesus to return just as he ascended on that day the disciples were told to stop 'staring at the sky'!

† *Holy Spirit, fall on me*
Holy Spirit, fill me
Holy Spirit, equip me
Holy Spirit, make me bold so that I will tell the world about Jesus

Friday May 10   **Luke 10:38–42**

TOO BUSY? As an evangelist I am often so busy demonstrating the gospel that I forget to dwell with Jesus and spend time with him! Can you relate to that? Church meetings and work are good, but they can distract us from the one thing Jesus desires of us, to spend time with him. Thinking of today's story, who are you more like – Mary or Martha? There are days when I become like Martha, rushing around being busy doing the things I think Jesus wants me to do.

> **[Martha] had a sister called Mary, who sat at the Lord's feet listening to what he said. But Martha was distracted by all the preparations that had to be made ... 'Martha, Martha,' the Lord answered, 'you are worried and upset about many things, but only one thing is needed. Mary has chosen what is better, and it will not be taken away from her.'**
> **(verses 39, 40a and 41–42)**

Whenever you feel under pressure to conform to going to meeting after meeting, say to yourself, 'I am a human being, not a human doing.' Break the tradition and spend some time alone with Jesus, just you and him. Our times with Jesus shape us, change us and equip us for acts of service. We can only freely give if we freely receive (*Matthew 10:8*), and unless we abide in Jesus we can do nothing (*John 15:5*).

† *Lord Jesus, help me to dwell with you. Help me to sit at your feet. Help me to listen to you. Help me to receive from you. In your name, Amen*

Saturday May 11   **Zechariah 8:1–13**

GOD WANTS TO BLESS US God is not stingy or tight-fisted! Today's reading tells us that he wants us to prosper in our mission and become a blessing to all people.

> **'The seed will grow well, the vine will yield its fruit, the ground will produce its crops, and the heavens will drop their dew ... As you have been an object of cursing among**

the nations, O Judah and Israel, so will I save you, and you will be a blessing.' (parts of verses 12–13)

Zechariah described literal, physical blessings for Israel, but as an evangelist, when 'fruit' or 'harvest' is mentioned I automatically think of people becoming Christians! God does want us to produce fruit (*John 15:1–11*), and in Acts we see how this was true of the early Church. These first Christians were 'enjoying the favour of all the people. And the Lord added to their number daily' (*Acts 2:47*). They were a blessing to their community, just as we can be a blessing to our communities.

✝ *Lord of blessing, place your hand upon me today and bless me so that I will see fruit and goodness in the place where I live. Lord of blessing, thank you that you want me to be a blessing to all those around me.*

For group discussion and personal thought

- Are there traditions in your life from which you need to break free?
- How can you reach out to people from other cultures and traditions?
- How can you spend more time with Jesus, simply to be with him, love him and learn from him?

BREAKING THE MOULD 2
Breaking expectations

Notes by Gillian Kingston

based on the New International Version

Gillian Kingston is a Methodist Local Preacher, living in Dublin, Ireland. She is married to Tom, with three sons and a daughter. She teaches Religious Education at Wesley College, Dublin, on a part-time basis. Committed to the vision of unity among Christians, she is Moderator of the Church Representatives' Meeting of Churches Together in Britain and Ireland.

Breaking the mould is not just about breaking with tradition, it may mean breaking with some of our dreams and plans, being ready to take on the *un*expected. Our God *is* a God of surprises who works through unusual people and circumstances, in ways which we often don't have the vision to imagine! This may sometimes upset us and those we love.

Text for the week: 1 Samuel 16:7b

Sunday May 12   Acts 1:12–14

WHY ARE WE WAITING?   It is so boring, waiting around for something to happen, especially when you're not quite sure when it *will* happen, like waiting for a bus or train. Is there time to go for a coffee... maybe not; is it worth buying a paper... probably not. What *are* you going to do with the time ?

They all joined together constantly in prayer, along with the women and Mary the mother of Jesus, and his brothers. (verse 14)

Jesus' disciples had come through a traumatic time: their leader and friend arrested, crucified, risen and then disappearing again with no promises about coming back in three days, just a vague instruction to return to Jerusalem... and wait! What could they do but pray... and wait? Sometimes we simply do not know what is going to happen next; things which had seemed so certain a few weeks, a few days, perhaps even a few hours, ago have evaporated. Dreams are shattered, but perhaps, *perhaps*, there is another vision waiting to burst upon us... We must wait and see.

† *Lord, when things are not working out as I had planned, give me the faith to wait and see what you have in mind for me.*

Monday May 13   1 Samuel 16:1–13

WHAT, HIM?   There are times when we wonder just what *is* happening... A political election and there has been a totally unexpected result; the selection of a football team and it is not the team *you* would have chosen; the announcement of scholarship places, and *look* who is at the top of the list!

But the LORD said to Samuel, 'Do not consider his appearance or his height, for I have rejected him. The LORD does not look at the things man looks at. Man looks at the outward appearance, but the LORD looks at the heart.'

(verse 7)

Who do you identify with here? Samuel, who was looking for the Lord's anointed, saw seven tall, handsome young men and knew that none of them was the one? Jesse, who summoned his older sons and wondered why none of them was chosen? David, called in from the field, who was utterly astonished? The seven brothers, probably resentful that the 'baby' of the family was selected? It is always difficult to deal with the unexpected, especially when personalities are involved. It tests relationships to the utmost, it demands all my reserves of grace, whether I have been singled out or left out. *Has* God got it right ? Time will tell.

† *Lord, when you make choices which I don't expect, protect me from resentment, protect me from pride. Help me to see things the way you see them.*

Tuesday May 14   2 Samuel 23:1–5

IT WASN'T THE WAY I THOUGHT IT WOULD BE!   It was the opportunity of a lifetime, everything had been provided but, somehow, it didn't quite work out as we expected and, now that it's almost over, we are left wondering. Perhaps it was a long-awaited holiday, a family get-together, a school leavers' ball...

Is not my house right with God?
Has he not made with me an everlasting covenant,
arranged and secured in every part?
Will he not bring to fruition my salvation
and grant me my every desire?

(verse 5)

David has come to the end of his life, and it has not always been happy. He has got many things wrong: personal relationships, family relationships, political relationships. And God has denied him the privilege of building a great temple. Yet he still has a sense of having been specially chosen and he does appreciate that righteous rule and peace go hand in hand (read *Psalm 85*). Through it all, the Spirit of God that he experienced when he was anointed *has* been with him. We all make a mess of things, we let ourselves down, we let others down, we let God down; life has not worked out as we would have liked or expected, but God has been there and he still is, in spite of everything.

† *Lord, give me the courage to face my mistakes, knowing that you are a loving and forgiving father and your promise to be beside me is sure.*

Wednesday May 15   Luke 1:1–6

A GOOD START   Here is a good start to the story: the writer knows what he is doing and why he is doing it, and the first people he introduces are law-abiding and godly in the best possible way; we know where we are (Judea) and when it is all happening (in the time of Herod).

> **Both of them were upright in the sight of God, observing all the Lord's commandments and regulations blamelessly. (verse 6)**

Zechariah and Elizabeth are good people, there is no doubt about that. Each of them is from a good family, with Elizabeth able to trace her line back to Aaron, the brother of Moses. But... they have no children. How this godly pair must have prayed and agonised: what sort of God was this who would not answer faithfulness with fulfilment? And then, when the miracle happened, what sort of son was this who turned their well-ordered lives upside-down? But God – and, later, the storyteller – could see that there was an order and a pattern which Zechariah and Elizabeth could never have seen.

† *Lord, help me to trust you when nothing seems to make sense and when all I have counted on does not seem to count any more.*

Thursday May 16   Matthew 11:7–15

WHAT *DID* YOU EXPECT?   Sometimes the most unexpected people do extraordinary and unexpected things: pop stars raise millions of pounds to help starving people; princesses get dirty in refugee camps – no reason why they should not, of course, but it is not what we expect.

> **What did you go out into the desert to see? A reed swayed by the wind? If not, what did you go out to see? A man dressed in fine clothes? No, those who wear fine clothes are in kings' palaces. Then what did you go out to see? A prophet? Yes, I tell you and more than a prophet.**
>
> **(verses 7b – 9)**

John was perplexed about Jesus and the crowds were perplexed about them both. Jesus sends an answer to John (*verses 4–6*), but he asks the crowd a series of questions which challenge their preconceived notions. John came from an impeccable background (*Luke 1:5–6*), but he has chosen a different way and is now in prison. His cousin Jesus says that he is the greatest prophet ever, yet even he has not seen the fullness of the kingdom that Jesus came to proclaim, the Upside-down Kingdom, where expectations are turned on their heads, just as Jesus' mother said they would be (*Luke 1:46–55*).

† *Lord, help me not to feel threatened when my expectations are turned upside down. Make me excited instead !*

Friday May 17   Luke 1:26–38

NOT **A GOOD START**   A humble family from a small up-country village; father a tradesman; mother pregnant before marriage; reports of angels and foreign visitors at time of birth; lived as refugees in Egypt.

> **He will be great and will be called the Son of the Most High. The Lord God will give him the throne of his father David, and he will reign over the house of Jacob for ever; his kingdom will never end.**   **(verses 32–33)**

An unlikely background for a god to choose for his only son: a backwater in an occupied country and an unmarried woman in a society where pregnancy before marriage could be punished by stoning! But this is not *a* god, this is God the Almighty and this child of humble birth is everything that the angel promised his mother. Even years later, people wondered what good could come from Nazareth (*John1:46*), but God can bring extraordinary things from what the world considers nothing!

† *Lord, open my eyes to see possibilities in the most humble and lowly and to recognise you where I least expect you.*

WHAT IS HAPPENING HERE?   We are most easily hurt by those we love and we most easily make assumptions about them. We sometimes make unreasonable demands and then expect them to make special allowances for us. We expect to be part of their group without making too much effort or giving much commitment.

> **My mother and brothers are those who hear God's word and put it into practice.**   **(verse 21)**

It is important to notice that Jesus is not *ex*cluding his 'blood' family here; rather, he is *in*cluding others, those who commit their lives to him. He is saying that *who* we are is not as important in the Kingdom of God as whether or not we are prepared to live obedient and faithful lives. It is all too easy to assume that we can succeed just because of who we are, but it is how we live which counts. And this new way of living calls for new relationships and a new perspective on 'old' relationships.

† *Lord, help me to hear what you are saying to me and then to put that into action.*

For group discussion and personal thought

● Think of a time when your expectations were shattered: how did you cope?
● Were you able to 'see' God in the way things turned out?
● When your preconceived notions are challenged, do you resent it or are you able to rise to that challenge?

BREAKING THE MOULD 3
Breaking and shaping

Notes by Val Ogden

based on the New Revised Standard Version

Val Ogden worked in training and broadcasting before becoming a Methodist minister. She has served in the United Church of Zambia and the Wolverhampton Trinity Circuit, England, and is now a Tutor in Mission Studies at the United College of the Ascension, Birmingham.

A broad selection of readings from Old and New Testaments this week invites us to focus on patterns of breaking and shaping. From the experience of Jeremiah at the potter's house through to the dynamic events of Pentecost, we sense the creative power of God as something which both shatters and shapes his people. The readings affirm both experiences as necessary elements in a life of faith, if we are truly open to receiving 'life in all its fullness'. As we trace this pattern through the biblical stories, we cannot help making links and connections with our own experiences of being broken and remade.

Text for the week: Jeremiah 18:6

Sunday May 19, Pentecost   Acts 2:1–21

WORD POWER   The Pentecost miracle is about speaking and hearing:

> **The crowd gathered and was bewildered, because each one heard them speaking in the native language of each. Amazed and astonished, they asked, 'Are not all these who are speaking Galileans?'**   **(verses 6–7)**

It was not that one, new, universal language for the world had suddenly been invented. Luke, the writer of Acts, wants to stress that everyone's own native language was being spoken and understood by each person present. How I would love that to be the case at the United College of the Ascension, where I teach! In the College we come from over twenty-five different countries, bringing with us many different languages. Out of necessity we all have to use English. Sadly, this can mean that we speak and hear on one level, but fail to communicate the life and meaning behind the words. Something is lost in translation. Second language speakers know this feeling only too well! We sometimes get much nearer to the experience of Acts 2 during worship, when we forget this 'universal language' of English and pray freely in the tongue that comes most naturally to us. Perhaps the words do sound strange to other ears, but the intensity and power of the prayer is heard and felt in the hearts of the hearers. And in this way, we sense the miracle of Pentecost.

† *Lord of all languages, hear our prayers.*

Monday May 20   Luke 2:41–52

LESSONS FOR LIFE At the age of thirteen, Jewish boys took on adult responsibilities. Here, Jesus is aged twelve and the family visit to Jerusalem for Passover is all part of his preparation for the coming year. Joseph, as a good father, would be keen to teach Jesus the traditional duties and rules of home and synagogue. Imagine his surprise to find him among the temple elders, taking extra lessons in spiritual matters:

> **After three days they found him in the temple, sitting among the teachers, listening to them and asking them questions. And all who heard him were amazed at his understanding and his answers. When his parents saw him … his mother said to him, 'Child, why have you treated us like this?'**   **(verses 46–48a)**

There is no hint that Jesus was summoned by the teachers. We assume he went to find them on purpose, wanting to receive wisdom from his heavenly Father's house as well as from his home in Nazareth. Some parents feel quite threatened when their children find sources of inspiration outside the home. They feel irritated when they keep quoting the words of a favourite teacher or a friend's parent! Jesus needed the parental love of Mary and Joseph, but he also needed the influence and challenge of other wise and godly adults. Our children need the same.

† *Pray for any godparents you know, for workers with children and young people in your congregation, and for adults who communicate the faith to the young, simply by being the people they are.*

BREAKING POINTS Some countries hold competitions to find their strongest man. Competitors pull cars with their teeth or try to lift impossible weights, sweating and straining in agony until it looks as though their bodies will burst. Eventually there is a breaking point. The strain is too much and they collapse. This is what happens to Peter; not physically, but mentally, he collapses under the weight of lies and denial.

> **Again he denied it. Then after a little while the bystanders again said to Peter, 'Certainly you are one of them; for you are a Galilean.' But he began to curse, and he swore an oath, 'I do not know this man you are talking about.' At that moment the cock crowed for the second time ... And he broke down and wept.**   (verses 70–71, and part of 72)

Perhaps we know of people living in denial; people who avoid facing up to difficult truths about themselves. Perhaps we recognise the tendency in ourselves. The longer we go on, the greater the strain. When Peter broke down and wept, it was a moment of total honesty but not of total collapse. That breaking point was also the making of him. Peter, the broken man who faced up to his failures, was later chosen and trusted by Jesus to feed his sheep, and inspire the early Church. We never want to see a total breakdown in someone's health, but there is no doubt that God can use moments of brokenness to make breakthroughs.

† *Loving God, I pray not for strength to achieve greatness but for weakness that I may feel my need of you.*

CHILD-SHAPED In 1 Corinthians 13:11, Paul says that he has 'put an end to childish ways'. Earlier, in chapter 3, he expresses sadness that the church members in Corinth are still not mature in the faith; they are behaving like babies fed on milk rather than adults eating solid food. Yet here in Mark 9, Jesus positively identifies himself with a little child:

> **Then he took a little child and put it among them; and taking it in his arms, he said to them, 'Whoever welcomes one such child in my name welcomes me, and whoever welcomes me welcomes not me but the one who sent me.'**   (verses 36–37)

The English language makes a useful distinction between being 'childish' and 'childlike'. It is childish to have petty arguments about things that don't matter – like the disciples' argument about greatness! Paul was urging the first Christians, rightly, to grow up in spiritual matters. But to be childlike is different. Little children need to be fed because they cannot feed themselves. They are vulnerable and need to receive adult love and protection. In the same way, adult Christians can leave behind childish ways, but still feel a childlike need of God and hold out their hands to receive grace and mercy from their divine parent.

✝ *O God, who came as a child to earth, cradle me in your love.*

Thursday May 23   Jeremiah 18:1–5

LIVES REWORKED In Europe people are encouraged to recycle household items they would normally throw away. For example, waste paper is made into pulp which can be used to make new paper. Glass bottles and tin cans are crushed and melted down for reuse. People put their waste items into special recycling bins at key points in the neighbourhood. We have one of these recycling stations just outside our College. Reading Jeremiah 18, perhaps we ought to call it 'The Potter's House'.

> **So I went down to the potter's house, and there he was working at his wheel. The vessel he was making of clay was spoiled in the potter's hand, and he reworked it into another vessel, as seemed good to him.**   **(verses 3–4)**

God is a natural recycler. Very few of the people he created turn out to be perfect pots! All of us fail and fall short of God's ideals. But just as the potter reworks and reshapes his spoiled pot, so God takes less than perfect people and, through the transforming love of Jesus, remakes us. How encouraging it is to know that God's kingdom has few scrapheaps, but many recycling points.

✝ *May my life be reshaped by your hand, Creator God.*

Friday May 24   Jeremiah 19:1–15

EVIL SMASHED This chapter records the people of Judah's complete rejection of God's ways. It results in appalling behaviour which shocks the very heart of God,

because they have filled this place with the blood of the innocent, and gone on building the high places of Baal to burn their children in the fire as burnt offerings to Baal, which I did not command or decree, nor did it enter my mind. (verses 4b – 5)

Here, in contrast to yesterday's reading, the image of the earthenware pot represents evil. God tells Jeremiah to go and smash it in public to make a dramatic statement: the sacrifice of children is the worst possible kind of evil and totally foreign to the God of Israel. A city which practises such horrors will face certain destruction. Smash goes the pot! The message is communicated. As a prophet, Jeremiah was called upon to denounce evil in no uncertain terms, using a visual aid to get his message across. What are the evils in our societies and communities which should be denounced in God's name? Are we brave enough to speak out against them and 'smash the pot' in the sight of our neighbours today?

✝ *Lord, give me strength to rise against evil in your name.*

Saturday May 25   **Ecclesiastes 3:1–8**

THE TIMES OF OUR LIVES   As I write this in October 2000, it is the season of autumn in England. That means that the leaves on our trees turn brown, red, gold and yellow and fall to the ground. Next it will be the bare, cold season of winter. When you read this, in May 2002, it will be the spring season in England. The trees will have new, fresh, green leaves on them once again and flowers will be blooming. I hope (though you never know in England!) that the sun will be shining.

For everything there is a season, and a time for every matter under heaven:
a time to be born, and a time to die;
a time to plant, and a time to pluck up what is planted.
(verses 1–2)

If autumn leaves fall onto soil, they break up and merge with it. In fact they enrich the soil, which then produces healthy plants in the spring. So the leaves which die in one season actually help the birth of new plants in another. The times and seasons form a God-given cycle which has sense and purpose to it. I believe that this is worth remembering because it can help us to put our own experiences of death and life in clearer perspective. Instead of picturing the life God gave us as a straight line with birth at one end and death at the other, we can imagine our life as a circle of seasons, with God present in each one. Think about it. You could even try to draw it. And in the drawing, thank God for seasons past and seasons to come. We are shaped by all of them.

✝ *Help me to love the seasons of my life and to trust in your timing, O God.*

For group discussion and personal thought

● As suggested in Saturday's note, try to draw a simple diagram to illustrate the seasons of your life. Identify the breaking and remaking times, the times of birth and death, waiting and hoping. At which times did God feel very close? Or very far away? Share your seasons with someone you trust and offer them to God in prayer.

BREAKING THE MOULD 4
Breaking bread

Notes by Rosemary Wass

based on the New Revised Standard Version

Rosemary Wass is a former Vice-President of the British Methodist Conference. She is a farming partner and wife to Howard and mother of two children. Rosemary is a Local Preacher and has been an Area President of the World Federation of Methodist Women and National President of the Women's Network of the Methodist Church. At the moment, she is President of Methodists for World Mission. Her hobbies include photography and crafts. Rosemary has always lived in a rural community and is a member of a small village church.

A loaf of bread offers a beautiful image for us to carry through this week's readings. It is created from a variety of ingredients of various amounts – all crucial to the finished product. It is attractive to look at, silky to the touch, mouth-watering to smell. Delicious to taste – it is even better when broken and shared. At communion in church or round a kitchen table, bread awakens all kinds of senses in us. So, this week, let us break bread together.

Text for the week: Ruth 3:17b

Sunday May 26   **John 6:35–40**

BREAD FOR BODY, MIND AND SPIRIT Here is one of John's 'I am' sayings – signposts within his Gospel. Everyone could relate to some kind of 'bread' – the staple food of the day. It was needed 'to keep body and soul together', to satisfy physical hunger. Here is Jesus, come to satisfy spiritual hunger in a different way from the norm, breaking the mould of tradition. Beginning where the people are, Jesus attempts to make them understand that daily feeding with God and the Holy Spirit will be a form of heavenly bread.

Whoever comes to me will never be hungry.   (verse 35b)

This bread will provide nourishment, feeding the soul and mind, cultivating a way of life that changes perspectives, and giving promises to last for ever. Jesus knows that it is hard for his listeners to believe. When Jesus says he is 'the Bread of Life', do we think about the implications of this? Every day we eat bread and the loaf is broken for us, just as Jesus' body was broken. He broke the mould so that we might know life.

✝ *Loving God, who gave your Son and allowed his body to be broken for us, forgive us for taking bread for granted. Teach us to treat bread well. Help us to share bread with others, just as Jesus shared his life with us. Amen*

Monday May 27   1 Corinthians 8:1–13

LIBERATING LIFE Can you think of something that you were forbidden to do as a young child? Can you remember what it felt like when you were old enough to make your own decisions and even, perhaps, to pursue what you were once forbidden? Perhaps you were forbidden it as a safety measure, though it may have been hard to understand or appreciate at the time. Right and wrong were very clear in Jewish law and this Jewish tradition was evident in every part of life. Jesus offered an alternative model for life, challenging the rigid laws of the day.

> **Indeed, even though there may be so-called gods in heaven or on earth ... yet for us there is one God.**
>
> **(parts of verses 5 and 6)**

Paul is writing to young Christians about the ethics of eating food that has been sacrificed to idols. It is an important issue. The act of 'breaking bread' – the eating of particular food – may have important repercussions for other people. Example is a strong tool of evangelism.

✝ *Help us to be sure why we do what we do. May what we do encourage other people to dare to break the mould of their lives and find you. Keep reminding us that bread is for breaking and food is for sharing today and every day. Amen*

Tuesday May 28   Exodus 16:4–6, 22–30

BREAD – A GIFT FROM HEAVEN Moses is dealing with a crowd of cross people. Things are not in his favour. A hungry crowd is an angry crowd. Somehow Moses convinces them of a promise from God. The people are not aware of the fact, but this will be a test of their obedience. Even God gives guidelines! Bread, manna, sustenance – fresh every day, except for the Sabbath when storing is allowed. Some people, now and today, will try to hoard more than their fair share – some things do not change. God has something else to stress to the people, enforcing one of the Ten Commandments, something of the pattern of creation. Six days for work and a holy day – space for a holiday! An opportunity to break the mould of work.

> **'Each of you stay where you are; do not leave your place on the seventh day.'** (verse 29b)

Perhaps we need to think again about how we use our gift of the seventh day of the week.

† *Thank you for bringing us face to face with reality in your guidelines. Forgive us if we abuse your gift of a particular pattern. Help us to break the mould of habit and expectation in order to take delight in your bread, which is available every day for each one of us. Amen*

Wednesday May 29   **Ruth 1:19–22; 2:8–13; 3:15–17**

BREAKING BREAD TOGETHER   You might like to read the whole book of Ruth. It is a moving story in which family, food, fellowship, faith and a future are interwoven. In the first section, Naomi returns to Bethlehem, but the community which welcomes her finds that her circumstances are very different. She changes her name to explain something of her experiences. Not everything is bleak, because the barley harvest is just beginning and there will be grain for flour for bread – the grain used by the poor to bake bread. There will be corners of the field for the strangers and the aliens to glean. Ruth will have an important part to play. The second section records a developing relationship between Boaz and Ruth. Her past has been made known to Boaz and she is surprised by his care for her. He has broken the mould of prejudice and expectation. The third section shows Boaz's generosity towards both Ruth and Naomi. He makes sure that they will not go hungry.

> **[Boaz] said, 'Do not go back to your mother-in-law empty-handed.'** (chapter 3, verse 17b)

† *Give us a generosity of spirit and a concern for the stranger in our midst, that will ensure bread and wellbeing each day. Amen*

Thursday May 30   **Matthew 15:29–39**

BREAD FOR ALL   This is a passage full of amazing events. The energy and enthusiasm generated are almost tangible.

Jesus is the flavour of the month! The hospitality of Jesus is truly amazing. He had no home, but he was host to thousands of people. He had no certificates of medical training, but he undoubtedly healed. He was not ordained, but he lived theology! This person, Jesus, was breaking the mould. His reputation went ahead of him. People were attracted – they wanted to experience being in his presence for themselves. Time passes quickly when your attention is fully caught. Jesus realised that his 'guests' needed succour before beginning their journeys home. Jesus' concern was for everyone present – regardless of who they were or where they had come from earlier in the day.

'I do not want to send them away hungry.'   (verse 32b)

When the story was told afterwards, many hard-pressed mothers must have wished that they had Jesus' secret of how to make the food go round! A simple act, basic food, the crowd fed and satisfied, ready to go to their homes and talk about the happenings of the day.

† *Help us to be more willing to accept people at face value, to accept the outstretched hand of a stranger and to offer ours, to be open to breaking the mould of what is usual and acceptable, and to offer bread to whoever crosses our path or doorway. Amen*

Friday May 31   **Luke 22:14–19**

SYMBOLIC EUCHARISTIC LIVING Luke underlines in this passage that this was a final, farewell act. The order in which the supper proceeds is worth re-reading. Cup and then bread, blood and then body. Jesus gives thanks for each of the elements separately.

Then he took a loaf of bread, and when he had given thanks, he broke it and gave it to them, saying, 'This is my body which is given for you. Do this in remembrance of me.'   (verse 19)

The meal, the Institution of the Lord's Supper, is in two sections, both with the command to 'do this in remembrance of me' – the beginning of a liturgy. Bread is a koinonia – fellowship, communion or sharing – of the body of Christ. We can imagine all these elements present round the table. The invitation of koinonia is personal – it is for you. Take and eat, you do this in remembrance of me. The communal sharing is a personal decision, but then becomes a corporate act, binding, covenanting to eternal life: 'we who are many are one body, for we all partake of the one bread' (*1 Corinthians 10:17*).

† *Whenever we take and eat bread, help us to take time to reflect on the breaking and the sharing. It may be through the lighting of a candle, or the conversation around the table, or it may be in silence, remembering the cost of love for a broken humanity, the supreme sacrifice made in order that we might know and remember. Bless us as we share bread this day. Amen*

Saturday June 1 — Luke 24:13–34

LIFE-CHANGING EXPERIENCES This is a Sunday experience! That in itself is mould-breaking: the special day for followers of Jesus is the first day of the week rather than the seventh. This is a unique account, found only in Luke. There is much for the two travellers to talk about, and a journey offers them the opportunity. It also gives them a sharing which leads to a greater sharing – of bread in a home in Emmaus. The guest becomes the host. He performs an act of breaking bread. Bread and hands provide the clue they need, and suddenly they know! Spirits are lifted, lives are changed, and suddenly, like 'the prodigal', they make their way 'home' to Jerusalem. Good news is for sharing, just as the breaking of bread begins the sharing of food. The mould is broken wide open. Life can never be the same again! Hallelujah!

'Oh, how foolish you are, and how slow of heart to believe all that the prophets have declared!' **(verse 25)**

† *Thank you that most of your disciples were as ordinary as us. Thank you that you never gave up on them and that, finally, they heard what you were saying and understood! Thank you that you still wait for us to catch a glimpse of your Kingdom. We ask that you will help us to continue to walk in your way, sit at your table, and share your bread in relevant ways with whoever we meet. Amen*

For group discussion and personal thought

- How important is the link between our daily bread and Communion bread?
- Can you think why Communion bread is sometimes called 'the Host'?
- We pray 'Give us this day our daily bread'. What does this really mean?

ROUGH PASSAGE TO THE PROMISED LAND (NUMBERS 20–36)

The route to Moab

Notes by Joy Pegg

based on the New International Version

Joy enjoys working as a library assistant in her hometown of Tewkesbury as well as being a tutor to many students from around the world engaged in a theology degree by distance learning. Leading a house group for those who are mainly new to the faith is immensely rewarding and hill-walking still brings much delight and endless opportunities for worship and meditation.

Sometimes our journey through life can be difficult. We can find many things to complain about. There are times when we feel as though we are going nowhere and even those people we look up to seem to make mistakes. Through their own disobedience the Israelites had wandered for 38 'wasted' years in the wilderness after their initial escape in the Exodus and we join them as their journey is about to start again and speed up.

Text for the week: Numbers 21:9

Sunday June 2   **Numbers 20:1–13**

MORE MOANING AT MERIBAH   Thirty-eight years earlier, the children of Israel had camped at the same place and moaned and quarrelled with Moses and Aaron because of the lack of water (*Exodus 17:1, 7*). God provided for them then but they had long forgotten that, and were now caught up in their current problems. Unfortunately the new generation followed in their parents' footsteps, and moaned again.

> If only we had... Why did you...? Why did you...? It has no...
> And there is no...   (parts of verses 3–5)

Sound familiar? Perhaps you can fill in the gaps. In the midst of the moaning, of course, there is the blaming. It's always someone else's fault! No wonder we read that

Moses and Aaron went from the assembly to the entrance to the Tent of Meeting and fell face down, and the glory of the Lord appeared to them. (verse 6)

This is where answers come from, along with all God's provision.

† *Holy Lord, may I learn to do all things without complaining and instead live to your glory.*

Monday June 3   **Numbers 20:14–21**

REPERCUSSIONS When working for a navigation certificate for walkers in the Welsh hills, I learned that there is a difference between a planned route and the conditions found on the ground. I discovered that there was a fairly extensive, unmarked, boggy area on our direct route. We made several attempts to cross it. Eventually I decided to keep our boots dry, but this involved a detour and delay. We always need to make some kind of compromise when we meet obstacles.

Moses sent messengers from Kadesh to the king of Edom, saying: 'This is what your brother Israel says ... we are here at Kadesh, a town on the edge of your territory. Please let us pass through your country ... But Edom answered: 'You may not pass through here; if you try, we will march out and attack you with the sword' ... 'We only want to pass through on foot – nothing else.' Again they answered: 'You may not pass through.' ... [So] Israel turned away from them. (parts of verses 14–21)

This action affected the Edomites for many centuries afterwards. Our decisions to help or hinder others will also have repercussions.

† *Guiding God, help me, as I make requests and offer or refuse help today, whether in large or small areas, to realise that there will be consequences.*

Tuesday June 4   **Numbers 20:22–29**

TRANSITION Four months after Miriam died *(verse 1)* it was Aaron's turn.

At Mount Hor, near the border of Edom, the LORD said to Moses and Aaron, 'Aaron will be gathered to his people. He will not enter the land I give the Israelites, because

both of you rebelled against my command at the waters of Meribah. Call Aaron and his son Eleazar and take them up Mount Hor. Remove Aaron's garments and put them on his son Eleazar, for Aaron will be gathered to his people; he will die there.' **(verses 23–26)**

God's word is certain, and just as God pronounced judgement so he also made provision for the future in Eleazar. At times of transition there can be much sadness and grieving for what is lost:

and when the whole community learned that Aaron had died, the entire house of Israel mourned for him thirty days. **(verse 29)**

This too is a gift and provision for the future and as we face changes in our lives, so we must also give time for this grieving process, whether it is for people, places or 'things' – even familiar routines. Don't rush ahead until you have dealt with the current issues.

† *Dear Lord, thank you for your love and graciousness to us as we face letting go of a variety of things. Give us courage to face the pain involved, and to know your love in it.*

Wednesday June 5 **Numbers 27:12–22**

PROVISION   Our God is a holy God. Even Moses, known as the 'friend of God', was not exempt from judgement.

Then the LORD said to Moses, 'Go up this mountain ... and see the land I have given the Israelites. After you have seen it, you too will be gathered to your people ... for ... you disobeyed my command to honour me as holy before their eyes.' **(part of verses 12–14)**

Moses was not concerned to defend himself but to make sure that the Lord made provision for his people.

'May the LORD, the God of the spirits of all mankind, appoint a man over this community to go out and come in before them ... so that the LORD's people will not be like sheep without a shepherd.' **(verse 16 and part of 17)**

Let us give thanks that eventually Jesus came and opened the way for us to 'come in' before God, for he is the ultimate answer to Moses' prayer and is our 'great Shepherd of the sheep' (*Hebrews 13:20*).

† *Thank you, Lord, for being our Shepherd.*

ANSWERED PRAYER – BUT NOT AS EXPECTED Yet again the people are moaning. Their route seems to be taking them south, away from the Promised Land and,

> **the people grew impatient on the way; they spoke against God and against Moses ... Then the LORD sent venomous snakes among them ... many Israelites died. The people came to Moses and said, 'We sinned when we spoke against the LORD and against you. Pray that the LORD will take the snakes away from us.' So Moses prayed for the people.** (verses 4b, 6–7)

It is always good when we come to our senses and realise where we have gone wrong. We think that if the Lord would just take the problem away, we could cope with life again and all would be well. But this is not always how the Lord works. He wants us to walk by faith and not by sight (*2 Corinthians 5:7*).

> **The LORD said to Moses, 'Make a snake and put it up on a pole; anyone who is bitten can look at it and live.'**
> (verse 8)

When Jesus said, 'Just as Moses lifted up the snake in the desert, so the Son of Man must be lifted up' (*John 3:14*) and 'I, when I am lifted up from the earth, will draw all men to myself' (*John 12:32*), he knew how he would die. He knew that God indeed 'made him who had no sin to be sin for us' (*2 Corinthians 5:21*) so that we could be saved from the effects of sin, if only we would look to him in faith.

✝ *Thank you, Jesus, that I can look to you and you will draw me to yourself.*

ONWARDS! At last there are real signs of progress. When a project or a dream that we have had for a long time starts to fall into place we feel energised, encouraged and more cheerful. The memories of difficulties begin to fade and we are more able to notice the good things in life. The Lord had provided for the Israelites all along, but now they recognise it.

> **From there they continued on to Beer, the well where the LORD said to Moses, 'Gather the people together and I will give them water.' Then Israel sang this song:**

'Spring up, O well!
    Sing about it,
about the well that the princes dug, that the nobles of
the people sank –
    the nobles with sceptres and staffs.'   (verses 16–17)

Be encouraged today on your pilgrimage. Take time to stop and recognise the many different ways in which the Lord is leading and providing for you. 'Sing about it'! Perhaps Jesus was thinking of this passage when he said that the water he would give would be a spring of water in you welling up to eternal life (*John 4:14*).

† *Lord, we rejoice in you as we hasten onwards on our journey.*

Saturday June 8   Numbers 21:21–35

OBSTACLES TO THE END   Israel was now at a crucial point, with Moab on one side and the Amorites on the other. Five months earlier, Edom had refused the Israelites passage through their land, and now they approached Sihon, king of the Amorites, with a similar request.

'Let us pass through your country. We will not turn aside into any field or vineyard, or drink water from any well. We will travel along the king's highway until we have passed through your territory.'   (verse 22)

Sihon, probably emboldened by Edom's success, refused them permission and mustered his whole army. This time, however, things were different.

Israel, however, put him to the sword and took over his land ... Israel captured all the cities of the Amorites and occupied them, including Heshbon and all its surrounding settlements ... So Israel settled in the land of the Amorites.
                    (part of verse 24, and verses 25 and 31)

Og, king of Bashan, was the next one to try to stop their onward thrust, but to no avail (*verses 33–35*) and again Israel 'took possession of his land' (*verse 35*). It had been a tough journey, a whole generation had perished, the new generation was learning to rejoice (*verse 17*) and trust (*verse 34*), and from here they could travel to the plains of Moab and camp along the Jordan across from Jericho (see *Numbers 22:1*). God's word to Abraham all those centuries before in Genesis 12:1, 7 ('Go to the land I will show you ... to your offspring I will give this land') was even closer to fulfilment. Consider how faithful God has been to you, bringing you through many difficulties and overcoming obstacles that seemed so firmly in your way. Take time to praise and thank him now.

† *Faithful Lord, no matter how hard the way has been, you are always true to your word.*

For group discussion and personal thought
- What things do you find it easy to moan about?
- Are you at a point of transition in your life? Where do you think your new direction will lead you?

ROUGH PASSAGE TO THE PROMISED LAND (NUMBERS 20–36)

Balaam and the Israelites

Notes by David Huggett

based on the Good News Bible

This week we become further immersed in the murky waters of ancient Middle Eastern power struggles. God's people, the Israelites, are on the verge of fulfilling their dream of entering the land God had promised them. But even after the forty years of wandering there are still problems to overcome and lessons to learn. It is a curious, yet dramatic, story. At first sight it may appear to have little to do with our modern world. On closer inspection, however, many of the issues raised for God's people then are issues that are still relevant today.

Text for the week: Numbers 23:19

Sunday June 9   **Numbers 22:1–20**

GOD IS ON HIS PEOPLE'S SIDE   On a human level Balak, the Moabite king, together with his Midianite allies, had good reason to be afraid. His territory and his own personal status and safety were all being threatened. The Israelites had a reputation and a string of victories behind them, and were now poised for their final thrust. Moab lay in their path. Had Balak realised the real situation, he might have been even more terrified. For God never stops protecting his people. As he said to Balaam,

'the people of Israel ... have my blessing.' (part of verse 12)

Instead of trying to buy the services of a dubious prophet, it would have been better if Balak had become an ally of Israel. Fear is, of course, a necessary part of human experience. It is important because it warns us of dangers and prepares us to meet them or flee from them. But fear can make fools of the best of us. Balak reacted in a way that is typical of a bully: he met threat with threat.

✝ *Thank you, Lord, that whenever I am threatened you give me the protection of your blessing. Thank you that your blessing is always stronger than any opposition.*

GOD SPEAKS TO BALAAM   We don't always want to hear what God has to say. Then he may have to use unusual means to get through to us. But he always starts from where we are. Balaam had faith although he was not an Israelite. He came from Abraham's homeland, by the great river Euphrates, and so he seems to have had some knowledge of God, although it had become mixed up with pagan magical ideas. Balaam was some kind of a prophet with an international reputation, so he ought to have known better than to try to bargain with God. Quite rightly, he had responded to Balak's initial request by insisting that he could only say what God permitted. But he also wanted the money that Balak offered him, and no doubt he would have argued that payment for his services was only fair. But his greed warped his judgement (see *2 Peter 2:15*). It took an angel and a donkey to bring him to his senses.

> **Balaam threw himself face downwards on the ground. ... 'I have sinned. I did not know that you were standing in the road to oppose me.'**   **(part of verses 31 and 34)**

Of course it is right that we should acknowledge when we have gone wrong. It is even better to develop a spiritual sensitivity so that we hear God's voice and obey it in the first place.

† *Give me a sensitive soul, loving Father, so that you can communicate easily with me without the need to shout or use strange methods. Teach me to silence my own heart that I can hear your still, small voice.*

BALAAM – A MAN OF PRINCIPLE   In spite of his mixed motives Balaam understood a fundamental principle that is true for all God's servants,

> **'I can say only what the LORD tells me to say.'**   **(verse 12)**

He was sufficiently convinced about it to repeat it several times to Balak. Perhaps it was because he was willing to do this that God, in spite of making his disapproval plain, allowed Balaam to travel about five hundred miles from his homeland into Palestine. But it is comparatively easy to pay lip service to a basic principle, and quite another matter to live out the practical implications – particularly when those hit your pocket. Balak, on the other hand, had no such scruples. Convinced that in politics money can buy anything – even God's co-operation – he was prepared to use any possible means to get what he wanted and secure Israel's defeat. We may think that trying to bring down a curse on someone is a very ineffective weapon, but in pagan Palestine more than 3,000 years ago it was regarded as powerful magic. Bullies like Balak use many different methods to try and undermine God's people. Sometimes it is open opposition; often it is much more subtle. But whatever method he used, Balaam could not escape the inevitable conclusion that the Israelites were God's people and therefore under his protection and blessing. They were the last people that God would curse. Neither Balaam nor Balak could go any further than God allowed.

† *Lord, help me to hold fast to your truth, and to live it out in my life.*

Wednesday June 12   Numbers 23:13–26

THE GOD OF INTEGRITY   Balak and Balaam were masters of the art of twisting and turning to avoid doing God's will. They refused to give up and tried looking at the situation from another point of view (*verse 13*). But although we should normally encourage perseverance in prayer, Balaam had no business to pray again, for God had already made his will clear on several occasions. Balaam may have hoped to change God's mind: instead, God uses him to make the great statement,

> 'God is not like men, who lie;
> He is not a human who changes his mind.
> Whatever he promises, he does;
> He speaks, and it is done.'   **(verse 19)**

How long it sometimes takes for us to learn that God cannot be manipulated. When we pray it is not to get him to change his mind, but to enable us to understand his mind and bring our wills into subjection to his.

† *Forgive me, Lord, when I think I know better than you. Help me to be true to you as you are always true to me.*

Thursday June 13   Numbers 23:27–24:19

NO PAYOUT FOR THE PROPHET

> By now Balaam knew that the LORD wanted him to bless the people of Israel ... The Spirit of God took control of him.   **(chapter 24, parts of verses 1 and 2)**

Like us, Balaam was a complex character. Much of the time he seems to have relied on his own skill in using ancient methods of divination rather like our fortune telling. At the same time he had prayed to God, and now, whether he was conscious of it or not, the Holy Spirit took over. But the message had not changed, and we must give Balaam credit for passing it on even though he knew it would be unpopular with his patron Balak. Although he had been stupid enough to try to change God's mind, he was also courageous enough to stand up to Balak even though it meant that he lost any chance of receiving payment for his services. Perhaps we think that at last Balaam has come to his senses. But an experience of the Spirit in our lives, however genuine and welcome, is no guarantee of future good behaviour, as Balaam will illustrate.

† *Give me courage, Lord, to speak the truth even when it is unpopular. Help me to rely daily on your Holy Spirit so that I may know when to speak and when to be silent.*

Friday June 14   Numbers 25:1–13

SPOTLIGHT ON GOD'S OWN PEOPLE Why bother with the expense of a prophet who doesn't do what you ask of him? The Israelites were quite capable of destroying themselves. Perhaps they had grown lax after a period of blessing and success – it can happen to us all. Not for the first time, Israel failed and discovered that sin brings its own inevitable response from God.

So the LORD was angry with them.　　　　　**(part of verse 3)**

The death of 24,000 people may strike us as harsh. But God's anger is always linked to his mercy. The Moabites and Midianites probably indulged in sexual immorality as part of their religion, and when some of the Israelites joined them in this it seems likely that the plague mentioned was some sexually transmitted disease like AIDS. If so, the only way to prevent the whole nation from being infected and possibly wiped out was to destroy those who had foolishly allowed themselves to be seduced. God mercifully intervened and stopped the disease from spreading.

† *Thank you, Lord, that your anger is not easily aroused, but that you prefer to show us your love, your faithfulness and your forgiveness (Numbers 14:18).*

FINAL PREPARATIONS The Israelites have at last almost achieved their objective – entry into Canaan. But before that can be completed they are required to inflict sharp justice on the nation that had led them into sin and near disaster. God's command was clear:

> **'Get ready for war, so that you can attack Midian and punish them for what they did to the LORD.'**   **(verse 3)**

In our more tolerant days this may seem rather drastic, but the later history of Israel showed how Israel's own religious faith was seriously compromised because they could not bring themselves to get rid of Canaan's tribes. Pagan customs, standards of behaviour and religious beliefs constantly undermined Israel's faith and allegiance to God. It turned out that Balaam was at the bottom of the trouble (*verse 16*). His wish to compromise, to be on both sides at the same time, cost him his life as well as the deaths of many Israelites and the destruction of a whole nation. Compromise can be spiritually disastrous for the individual and the community.

† *Lord, protect me from the folly of compromise. Give me strength to be gracious yet firm in my stand for you.*

For group discussion and personal thought

- What different ways may God use to communicate with his people today? Are there any particular things that you believe he is saying to you just now? What actions could you take to ensure that you carry out any practical aspects of what God is saying?
- What are the specific issues in your own life and community which demand that you make a clear and uncompromising stand? Are there also matters on which you need to be more tolerant?

ROUGH PASSAGE TO THE PROMISED LAND (NUMBERS 20–36)

Getting ready to arrive

Notes by Alec Gilmore

based on the Revised English Bible

The plane is about to land. Your tray is folded away. Your seat is in the upright position. All you have to do is sit and wait – with perhaps a twinge of anxiety. You begin to think about arrival. Is your baggage safe? Will you be met? What is the weather like? And so on. The questions for the Children of Israel when they entered Canaan were different. But the feelings were much the same. And these feelings are not confined to arrival in a foreign country. They are there every time we find ourselves facing a new situation.

Text for the week: Numbers 32:13

Sunday June 16   **Numbers 27:1–11; 36:1–12**

THE WIDER WHOLE   The daughters of Zelophehad bring to light an anomaly in Israelite practice. On the one hand, land is important. It is a gift from God and not something from which a family can be separated. On the other hand, only males can inherit. So what happens when there are no males? In the absence of precedents, Case Law comes into operation. Daughters can inherit. But that only creates another anomaly, because if they marry their land goes to the husband's family. So the circle is squared. They can inherit and marry, but only within their own family.

> 'The claim of the daughters of Zelophehad is good: you must allow them to inherit on the same footing as their father's brothers ... This is the Lord's command for the daughters of Zelophehad: They may marry whom they please, but only within a family of their father's tribe.'
>   **(chapter 27 verse 7 and chapter 36 verse 6)**

Thus the family's land is kept intact. Identity is maintained. Property rights are safeguarded. God's promise will find fulfilment in future generations. The daughters of Zelophehad have won their battle for equality and human rights, but this was only possible when they were able to see those rights as part of a wider whole.

✝ *Father, when I fight for my rights help me always to see those rights as part of a wider whole.*

A SENSE OF BELONGING   The Reubenites and the Gadites know a good deal when they see one. The land east of Jordan is high (over 600 metres), enjoys good rainfall and is ideal for flocks and herds. True, it is not the end of the journey. It is not even inside the Promised Land. But once you have found what you are looking for, why go further? So no wonder the Reubenites and Gadites say,

> **'If we have found favour with you, sir, then let this country be given to us as our possession, and do not make us cross the Jordan.' Moses demanded, 'Are your kinsmen to go into battle while you ... stay here?'**   **(verses 5–6)**

And that is not the only consideration. Forty years before, their fathers had done something similar and the price they had paid for that was forty years wandering in the wilderness. If they behave like that, they are no better than their fathers. And for two reasons: one, you cannot settle for a comfortable life before you have obtained your objective. And two, if you opt out you weaken the determination of the rest.

✝ *Father, when I am tempted to grab something for myself, help me to ensure that I am not failing in my responsibility to others or losing a sense that we all belong to one another.*

PROMISE AND ENCOURAGEMENT   A deal is struck! The Reubenites and the Gadites begin to see things differently and closer examination suggests that some of their concern is for the safety of their families, so they make an offer.

> **We shall build pens for our livestock here and towns for our dependants. Then we can be drafted as a fighting force to go at the head of the Israelites until we have brought them to their destination. Meanwhile our dependants can live in the fortified towns, safe from the natives of the land.**   **(verses 16–17)**

Moses agrees. They can have what they want as long as they are prepared to fight until other people have got what they want too. And to their credit that is exactly what the Reubenites and Gadites did. They stayed in the fight as long as they were needed, and no doubt discovered through the experience that they were really only able to enjoy their own families, pleasures and possessions to the full once their responsibilities to others had been fully discharged. Christian living is not about finding the loot you want and settling down with it. It is acknowledging our relationship to others – those who depend on us and those on whom we depend.

† *Father, keep alive in me that promise which enables me to feel your encouragement and to convey that encouragement to others.*

Wednesday June 19   **Numbers 35:1–15**

SPECIAL TREATMENT Some people (the Levites) are getting special treatment! They are deprived or privileged, according to your point of view, but they are not to have any land (*Numbers 18:21–24*). Instead, in return for maintaining the Tent of Meeting, they are the responsibility of the people and will receive tithes. Safe, because they have nothing to worry about. Insecure, because they depend on others.

> **[The Lord] said, 'Tell the Israelites to set aside towns in their holdings as homes for the Levites, and give them also the common land surrounding the towns. They are to live in the towns, and keep their animals, their herds, and all their livestock on the common land.'** (verses 2–3)

But then even those who supposedly have nothing have to give some of it up, because out of the 48 towns allocated to them, 6 are to be set aside as Cities of Refuge. Cities of Refuge were a way of handling the law of blood revenge in cases where death had been accidental (*verse 15*) by offering a place of sanctuary to potential victims of mob rule until community justice could be discharged.

† *Father, never let me forget my responsibilities to those who have no means of helping themselves and help me always to protect those in danger of becoming victims of violence.*

Thursday June 20   **Numbers 35:16–28**

REFINED JUSTICE The Israelites appear to have had no difficulty with blood revenge. Murder called for the death penalty and it was the duty of the next-of-kin to discharge it. But it had to be clear that it was murder. Hence this series of refinements to distinguish murder from manslaughter, and each judgement was the responsibility of the community.

The community is to judge between the attacker and the next of kin according to these rules. The community must protect the homicide from the vengeance of the kinsman and take him back to the city of refuge where he had taken sanctuary. He must stay there till the death of the duly anointed high priest. (verses 24–25)

But the homicide does not go free. He must stay in the City of Refuge and if he does not, he forfeits his right to protection. Release comes only with the death of the high priest; then he can return home. Such refinements seek to balance the rights and feelings of the criminal with those of the victim; this is still a very live issue.

† *Father, when I am confronted with any crime or offence, whether personally or in society, let me pause long enough to understand the story from both points of view before I open my mouth or come to a judgement.*

Friday June 21   **Numbers 34:1–15**

BOUNDARIES   The Promised Land is now just around the corner. The Children of Israel have never been here before. Wandering in the wilderness was so different. So was slavery in Egypt, and in any case most of them cannot remember it. They face a totally new situation and there are all sorts of problems to be sorted out – to begin with, who lives where and who owns what. Boundaries are crucial. And the most important thing to remember is that the land is not theirs. It belongs to God.

Moses gave these instructions to the Israelites: 'This is the land which you are to assign by lot as holdings; it is the land which the Lord has commanded to be given.'
(verse 13)

After the land come the people. Once they are in this new situation, how are they going to relate to one another, to the people whose land they are entering, and to those who begin to come across their threshold? These 'other people' do not belong to them either – they too belong to God. Boundaries call for courtesy before ownership, whether the boundaries are between nations, churches, groups in societies, families, parents and children.

† *Father, teach me to remember that all my possessions, my family, my friends and relationships belong to you before they belong to me, and to treat them as I would treat you.*

Saturday June 22   **Numbers 34:16–29**

FLEXIBLE LEADERSHIP   On the surface this is not a very inspiring or stimulating passage, but what is there is both important and significant.

> **The Lord said to Moses, 'These are the men who are to assign the land for you: Eleazar the priest and Joshua son of Nun. You must also take one chief from each tribe to assign the land.'**   **(verses 16–18)**

Hardly the foundation of democracy! The land is to be 'assigned'. But neither is it a dictatorship. Moses is not to do it by himself. Leadership is to be given and received, not grabbed. It is also representative: Moses is to delegate it to two leaders together with the tribal chiefs, each of whom is named, so that it is quite clear who is responsible and an opportunity is provided for everyone to be involved through their chief. The result is a society of 'things given' and 'things left open', of specific instructions with room for negotiation, of clear instructions about what is to be done which leave the chiefs to exercise their responsibility as seems best.

† *Father, help me to find a balance in my life – what to 'believe' and what to question, when to 'know' and when to trust, how to be definite and how to be flexible, how to be sure of myself and how to be open to others.*

For group discussion and personal thought

- Think of some of the crimes and criminals which have hit the headlines recently. How might they have been treated differently if we had observed some of the principles of the Cities of Refuge?
- Think of some examples of Human Rights (or their violation) and look at those who support or oppose them. How far are they 'seeing things whole'? And how far are you 'seeing things whole' when you make your evaluation?

DIFFERENT WAYS OF LEARNING 1
Learning from each other

Notes by Marian Strachan

based on the New Revised Standard Version

Marian Strachan has taught in Papua New Guinea, Western Samoa and Britain. She is a part-time lecturer and freelance writer. Marian is the wife of a minister of the United Reformed Church, and in her spare time works with international students, children and young people in the church.

A special joy of our lives today comes from the variety of opportunities we have to learn from each other. Through mixing with people of different ages, backgrounds and nationalities, and from what we learn about others through the media, our lives can be enriched and blessed. We benefit from our contacts with others if we are willing to receive, share and grow, and to hear the truth of God in our encounters.

Text for the week: John 13:15

Sunday June 23   **1 Peter 5:1–10**

OUR DEALINGS WITH ONE ANOTHER There is a gentleman in our church who is an elder. Although he is 95 years old, he seems very young. He greets everyone with a smile, then listens or talks expectantly as though he is discovering something new and exciting just by being with you. To be in his presence is a pleasure and an adventure. Fellowship within the Church is a wonderful experience. But it does not always come easily. Pride sometimes causes divisions and rivalries. This is why this letter appeals to young and old for humility and mutual respect:

> [Elders,] do not lord it over those in your charge, but be examples ... In the same way you who are younger must accept the authority of the elders. And all of you must clothe yourselves with humility in your dealings with one another, for
>> 'God opposes the proud,
>> but gives grace to the humble.'   (parts of verses 3 and 5)

The Church is dynamic and exciting partly because we are often thrown together to worship and work with people who are very different. Christ challenges and invites us to love one another. We grow as we learn to accept and value each other, sharing the understanding and insights that are God's gift to us.

† *Loving God, help us to respect and care for one other as we work together in your service.*

Monday June 24   Proverbs 2:1–5

STRIVING FOR KNOWLEDGE AND UNDERSTANDING

Every country in the world has its proverbs, or wise sayings. They are the gathered wisdom of many generations and of the culture from which they come. In the book of Proverbs the wise sayings of the nation of Israel and of other communities and countries were collected to provide teaching and guidance. For the people of Israel, to search for wisdom was to search for God.

If you indeed cry out for insight,
   and raise your voice for understanding...
then will you understand the fear of the LORD
   and find the knowledge of God.   (verses 3 and 5)

It is a privilege to be able to learn from former generations and the peoples of other countries, not only from their accumulated wisdom but also about their understanding and experience of God. Learning across cultures can be hard work but it is rewarding and enriching. When our family lived in Samoa, I was thankful for the wisdom and challenge – not of a proverb, but of the country's motto, 'Samoa is founded on God'. We learned so much from these words, especially when we saw them reflected in the daily prayers and life of Samoan Christians. They continue to be a constant reminder to us of the need to ensure that our lives are centred on God.

† *Lord, open our minds and hearts to be receptive to the wisdom and understanding of different nations and cultures.*

Tuesday June 25   Romans 10:14–17

FAITH AND WHAT IS HEARD   At a church weekend, we were each invited to look back over our journey of faith and to write down the good and difficult times, plotting these like a graph from the time we began to love and serve Christ until the present. My graph started at a high point, as I recorded the period

in my life when I began to understand the good news of God's love, through the preaching of a young minister. Most of us are thankful for those who faithfully challenge, inform and encourage us through the preaching or proclamation of the word of Christ.

> But how are they to call on one in whom they have not believed? And how are they to believe in one whom they have never heard? And how are they to hear without someone to proclaim him? And how are they to proclaim him unless they are sent? ... So faith comes from what is heard, and what is heard comes through the word of Christ.
>
> (verses 14–15a and 17)

Sadly, we often assume that we can leave the sharing of God's word to the minister. Having learned of God's love, we need to ask ourselves frequently how we can share the good news that we have received with those we meet every day.

† *Enable me, Lord, to live in such a way that others will learn about your love through what I say and do each day.*

Wednesday June 26   **John 13:1–17**

DO AS I HAVE DONE   'My feet are the wrong shape,' the old man said as he struggled to pull his socks over bunions and toes twisted from years of walking and tight shoes. Feet are strange shaped and often smelly parts of the body. In the time of Jesus, Jewish slaves did not have to wash the feet of visitors. However, someone had to do it, because good manners required that this service was performed in Jewish homes to refresh and welcome guests. At the last meeting with his disciples, it was Jesus who willingly took on this service and said,

> 'if I, your Lord and Teacher, have washed your feet, you also ought to wash one another's feet. For I have set you an example, that you also should do as I have done to you.'
>
> (verses 14–15)

In serving each other we can learn very important lessons about true Christian lifestyle. Like the disciples, who argued about who was the greatest and most important amongst them (*Luke 22:24*), we are sometimes tempted to look for, and expect, positions of importance in our churches and communities. But if we are too proud or reluctant to serve, others will never learn from us the importance of Christian love and concern.

† *Teach us, Lord, to serve one another with true humility and love, in your name.*

YOU MAY LEARN THEIR WAYS   When children and young people go off to new schools, or university, or away from home to work, parents are usually anxious, wondering what attitudes and behaviour they will learn from their new companions. Recently, during a discussion with a group of teenagers, they told me that they felt that the strongest influence on them at this stage of their life came from their peer group, rather than their parents. We all know the pressures to conform and how much our friends influence us, and so did the writer of this proverb:

> Make no friends with those given to anger,
>   and do not associate with hotheads,
> or you may learn their ways
>   and entangle yourself in a snare.   **(verses 24–25)**

We know how easy it is to absorb the outlooks of others almost unconsciously. There is a tendency to become more like those with whom we spend time, as we adopt similar attitudes. The positive re-writing of the proverb would be to choose friends wisely so that we have good influences in our lives. We should also consider what others learn from spending time with us, and what behaviour they may copy. We have an awesome responsibility if we are involved with children and young people, who may look to us for examples of Christlike living.

† *Living Lord, guide us in our friendships, direct us in our behaviour, and help us to reflect your love in our influence over others.*

LEARNING MORNING BY MORNING   The Old Testament prophets spoke with the authority of God because it was the Lord himself who poured his message onto their lips. In order to speak and teach God's word, they first had to listen. 'The tongue of a teacher' can be translated as 'the tongue of a learner'. Their understanding of what God was doing came from their daily waiting on God. They sought to understand and learn God's wisdom and truth in the voices and events of each new day.

> The Lord God has given me
>   the tongue of a teacher,
> that I may know how to sustain
>   the weary with a word.
> Morning by morning he wakens –
>   wakens my ear

> to listen as those who are taught.
> **The Lord God has opened my ear,**
> **and I was not rebellious.** (verses 4–5a)

By listening to God morning by morning the prophets were able to respond to life in a fresh and helpful way that had relevance for those who were weary, or pressured by injustices. If we listen to God regularly, he is able to teach and guide us, so that we really do have something relevant to offer to our own situations and in our world today.

† *Speak, Lord, for your servant is listening.*

Saturday June 29 Job 2:11

FRIENDS We often learn more from people's actions than from what they say. It takes time and effort to visit and help when friends are ill or in trouble. Perhaps that is partly why visits are usually appreciated so much. Having visits from friends who will sympathise, support, and listen is usually enormously encouraging and comforting.

> **Now when Job's three friends heard of all these troubles that had come upon him, each of them set out from his home ... They met together to go and console and comfort him.** (part of verse 11)

The three friends certainly had warm hearts and good intentions. Unfortunately, during their visit, they were more eager to express their own views and opinions than they were to listen. In despair, Job eventually says, 'Miserable comforters are you all. Have windy words no limit?' (*Job* 16:2–3). The friends we really learn from and grow with are usually non-judgemental, supportive and ready to offer their full attention. They are also honest enough to cut us down to size when necessary, but they help us accept and value ourselves too.

† *For loving friends and for your friendship, we thank you, Lord. Forgive us that in our busy lives we sometimes neglect to make time for friendships to grow.*

For group discussion and personal thought

- What difficulties do you encounter in trying to share your faith today?
- Are you selective in what you want to learn and who you will learn from?

DIFFERENT WAYS OF LEARNING 2
Learning from the past

Notes by Kate Hughes

based on the New Revised Standard Version

In the past, Kate Hughes has been an Anglican nun for 20 years and then spent 14 years working with the Church in Southern Africa. Today, she works from her home in an Urban Priority Area council estate, editing books and writing and editing distance learning courses in theology. Currently she edits *Light for our Path* and *Sharing God's Word* for IBRA.

History is important. The history of a nation or a people, or even of a small group, makes it what it is. History explains why people live as they do, why they have certain customs, why they hold certain beliefs. The past, our history, can hold us back if we make it too important and refuse to change or grow. But the past can also guide us into the future, and give us enduring values which will help us to change and grow. Our readings this week look at different ways in which people can learn from their past.

Text for the week: Deuteronomy 6:6–7

Sunday June 30   Deuteronomy 6:4–12

TEACHING THE CHILDREN

Keep these words that I am commanding you today in your heart. Recite them to your children and talk about them when you are at home and when you are away, when you lie down and when you rise.   **(verses 6–7)**

Today's reading includes one of the most important texts in the Bible for Jews. Written down several thousand years ago, verses 4 and 5, known as the *Shema*, are still used in daily prayer by devout Jews, especially as a bedtime prayer for children. They sum up the two sides of the covenant: the Lord is our God, and we must love him. This is the core of the faith that has been handed down from generation to generation, the declaration of faith which Jesus made his own and handed on to his followers (see *Mark 12:29–30*). What we believe about God has been given us by the past, and we are responsible for handing it on to the future, even though it may need explaining in new ways for new generations.

† *Thank you for the faith which we receive from the past and can hand on to the future.*

Monday July 1   2 Kings 22:10–13

REDISCOVERING THE LAW

'The priest Hilkiah has given me a book.' (part of verse 10)

As the prophet Samuel warned the people of Israel when they demanded to have a king like their neighbouring nations (*1 Samuel 8*), many of their rulers were tyrants who led the people away from God. Some of the kings turned away from the worship of God and followed other religions. Many of the kings were murdered. The people became careless in keeping the law, and the priests did not teach them. So the discovery of a book of the law was a revelation. This survival from the past showed King Josiah just how far the nation had wandered away from its commitment to God. But the book was also a gift from the past, because it enabled the king to begin to lead the people back to the true way. The book of the law was a guide book for the future. The written word of Scripture can indeed be, in the words of Psalm 119:105, 'a lamp to my feet and a light to my path'.

† *Help us to treasure the words of Scripture and to use them as a guide for our journey.*

Tuesday July 2   Romans 4:7–13

THE REMINDER OF THE COVENANT

He received the sign of circumcision as a seal of the righteousness that he had by faith while he was still uncircumcised.   (verse 11a)

The word 'tradition' means literally 'something that is handed over'. So traditions are actions and events which are handed down to us by the people who lived before us. Not all traditions are worth keeping; some schools, for example, have initiation traditions for new pupils which are simply cruel bullying and need to be stopped. But other traditions reflect the good values of a social group or nation, and remind the people of things which are important to them. The tradition followed by many Christians of renewing their baptismal vows at Easter is an example of a useful tradition. It reminds us of the promises we made to God (or which were made to God on our behalf, if we were baptised as babies) and gives us an opportunity to commit ourselves to God again and to thank him for the journey of our life so far. In the same way, circumcision was a useful tradition which reminded the Jews of their special relationship with God and their faith in him. But traditions simply remind us of values – they are not the values themselves. They are signs, not the reality; it is up to us to make sure that the values they represent are preserved.

† *Thank you for the traditions that enrich our lives; help us to pass on to others not just the outward event but also the values that they represent.*

Wednesday July 3   **Jeremiah 12:7–13**

WE NEED TO LEARN   History reminds us how difficult it can be for human beings to learn from the past. We seem to need to be taught the same lessons over and over again. Suffering does not necessarily make us more compassionate to other people. Our success and prosperity do not necessarily make us more generous. However much harm has been done by greed for power in the past, people still bribe, cheat, fight and kill their way to the top.

The whole land is made desolate,
but no one lays it to heart.   **(verse 11b)**

God is a good teacher: if we do not learn the lessons we need the first time, he will teach us over and over again until we do learn. We need to read 'the signs of the times' (*Matthew 16:3*) and learn from the experience of the past, to listen to God and hear what he is saying to us through the events of history and the present.

† *Help us, O God, to learn from the experience of the past and the events of the present.*

WE NEED REMINDERS

'This song will confront them as a witness.'

(part of verse 21)

We do not always understand God. It is not always clear to us
why he acts as he does – or whether he is doing anything at all.
We cannot always interpret 'the signs of the times' and it is not
always obvious that he has our best interests at heart. This is
why it is so important that we build up our own history with
God. If we maintain contact with God through prayer; if we
read about his dealings with other people, both in the Bible and
in other books; if we talk to other people about their experience
of God; if we expect him to be present and active in our own life
– then, when we encounter difficulties, danger or tragedy, our
past experience of God 'will confront us as a witness'. If we
already know him as loving, caring and powerful, we will be
better able to trust him at those times when we do not
understand what he is doing and are tempted not to believe in
him.

✝ *Thank you for my past knowledge of you and your love which
enables me to trust you in the present, even when I do not
understand what you are doing.*

THE NEED FOR GUIDANCE   If we are to learn from the
past, we need guidance. No one person can interpret and
understand everything, or do everything required to hand on
traditions. This needs to be a community effort.

So Philip ran up to [the chariot] and heard him reading the
prophet Isaiah. He asked, 'Do you understand what you
are reading?' He replied, 'How can I, unless someone
guides me?'   (verses 30–31a)

Philip interpreted the words of the prophet Isaiah for the
Ethiopian eunuch, who then went on his way, presumably on
the long journey back to Ethiopia. Today, Philip would
probably have tried to link him up with a local Christian group,
so that he could continue to receive guidance in learning from
the past. For Christians, the past is important; it is where our
faith begins. Jesus was born, lived and died at a particular time
in a particular place, nearly 2000 years in the past. However
much he is alive and active today, we need to understand his

past, which is also our past. It is in the Church, in the Christian community, that we find the help and guidance we need, and can ourselves become guides to others.

✝ *Thank you for all those who have guided me and helped me to learn from the past which is the story of our salvation.*

Saturday July 6   Hebrews 12:1–2

THE CLOUD OF WITNESSES   Our Christian past is not only the past of the life and death of Jesus Christ. It is also the past of the continuing Body of Christ, the Church. In chapter 11 the letter to the Hebrews lists the important people of the Old Testament: Abel, Enoch, Noah, Abraham, Isaac, Jacob, Joseph, Moses, and many others. We can add the outstanding people of the New Testament: the Apostles, the writers of the Gospels, Paul, Timothy, Barnabas, Dorcas, and others like them.

We are surrounded by so great a cloud of witnesses.
(part of verse 1)

We can add to this cloud those from the past who have helped us on our own Christian journey: saints and leaders, teachers, preachers, writers, members of our local congregation. All of them reinforce our own experience of God and increase our understanding. Our belief in the resurrection means that we are part of a great community of those from every age and every country who can witness to the truth and love of God – a living past from which we can learn to love him more.

✝ *May all who love God, living and departed, on earth and in heaven, witness with joy to his greatness.*

For group discussion and personal thought

● Apart from Jesus, what events or people in the past have taught you most about God?

DIFFERENT WAYS OF LEARNING 3
Learning through stories

Notes by Colin Hurford

based on the New International Version

Colin Hurford, an Anglican priest, has worked in England in urban and rural parishes. He spent seven years in Sabah, Malaysia, at a Secondary School as teacher and school Chaplain. He also spent some months in Tanzania lecturing at a Theological College. Now retired, he is working on a book about Christian Adult Education.

Jesus was a very great teacher and loved telling stories. Telling a good story is an excellent way of teaching. A very helpful way of learning is to imagine that you are one of the people in the story. For example, in the parable of the Good Samaritan, imagine you are the priest – what would it have been like on that road? Why would you have passed by? Or put yourself in the place of the Samaritan or the wounded man or even the innkeeper. What would you think and feel?

Text for the week: Luke 10:37

Sunday July 7   2 Samuel 1:17–27

DAVID'S GRIEF   King Saul and his son, Jonathan, have been killed in battle against the Philistines. Although this means that David can now become king, he is desperately sad. He is especially sad at Jonathan's death because Jonathan had been such a dear friend, taking David's side against Saul. Can you put yourself in David's place? David expresses his grief by writing this wonderful song, or lament.

> **I grieve for you, Jonathan my brother;**
> **you were very dear to me.**   **(verse 26)**

This very moving story shows that even great men can feel the deepest emotions. Like David, we should not be afraid of sharing our sadness with others.

† *Heavenly Father, please be with all who are mourning the loss of a dear friend and give them your comfort, for Jesus' sake.*

JESUS TELLS A STORY   This is probably the best known story in the world. Think how many Christians of all races, throughout the centuries, have been inspired by this story. And more! It speaks to us throughout our lives. After forty years in ministry, I can still learn new things from this parable.

> **[The expert in the law] asked Jesus, 'Who is my neighbour?'**   **(verse 29b)**

The Jews had been arguing for many years about this very question. Is our neighbour a fellow Jew, or one sympathetic to the Jewish faith, or anyone? The Jews and Samaritans were enemies – in fact some Jews called Samaritans 'dogs'. So Jesus teaches us that our neighbour includes everyone – even those we do not like, perhaps of another race or tribe. If you would like to imagine the story (see the introduction), the road from Jerusalem to Jericho passes through very dry, arid country with twists and turns and rocky hills – ideal for an ambush. The story is about loving our neighbour, but we must not forget the first commandment. Let us ask God to give us a deeper love for him and we will find that we love others more.

† *Heavenly Father, help us to follow the example of the good Samaritan in loving and caring for all who are in need.*

KING DAVID THE SINNER   The full story is told in chapter 11. David, even though he has wives and concubines already, lusts after Bathsheba, the wife of Uriah, a loyal officer. Bathsheba becomes pregnant. David attempts a cover-up but this fails. So he sends a message to the general, Joab, to put Uriah into the frontline of the battle. Uriah is killed and David gets Bathsheba. David breaks four of the ten commandments! Imagine you are at court when Nathan approaches David. Imagine the approval of the bystanders when David condemns the rich man – and then the gasp of horror and utter silence at Nathan's words.

> **Nathan said to David, 'You are the man.**   **(verse 7)**

Notice that Nathan does not accuse David directly, but cleverly gets David to condemn himself. The Bible is not afraid to show up its heroes' weaknesses as well as their strengths. Kings of nearby states would have got away with that kind of conduct but the Jews had standards which other countries did not have.

For Israel, God was in charge – even of kings.

† *Lord, help us to see our sins clearly and to be truly sorry for them.*

Wednesday July 10   Luke 24:1–12

THE STORY OF THE EMPTY TOMB

'He is not here; he has risen!'   **(verse 6a)**

Belief in the resurrection did not come easily even to those closest to Jesus. The women were puzzled and afraid. The apostles thought that what the women said was nonsense – but at least Peter went to see for himself. The best way to learn from this story is to put yourself in the place of one of the people: Mary, Joanna, Peter. Imagine the garden that first Easter morning – everything hushed as dawn breaks. See the stone rolled away – what can have happened? Hear the angels and let their words sink deeply into your heart. Then face the questioning and unbelief of the apostles as you tell your story. Or think of Peter. Imagine yourself out of breath as you reach the tomb. What thoughts go through your mind when you see the tomb empty and the grave cloths lying by themselves? The apostles really believed only when they actually saw their risen Lord. We too need to find the living presence of Jesus in our own lives for our faith to become real.

† *Father, grant that I may know Jesus ever more fully as my risen Lord. Help me to share this truth with others.*

Thursday July 11   Matthew 28:11–14

THE SOLDIERS' STORY

They gave the soldiers a large sum of money.   **(verse 12b)**

The chief priests had to have some explanation about what had happened, so they bribed the soldiers. Don't be too hard on the soldiers! They would be members of the temple guard. Their jobs and the welfare of their families would depend on doing what they were told. And, naturally, they wouldn't mind the extra money! Also they themselves could not be certain what had happened. What would you have done if you had been in their place? After all, dead men do not come back to life – you're a soldier and you know it. Should you ever accept a bribe – even if your children are going hungry? Can we trust Jesus to see that things work out all right if we stick to what is true? A hard question! But can anyone who tells lies really have an easy conscience? Let's hope that one or two of the soldiers did realise the truth and join the Christians despite the cost.

† *Dear Father, help all those who are tempted to cover up the truth for money. Help me to resist the temptation to lie.*

Friday July 12   **Acts 2:22–24, 32–38**

ONLY 9 O'CLOCK IN THE MORNING!   The Holy Spirit can work wonders even early in the morning! Imagine you are in the crowd listening to Peter – what would you feel? Many years ago, I was at a conference centre in England and was told a story about the Chaplain, who had spoken to a roomful of young people. It seemed a fairly ordinary address, but there was much prayer behind it. Suddenly the Holy Spirit touched the hearts of the young people. They started to cry, wanting to follow Jesus. The leaders sent the teenagers to bed, afraid that some might be too emotional. But early the next morning, there were queues outside the rooms of the leaders – young people wanting to find forgiveness and give their lives to Jesus! It is the Holy Spirit who inspires both our speaking and the hearts of those who listen.

'And you will receive the gift of the Holy Spirit.' (verse 38)

The following verse underlines that this gift is available to everyone: 'The promise is for you and your children ... for all whom the Lord our God will call' (*verse 39*).

† *Heavenly Father, please fill me more and more with your Holy Spirit so that I may play my part in building up your kingdom.*

Saturday July 13   **Psalm 19:1–4**

DAY AND NIGHT WITNESS TO GOD   Notice again (as in David's song of lament which we read last Sunday) the parallelism found in all Hebrew poetry – that is, the thought of one line is repeated in different words in the next line. It is this which makes Hebrew poetry such as the Psalms so strong and appealing:

The heavens declare the glory of God;
    the skies proclaim the work of his hands.   **(verse 1)**

Look up to the sky and let your heart be filled with praise. And

at night, when the stars are shining brightly, look up in awe –
God created all that. No words are needed – just a lifting of our
hearts to God. Not easy, though, when the sun shines brightly
for months, crops fail, and people are hungry. Or when the rain
never stops, rivers flood and crops are ruined. How can people
who are suffering in that way praise God? Are these times
really God's will? But God is not responsible for global
warming and changes in climate caused by the selfishness of
wealthy nations. If only those of us in industrial countries
would stop polluting the world so much and share our
resources, there would be far fewer natural disasters and
enough for everyone.

† *Father, give us open and caring hearts, that those who are unable to
see your glory in the heavens because of hunger or hopelessness
may find enough for their needs and the knowledge that you do care
for everyone.*

For group discussion and personal thought

- Imagine Jesus telling the story of the Good Samaritan to
  your local congregation today. Who would be the Samaritan
  (i.e. what tribe, race or group)? What implications does this
  have for you?
- To what extent is your faith in the resurrection of Jesus based
  on your experience of the risen Lord? Is Jesus truly among
  you?

DIFFERENT WAYS OF LEARNING 4
Learning through precepts

Notes by Borlabi Bortey

based on the New International Version

Borlabi Bortey is a minister of the Methodist Church Ghana. He works as General Manager for Asempa Publishers, the publishing house of the Christian Council of Ghana.

Rules and regulations are indispensable tools for ensuring the maintenance of peace and order in human society. One of the principal tools of governance employed by governments all over the world is the enactment of legislation. Rules are essential for learning to observe the norms of society and for shaping our conduct. This week's readings show us how the scriptures, and the laws of God revealed in them, serve as precepts – principles for good conduct – which help us to learn to do what God expects of us.

Text for the week: Isaiah 2:3

Sunday July 14   **Matthew 9:9–13**

RECOGNISING THE NEED TO LEARN   Jesus' willingness to relate to all classes of people was a shocking revelation for the Pharisees, who could not help questioning the disciples about Jesus' strange behaviour.

> **'Why does your teacher eat with tax collectors and "sinners"?' On hearing this, Jesus said, 'It is not the healthy who need a doctor, but the sick. But go and learn what this means: "I desire mercy, not sacrifice." For I have not come to call the righteous, but sinners.'**   **(verses 11b – 13)**

Jesus challenged the Pharisees to reflect on the meaning of a well-known prophetic saying on mercy and sacrifice. The Pharisees could miss the import of this saying because they were confident about their own position on how a religious person should behave: ritual observance, to them, was more important than relationships. A closed mind cannot discover anything new from familiar terrain. However, when we realise that it is always possible to learn, even from those we least expect can teach us anything, we can discover new and refreshing truths which can change our attitudes, perceptions and values. Unless we appreciate the need to be open to learning new truths, we shall probably – like the Pharisees in Jesus' time – miss opportunities for exciting discoveries.

† *Lord Jesus, grant us the humility to be willing to learn whenever and wherever your truth is revealed.*

Monday July 15   Isaiah 2:1–4

LEARNING THE WAYS OF GOD The law of God is an indispensable means for us, humankind, to discern how God wants us to behave towards each other in his world. Isaiah looked forward to a time when human beings will eagerly search for God.

'He will teach us his ways,
  so that we may walk in his paths.'
The law will go out from Zion,
  the word of the LORD from Jerusalem...
They will beat their swords into ploughshares
  and their spears into pruning hooks.
Nation will not take up sword against nation,
  nor will they train for war any more.
                              (part of verses 3 and 4)

For Isaiah, an inevitable outcome when human beings are taught the ways of the Lord, is that conflicts will be banished from our world. The resources we waste on weapons for destroying ourselves will be channelled into more productive ventures for eliminating hunger from the world. How can we contribute towards the realisation of this vision from Isaiah? We must help the world – the whole of humanity – to see how much we shall gain if we learn to live by the laws of God as revealed to us in the scriptures. We must work and pray for a time when learning the ways of God will become an urgent desire for all nations and people.

† *Lord, we pray for the time when 'war shall be no more, and lust, oppression, crime shall flee thy face before', when all people everywhere will learn to live by your law.*

WE MUST TEACH BY PRECEPT AS WELL AS BY EXAMPLE We learn best through the things we do. It is said that 'practice makes perfect'; many disciplines are best learnt through constant practice. Children learn best by imitating what they see and hear. How confusing then, for a learner, when a teacher's behaviour or practice contradicts what he tells his learners to do. This is the dilemma experienced by those who listened to the teachers of the law and the Pharisees.

> **Then Jesus said to the crowds and to his disciples: 'The teachers of the law and the Pharisees sit in Moses' seat. So you must obey them and do everything they tell you. But do not do what they do, for they do not practise what they preach.'**   **(verses 1–3)**

It is said that 'actions speak louder than words'. The challenge we face as the Church and as Christians in the modern world is to *demonstrate* the love of God, rather than *talk* about it as a precept from God. The world needs to see love rather than hear about love. Precept and example must go hand in hand to reinforce each other. So in every community the Church, as well as individual Christians, must take the lead in challenging oppressive structures and dehumanising systems by offering some practical support to the oppressed and marginalised people in our societies.

✝ *Lord, help us to learn the precepts you teach us in the scriptures, so that we can demonstrate them in our daily conduct.*

LEARNING TO OVERCOME SIN Today's reading is a song dedicated to extolling the virtues of the laws of God. The psalmist is excited by what he discovers in the word of God and this stirs him to express joy and praise to God.

> **I will praise you with an upright heart**
> **as I learn your righteous laws...**
> **How can a young man keep his way pure?**
> **By living according to your word ...**
> **I have hidden your word in my heart**
> **that I might not sin against you ...**
> **I rejoice in following your statutes**
> **as one rejoices in great riches.**   **(verses 7, 9, 11 and 14)**

From his study of the word of God, the psalmist has discovered a formula for overcoming sin and he enthusiastically recommends this to his readers: purity of life or righteous living is possible when we make the word of God the guiding principle in every aspect of our daily life. This comes through *internalising* the word of God – allowing God's laws to fill our hearts (direct our will) and fill our minds (direct our thinking). The word of God is a powerful weapon for overcoming sin. We can appropriate its benefits for ourselves through diligent study, so that the principles for life which God teaches us through his word become ingrained in us.

† *Divine word of God, abide in me always to keep me in the paths of righteousness which glorify your holy name.*

Thursday July 18   **Ecclesiastes 12:9**

LEARNING THROUGH PROVERBS The writer of Ecclesiastes is introduced to readers as the Teacher (see *1:1*). In today's reading we learn that the teacher used proverbs as one of the means by which 'he imparted knowledge to the people':

> **Not only was the Teacher wise, but also he imparted knowledge to the people. He pondered and searched out and set in order many proverbs.** **(verse 9)**

All over the world, proverbs are regarded as effective means for communication. However, in societies like Africa, which are dominated by oral culture, proverbs assume an even greater significance. They enable the people to preserve traditional philosophies, values, knowledge, ethics and morals. The mark of a good African linguist (the spokesman for a chief) is his ability to use proverbs: to communicate profound truths in a few words which are easy to remember because of the symbolic and graphic images in which they are expressed. The Bible celebrates the value of proverbs by dedicating a whole book to a collection of them. Proverbs can enable us to know God better: a Ghanaian proverb, for example, expresses God's invisibility and omnipresence: 'If you want to speak to God, speak to the winds.'

† *Heavenly Father, thank you for the gift of language and for the wisdom you impart to us through the gift of proverbs.*

KNOWING THE NATURE OF GOD The Exodus account of God giving the Ten Commandments to Israel shows that God took the initiative in revealing these laws. Similarly, in today's reading we have an account of God's self-revelation to Moses.

> **And he passed in front of Moses, proclaiming, 'The LORD, the LORD, the compassionate and gracious God, slow to anger, abounding in love and faithfulness, maintaining love to thousands, and forgiving wickedness, rebellion and sin. Yet he does not leave the guilty unpunished; he punishes the children and their children for the sin of the fathers to the third and fourth generation.' (verses 6 and 7)**

Can we know who God is? Moses' own intelligence could not discover who God is. Knowing God is a gift from God. Thank God that he is so willing to make himself known to us through his self-revelation recorded in the scriptures. From the recorded experience of Moses we learn what God is like: he is loving as well as just; he forgives our sins, but also punishes us when we go wrong. The deeper our understanding of the nature of God, the better we are able to respond to him in the true worship and praise which are best seen in obedience.

† *Heavenly Father, we thank you for the gift of the scriptures, through which we get to know who you are and so can worship you as we ought.*

RULES FOR GOOD NEIGHBOURLINESS The Ten Commandments are traditionally summed up as two commandments: love God and love your neighbour (see *Luke 10:27*). These two commands are inseparable and represent two sides of the same coin: true love for God is best expressed in how we relate to those we encounter in our day-to-day activities.

> **'You shall not murder.**
> **You shall not commit adultery.**
> **You shall not steal.**
> **You shall not give false testimony against your neighbour.**
> **You shall not covet your neighbour's wife. You shall not set your desire on your neighbour's house or land, his manservant or maidservant, his ox or donkey, or anything that belongs to your neighbour.'**   **(verses 17–21)**

The commandments teach us to avoid conduct which can mar relationships and create tension in society. We can live in peace if we avoid offending or hurting our neighbours. However, Jesus' emphasis on love is more positive: it is not enough merely not to hurt your neighbour; we must be concerned for each other's welfare and look for opportunities to show love and service to our neighbours and actively promote their wellbeing. Trying to do good effectively to your neighbour is the best way of resisting the temptation to break the divine laws.

† *Lord, fill our hearts with your love that we may learn to do good to all people and promote peace in our world.*

For group discussion and personal thought

- What should be the relationship between precept and example?
- How can we ensure that we live by the precepts (the ways of the Lord) that we learn from the scriptures?

DIFFERENT WAYS OF LEARNING 5
Learning by doing

Notes By Philip Wetherell

based on the Revised Standard Version

Philip Wetherell is the director of Christians Abroad, an ecumenical agency working to encourage people to find their place in international mission and development work. Previously he led the overseas personnel section of the United Society for the Propagation of the Gospel, worked as a missionary teacher in Namibia, and directed a Religious Education Centre in the south of England.

It is said that we learn only a small amount from what we read (be warned!), more from what we see, but the most from what we do or take part in. Those who heard Jesus (or Paul for that matter) were lucky to have heard, seen and been part of the greatest revolution in learning. But, as we shall see, the book-wise found the revolution hard to take because its basis was not logic but action.

Text for the week: Matthew 11:28–30

Sunday July 21   **Matthew 11:25–30**

LEARNING BY BEING SIMPLE? In a family discussion, when perhaps we have been going round in circles or not saying what we really think, it is often a child who says something clear and direct which brings us to our senses. Jesus was also aware of this. He invites everyone who is worn down by the cares of the world – but the 'wise' refuse the invitation because they cannot appreciate the real nature of God in Jesus. He is gentle and humble-hearted, and the way to God is to become like him:

> 'Come to me, all who labour and are heavy-laden, and I will give you rest. Take my yoke upon you, and learn from me; for I am gentle and lowly in heart, and you will find rest for your souls. For my yoke is easy, and my burden is light.'
> **(verses 28–30)**

The 'un-learned' – the simple – can learn what is truly important by casting their load on Jesus. To learn about Jesus requires us to give up our dependence on ourselves and our home-grown wisdom and instead become vulnerable and open to new things. The wise, in their arrogance, set themselves apart and continue to argue about the meaning of past events, rules and regulations. The 'simple' have open minds – the most important characteristic of real learning.

✝ *O Lord, help me to have an open mind, to put aside all barriers that stop me from being vulnerable – so that I can bear your lighter yoke.*

Monday July 22   Psalm 111:10

LEARNING BY FEAR? Fear is part of our survival instinct: dark places can be dangerous, and it is sometimes right to fear the unknown. We may be afraid of illness, old age and dying; or, according to our circumstances, of civil war, hunger or unemployment. Fear can educate us: as we grow up we learn that fire is dangerous. Fear also affects our decisions: when we get older we learn to mistrust politicians who promise us everything. We get wise to such people. So it is sometimes wise to be fearful – but isn't it going too far to say that fear is the beginning of wisdom itself?

> **The fear of the LORD is the beginning of wisdom;**
>   **a good understanding have all those who practise it.**
> **His praise endures for ever!**   **(verse 10)**

If God were human we would be right to be afraid of his power and how he might misuse it. But God is love. How can we be afraid of love? There is no need – this 'fear' is different. It means all that we feel in the presence of God – the effect God has on us if we give him his due. It needs a positive decision. It gives God his worth. It is worship – and what can be wiser than that? That is true understanding.

✝ *O Lord, let me be truly fearful of you, worship you and praise you in everything I do.*

Tuesday July 23   Ephesians 4:17–24

LEARN A LIVING PERSON   I have good friends who would not want to be called Christian, but they are good and kind people who would be deeply offended at the suggestion made here that they are pagans who are

alienated from the life of God ... they have become callous and have given themselves up to licentiousness.
(part of verses 18–19)

In their own lives my friends are clearly not like that. But as Christians we are told here to give up living like them in a supposed life of vice, and instead to 'learn Christ'. What difference will it make? What difference would it make to my good and kind friends to 'learn Christ'? How would they change? Do my Christian friends behave any better? The clue is in the nature of what is being learned. Christ is not a book, an idea, or even a way of life. Christ is a living person, alive and with us. By learning Christ we are

renewed in the spirit of [our] minds, and put on the new nature, created after the likeness of God in true righteousness and holiness. **(verses 23–24)**

Christ not only taught a new law, but lived it. To learn Christ is to become part of a life with different motives and ideals, and to act from an abandonment to God's will. It is to have the freedom to act as a result of that new nature and not from human motives, however good they may be. It is to abandon human goodness and give ourselves over to God's direction. Far harder than being a good pagan!

† *Lord, help me to learn Christ and to abandon myself to your will.*

Wednesday July 24   **Hebrews 5:1–10**

OBEDIENCE LEARNED IN SUFFERING Armies, some religions, some churches, and some families work as units because members obey their leaders, almost without question. Otherwise, they fall apart. In traditional Christian marriage services, the new bride is required to be obedient. In some families violence was (and still is) used to force obedience – and for many years in many cultures, the more powerful members of society (usually male) saw this as an essential tradition. Some people still see God as that kind of powerful figure: he must be obeyed, and if this means suffering, well, pain was good enough for Jesus so it must be good for us too.

In the days of his flesh, Jesus offered up prayers and supplications, with loud cries and tears, to him who was

able to save him from death, and he was heard for his godly fear. Although he was a Son, he learned obedience through what he suffered. **(verses 7–8)**

But there is a difference. Jesus' suffering was not imposed, to maintain superiority and obedience through fear. This is the action of the Son who is equal to his Father, who voluntarily accepted the suffering of becoming human. He lived through the double agony of seeing people misunderstand and fail him and the physical suffering of voluntary death. This, he learned, was the only way of hope for the rest of us. It was an act of love, which obedience imposed from above can never be.

† *Lord, help me to be prepared to love enough, and give all that is demanded of us for your sake.*

Thursday July 25   John 7:14–17

KNOW WITHOUT LEARNING?   We dislike the 'know-alls': the people who have done it or seen it or heard it before we have – and tell us so; the people who 'know' they are right. In this story, the opponents of Jesus seem to suggest that he is such a person; he has no learning or qualifications and therefore no right to stand up and spout his opinions. That is the job for those who have studied long and hard. Jealous and concerned about their own position as teachers, they wonder how they can deal with this upstart:

About the middle of the feast Jesus went up into the temple and taught. The Jews marvelled at it, saying, 'How is it that this man has learning, when he has never studied?' **(verses 14–15)**

This man is arrogant as well – he claims his teaching comes from God who is his Father! But his opponents dare not put his teaching to the moral test: anyone who does the will of God will know that Jesus' teaching is from God; so if they say that this teaching is not from God, they are also saying that they themselves do not know or obey God's will. No wonder they attack him, not for his learning, but for the fact that he had no teacher. But they get it wrong again:

'My teaching is not mine, but his who sent me.' **(verse 16)**

† *Lord, help me to know what is from God, and to do the will of him who sent Jesus.*

DEEDS AND NOT WORDS   Today we have instant news, radio and television replays and journalists who dig deep into the private lives of politicians. As a result, we have far less respect for our leaders. Our politicians are 'packaged' by marketing people and seem to speak only the words which will catch the next news headlines. 'Sound-bite' and 'news-speak' are the only ways they can catch our attention. The fine words and oratory which, we are told, characterised the great preachers and leaders of previous generations don't work any more. Is it just the effects of our technological age – or are we tired of words? We may have some sympathy with those in Jesus' time who wanted to see action, not words. Jesus has perhaps sensed this:

> **'If I am not doing the works of my Father, then do not believe me; but if I do them, even though you do not believe me, believe the works, that you may know and understand that the Father is in me and I am in the Father.'**
> **(verses 37–38)**

For many people who look at our faith from the outside, the test is the same as for the politicians. Do the fine words mean anything? Are they matched by how we act? How do we live out our faith?

✝ *Lord, help me to live out my faith, so that others may see the truth in works and word.*

LEARNING BY FAITH   The Christians in Galatia were what we might call middle class – the sort of people who might live in the university area of a modern town. They were educated and sophisticated – but they were foolish.

> **O foolish Galatians! Who has bewitched you ... ? Let me ask you only this: Did you receive the Spirit by works of the law, or by hearing with faith? Are you so foolish?**
> **(parts of verses 1–3)**

Paul's preaching had led them to an experience of the Spirit which made their detailed, piece by piece discussion of fragments of Old Testament law seem insignificant. Learning is important – Paul was 'learned' himself and could argue with the best of them. But compared with what the Spirit brings, learning is nothing. The Spirit comes when we hear with faith. No exams are needed.

Does he who supplies the Spirit to you and works miracles among you do so by works of the law, or by hearing with faith?
(verse 5)

The miracles and the experience are real. We learn by what happens to us and to those we meet as the Spirit works in us all – preaching, healing, befriending, leading, praying. Learning is part of this, but it is only one experience of God at work planting the possibility of faith in us – if we care to listen.

† *Lord, help me to listen to your Spirit, that I may come to a true faith and bring others to know you.*

For group discussion and personal thought

- How much does our 'learning' prevent us from true understanding?
- How important to you is your experience of Jesus, compared with what you read about him?
- Do our friends know we are Christians because of our deeds or because of what we say?

DIFFERENT WAYS OF LEARNING 6
Learning through worship

Notes by Aileen Khoo

based on the New International Version

Aileen Khoo has worked in the Methodist Church in Malaysia for 28 years. Currently she is Director of Christian Education at Trinity Methodist Church, Petaling Jaya. She particularly enjoys leading Bible studies, especially experimenting in participatory Bible study methods.

As the people of God we gather to face up to ourselves and to one another, to hear the word of God, to call to remembrance who we are, to celebrate the God from whom all blessings flow and to fellowship with one another. These acts of worship are made more meaningful through our orderly participation and God-inspired demeanour. Our worship can be described thus:

> To worship rightly is to love each other,
> Each smile a hymn, each kindly deed a prayer.
> (from 'O Brother Man' by J G Whittier)

Text for the week: Isaiah 6:5

Sunday July 28   Isaiah 6:1–9a

CONFESSION IN WORSHIP

'Woe to me!' I cried. 'I am ruined! For I am a man of unclean lips, and I live among a people of unclean lips, and my eyes have seen the King, the LORD Almighty.' (verse 5)

The king is dead. Isaiah may have gone to the temple to pray for the departed king, but he meets the King of kings. Some of us are deeply religious and come to worship regularly, but only practise the outward rituals of religion until one day we are surprised to meet God face to face. When we stand before the holy God we realise our sins and inadequacies, we are changed and made ready for guidance. When we confess our failure to obey, God forgives, renews and empowers us for service. Repentance is more than just feeling sorry for our wrong-doings, it is more than reform in worship. It is turning back to God, placing the Lord first in all our ways. This requires a radical change. Worship is not merely a matter of hearing truth and receiving a message; it is being encountered by God and gripped by God. Our acts of worship are significant only in so far as they include true repentance and a desire to do God's will.

† *Keep your promise, Lord, and forgive my sins, for they are many. (Psalm 25:11, GNB).*

Monday July 29 — Luke 4:14–30

PROCLAMATION IN WORSHIP   Worship in Judaism took two forms in Jesus' day: worship through sacrifices in the temple, and worship in the synagogue where men studied and discussed the law and taught the tradition to the children. Jesus was deeply rooted in the Jewish tradition. His parents brought him up so that worship and teaching/learning from Scripture were his way of life.

He went to Nazareth, where he had been brought up, and on the Sabbath day he went into the synagogue, as was his custom. (verse 16)

All too often at worship services we know the familiar stories, but do not want to be reminded of them. The good news is sometimes bad news for us because we are reluctant to face the truth or be obedient to it. We get angry when we hear things we don't want to hear. We react negatively to criticism. Sometimes we don't want to listen in case God asks us to do something we don't really want to do. But Jesus spoke with authority and those who are willing to listen will hear the secrets of the Kingdom. Proclamation in worship is the Emmanuel event – the event of God-with-us. It is God communicating to us and in communion with us.

† *Teach me, Lord, the meaning of your laws, and I will obey them at all times. (Psalm 119:33, GNB)*

Tuesday July 30 — 1 Corinthians 11:17–33

FELLOWSHIP IN WORSHIP   Paul wrote several letters to this very troublesome church, which lacked fellowship, love and concern. There was constant bickering within the church and division among them. In those days the Lord's Supper was a love feast with a full meal. The wealthy arrived first and ate up the best! Late-comers and servants were left with nothing to eat. Paul was shocked and angry at their arrogant and undisciplined behaviour.

> **When you come together, it is not the Lord's Supper you eat, for as you eat, each of you goes ahead without waiting for anybody else. One remains hungry, another gets drunk.**
> **(verses 20–21)**

Paul reminds them that the Lord's Supper is a means of Christian fellowship. 'Do this in remembrance of me', said Jesus. What do we remember about Jesus? We remember his character and teachings, and proclaim his death until he comes again. Don't come with arrogance and hatred but with humility, penitence and love. Wait for one another and make the Lord's Supper truly a love feast, the main meal where the whole family of God gathers together. In fact, every meal ought to be a holy communion where you celebrate your love for God and for each other.

† *Praise the Lord, all nations!*
Praise him, all peoples!
His love for us is strong
And his faithfulness is eternal. (Psalm 117, GNB)

Wednesday July 31   **Deuteronomy 26:1–11**

REMEMBRANCE IN WORSHIP What made the Hebrew faith was the stories that were passed on in every Jewish home: Remember! Give thanks! We give thanks because we remember what God has done for us. The offering of the first fruits is an essential part of the covenant people. It is the mark of belonging to God. Both the Old and New Testaments emphasise the tithe as the standard of faithful worship.

> **He brought us to this place and gave us this land, a land flowing with milk and honey; and now I bring the firstfruits of the soil that you, O LORD, have given me.**
> **(verses 9–10a)**

At worship we gather to remember who and whose we are and to give thanks. Proportionate giving, regular offerings and joyous worship characterise Christian worship. Thanksgiving is a way of life, not something that Christians do only occasionally. The person who remembers is the person who is grateful. Remembering is also a means of affirming and reaffirming our faith. Part of remembering is to remember collectively. The task of community recall is an unending recital of the faith lest we forget. Remember it, teach it to your children! When this happens, memory becomes a vision. We remember to give thanks – we remember, we give thanks!

† *I will remember your great deeds, Lord;*
I will recall the wonders you did in the past.
I will think about all that you have done;
I will meditate on all your mighty acts.

(Psalm 77:11–12, GNB)

Thursday August 1   **Genesis 22:9–13**

OFFERING IN WORSHIP God wanted Abraham to be willing to offer up the one thing dear to him. Is Abraham willing to do that? God made a discovery:

Now I know that you fear God, because you have not withheld from me your son, your only son.'   **(verse 12b)**

The story tells us that God provided the lamb for the burnt offering. God did not want to bankrupt the people. God just wanted the people to be generous with their giving. God wants a grateful heart – our best. Offering is what we make of our lives, not something we take. Worship demands our whole self, as Isaac Watts wrote in the last stanza of his hymn 'When I Survey the Wondrous Cross':

Were the whole realm of nature mine,
That were an offering far too small;
Love so amazing, so divine,
Demands my soul, my life, my all.

Worship demands a complete response to the love of God. The sacrifice God wants is a living sacrifice. When the Son of God was offered, there was no lamb in the thicket to be offered as a substitute.

† *I call to you, Lord, help me now!*
Listen to me when I call to you.
Receive my prayer as incense,
my uplifted hands as an evening sacrifice.

(Psalm 141:1–2, GNB)

Friday August 2   **1 Corinthians 14:26–32**

ORDERLY PARTICIPATION IN WORSHIP The increasing popularity of spectator sports seems to be a sign of our times.

But the biggest spectator sport of them all has been around for a long time – the traditional Sunday morning worship. Too often, we have gone to see others 'perform' and been content to be anonymous 'spectators', taking a back seat. When the early disciples assembled for corporate worship, they did not 'go to church'. They *were* the Church.

When you come together, everyone has a hymn, or a word of instruction, a revelation, a tongue or an interpretation. All of these must be done for the strengthening of the church.
(verse 26)

Liturgy is meant to be a corporate action – one in which we, together with the ministers, share, co-operate and participate in a common experience. This makes us a community of believers. Order, decorum, decency and mutual respect are important in the corporate body of Christ. The Spirit of God works in an orderly way, building up the Church, edifying the community of believers. Sometimes we become spiritually arrogant, thinking we have the truth, the better way; but love is the answer, the sign of spiritual maturity.

† *Fill us each morning with your constant love,*
  so that we may sing and be glad all our life. (Psalm 90:14, GNB)

Saturday August 3   **2 Samuel 6:15–23**

CELEBRATION IN WORSHIP   David brought the ark of the covenant back to Jerusalem with great ceremony. To celebrate this event he danced:

David, wearing a linen ephod, danced before the LORD with all his might, while he and the entire house of Israel brought up the ark of the LORD with shouts and the sound of trumpets.
(verses 14–15)

Worship is always an act of celebration. In worship we pay homage and reverence to God, because of who God is and what God has done for us and for the world. Christian worship celebrates what God has done in Christ, who has given hope and new life. It celebrates the exciting, exhilarating assurance of a living Lord, in thanksgiving for the life God gave us. Just as David gave a loaf of bread, a cake of dates and a cake of raisins to each person in the whole crowd (*verse 19*), so worship celebrations should move us to feed the hungry and help the poor. J G Whittier expressed this in his hymn, 'O Brother Man':

The holier worship which he deigns to bless
Restores the lost, and binds the spirit broken,
And feeds the widow and the fatherless.

† *How good it is to give thanks to you, O LORD,*
to sing in your honour, O Most High God,
to proclaim your constant love every morning
and your faithfulness every night. (Psalm 92:1–2, GNB)

For group discussion and personal thought

- What characterises a vital, 'learning' congregation?
- How can we make the Holy Communion truly a time of fellowship?
- What means and opportunities do we have for remembrance as a part of worship?
- Is there a perfect structure in worship? How much freedom can we have in our order of worship?

UNCOMFORTABLE WORDS 1
Difficult texts

Notes by Peter Cotterell

based on the Good News Bible

Peter Cotterell is a Uniting Church parish minister in Wynyard, on the north-west coast of the beautiful island of Tasmania, Australia. Ordained in 1977, he has ministered in a number of rural parishes. He has also served the Uniting Church on local, regional, state and national committees and was Moderator of the Synod of Tasmania for 1993–95. Married to Sally, he has four young children.

There is a great deal of conflict and pain in our world. Throughout the Bible God's people respond honestly, though not always appropriately. In the midst of the pain our Lord reminds us of his presence and asks us to trust that his kingdom will prevail.

Text for the week: Genesis 22:14

Sunday August 4   **Genesis 22:1–14**

TERRIBLE TIMES OF TESTING As the father of four vibrant, healthy children I well remember the wonderful sense of anticipation that accompanied the birth of each of them. Abraham had to wait decades longer than I did for the birth of his 'child of promise', Isaac. Then God called him and commanded him to sacrifice this son, 'whom you love so much'; it came as a terrible test of his loyalty. How could God expect so much of him? Yet Abraham obeyed and made preparations. I'm not sure that I could have done the same.

Abraham made Isaac carry the wood for the sacrifice, and he himself carried a knife and live coals for starting the fire. As they walked along together, Isaac said, 'Father! ... I see that you have the coals and the wood, but where is the lamb for the sacrifice?' Abraham answered, 'God himself will provide one.' And the two of them walked on together.
(verses 6–8)

At the last moment God spared Isaac's life and provided a ram for the sacrifice. Abraham was not, in the end, required to offer his son. But God did! God offered his Son, our Lord Jesus, on the cross as a sacrifice for our sins.

✝ *Lord, thank you for the ultimate sacrifice which you made on our behalf.*

Monday August 5   2 Samuel 13:1–22

SOMETHING ROTTEN IN ISRAEL   I don't like this story! Amnon, King David's son, confused his lust with supposed love for his half-sister, Tamar, and destroyed her life in the process.

> **Then he said to her, 'Bring the cakes here to my bed and serve them to me yourself.' She took the cakes and went over to him ... he grabbed her and said, 'Come to bed with me!' 'No,' she said. 'Don't force me to do such a degrading thing! That's awful! How could I ever hold up my head in public again? And you – you would be completely disgraced in Israel. Please, speak to the king, and I'm sure that he will give me to you.' But he would not listen to her; and since he was stronger than she was, he overpowered her and raped her.**   **(verses 10 –14)**

I hate the very thought of rape! It is a monstrous crime! It is never an act of love, it is an inexcusable act of domination and violation. King David, though furious, was weak and did nothing to punish his shameful son. Absalom, Tamar's brother, was calculating in his anger and bided his time. After two years of waiting he murdered his half-brother and was subsequently murdered himself. The House of David was disintegrating. The sin which had not been dealt with immediately and appropriately had begun to destroy it from within like a cancer.

✝ *Lord, help us to recognise our sin, confess it and deal with it immediately before it works its destructive power.*

Tuesday August 6   Psalm 17:1–15

THE CONFIDENCE OF INNOCENCE   It is very rare for us to proclaim our innocence with complete confidence. There is usually some lurking doubt. Perhaps our motives are not as pure as we maintain, or perhaps we could have acted differently and avoided the pain. The psalmist, however, remains confident even before the searching gaze of the Lord.

You know my heart.
  You have come to me at night;
  you have examined me completely
  and found no evil desire in me.
I speak no evil as others do;
  I have obeyed your command
  and have not followed paths of violence.
I have always walked in your way
  and have never strayed from it.   (verses 3–5)

In his confidence the psalmist expects to be declared 'not guilty'
and delivered from his enemies. In the embarrassing honesty of
the scriptures, we then find his suppressed anger bubbling
over. He calls for the destruction of those same enemies, even
down to their children's children! Jesus, however, has shown us
a better way: though innocent and falsely accused, he forgave
his enemies from the cross.

† *Forgive us our sins as we forgive those who sin against us.*

Wednesday August 7   Joel 3:9–21

THE FUTURE IS THE LORD'S I remember driving between
Canberra and Melbourne and coming across a great swarm
of locusts. It was an amazing sight! Thousands upon
thousands of voracious insects ate their destructive way
across the countryside. When Joel saw a similar plague sweep
across Israel, he recognised the judgement of God upon his
people. Nations would come swarming and devour the land.
Joel also recognised that after the locust plague God would
renew the land. Joel anticipated that in the future these
nations would be judged. He mockingly reversed the words of
Isaiah and called upon the nations to gather for war in the
Valley of Judgement (*verses 10–13*), after which Israel would be
blessed.

'Then, Israel, you will know that I am the LORD your God.
  I live on Zion, my sacred hill.
Jerusalem will be a sacred city;
  foreigners will never conquer it again.
At that time the mountains will be covered with vineyards,
  and cattle will be found on every hill;
    there will be plenty of water for all the streams of Judah.
A stream will flow from the Temple of the LORD,
  and it will water the Valley of Acacia.'   (verses 17–18)

The war in the valley and the subsequent blessing of Israel did not happen in Joel's lifetime, which leads some scholars to suggest that Joel was mistaken; others suggest that this prophecy is still to come. One point, however, is agreed: the Lord our God is the Lord of all nations and the final arbiter of all history.

† *Lord, in these times when nations seem able to go their own destructive way, continue to remind us that all nations will bow before you, the Lord of all the earth.*

Thursday August 8   Mark 13:7–20

HOLD FAST TO THE END The Gospel of Mark was probably written in AD 68 or 69 at a time when the Judean revolutionaries (Zealots) were enjoying victories over the Romans. Mark anticipated that this success would be short-lived and that a time of terrifying war would follow in which the Romans ('The Awful Horror') would crush the rebellion and destroy Jerusalem. War is always terrible, especially for non-combatants: women and children. It is a time to flee to the hills.

'You will see "The Awful Horror" standing in the place where he should not be.' (Note to the reader: be sure to understand what this means!) 'Then those who are in Judea must run away to the hills. Someone who is on the roof of his house must not lose time by going down into the house to get anything to take with him. Someone who is in the field must not go back to the house for his cloak. How terrible it will be in those days for women who are pregnant and for mothers with little babies! Pray to God that these things will not happen in the winter!'

(verses 14–18)

In chapter 13 Mark encouraged his church (and ours) to stand fast for the non-violent way of Jesus in the face of such nationalistic fervour. Jesus' way would lead some people to be betrayed as 'traitors' by their own families. They were to trust in the ministry of the Holy Spirit among them and be encouraged to look beyond the present tensions to the future dawning of God's kingdom.

† *Lord, thank you for the gift of the Holy Spirit who leads us in the way of Jesus.*

HOW CAN WE SING? Grief can be a very deep and distressful experience. We cry out in our pain and the things which would normally bring us joy are sometimes avoided. In our grief we can often become very angry. The people of Israel were deeply hurt by their exile and expressed their grief and anger in terrible curses against Babylon, their captors.

> By the rivers of Babylon we sat down;
> there we wept when we remembered Zion ...
> How can we sing a song to the LORD
> in a foreign land? ...
> Babylon, you will be destroyed.
> Happy are those who pay you back
> for what you have done to us –
> who take your babies
> and smash them against a rock.   (verses 1, 4 and 8–9)

I have found that it is OK to be angry and cry out in our pain. God understands and bears with us patiently. He whispers gently to our spirit, comforting us and reminding us of his presence. As the pain eases he also reminds us that there is a better way, and through the resurrection of Jesus Christ he offers hope and life.

† *Lord, comfort the sorrowing, the angry, the bewildered and the dying with your gentle embrace and tender whispers.*

APOCALYPTIC IMAGES   I love political cartoons! They are often clever, witty and to the point, using symbols or images with a minimum of words. However, the reader needs to know the context or background to appreciate them fully. Apocalyptic writings, such as Daniel and Revelation, have much the same characteristics. They use symbols and images like a code which is understood by the reader. Apocalyptic letters were written first and foremost to encourage the Church to stand fast in times of persecution.

> Then a great and mysterious sight appeared in the sky. There was a woman, whose dress was the sun and who had the moon under her feet and a crown of twelve stars on her head. She was soon to give birth ... Another mysterious sight appeared in the sky. There was a huge red dragon with seven heads and ten horns and a crown on each of his

heads ... He stood in front of the woman, in order to eat her child as soon as it was born. Then she gave birth to a son, who will rule over all nations with an iron rod. But the child was snatched away and taken to God and his throne.
(parts of verses 1–5)

Who is this woman? She is not Mary the mother of Jesus but the true Israel from whom the promised Messiah was to come. Who is the red dragon? The age-old enemy of God's people, reminiscent of Daniel's beast. From the beginning he threatens the very existence of the Christ Child who will 'rule over nations with an iron rod'. But the Christ is victorious, a reminder that the purposes of God cannot be overthrown, no matter how threatening the circumstances. God will prevail! Hallelujah!

† *Lord, in these troubled times we are again reminded that your purposes will prevail. Praise be to the Lord!*

For group discussion and personal thought

- Have you ever been tempted to depart from your faith in Jesus Christ? Or do you know of someone who has? What circumstances brought this about?
- How have you been most encouraged to 'hold fast your faith'?

UNCOMFORTABLE WORDS 2
Difficult sayings

Notes by Tom Arthur

based on the New Revised Standard Version

Tom Arthur, an American Presbyterian, was recruited from his home denomination to serve three churches on a large Cardiff council estate. After nine years as minister of Weoley Hill Church in Birmingham, England, he is now back in Cardiff, where he serves as minister of City United Reformed Church, together with his Dutch wife Marieke and the youngest of the three children they adopted when first in Wales.

I have a large collection of books and tapes that attempt to teach me Dutch. One time I came home with a book titled *Dutch Without Pain*. My father-in-law saw it, shook his head, and said, 'Ach! There is no Dutch without pain.' And so it is with the gospel. The good news is supposed to be comforting. But it can also be very un-comforting, challenging, even threatening. It nevertheless remains good news. These texts, our second set of 'uncomfortable words', are like doorways into a new world, invitations to anguish and discomfort that lead paradoxically to joy. Be not afraid. In the end it will be like being able to speak with your spouse, for the first time, in a language you both understand.

Text for the week: Luke 9:23

Sunday August 11   **Matthew 19:16–26**

ALL OR NOTHING   The exam was to be a series of short quotations from the Shakespeare plays we had been studying. We were to write analytical comments on as many as we could get through in an hour. 'Sir,' I asked, 'Will these be significant quotations?' I will never forget my embarrassment as Professor Forker leaned forward over the lectern to remind me of what should have been obvious: 'Mr Arthur, *everything* in Shakespeare is significant!' The young man in today's reading asks what he has to do to get eternal life. Keep the commandments, Jesus says. Which ones? And when Jesus lists a representative string of commandments, the young man protests that he has kept these since youth. Jesus says to him,

> **'If you wish to be perfect, go, sell your possessions, and give the money to the poor, and you will have treasure in heaven; then come, follow me.'** (verse 21)

Ah! This the young man can't do. It is harder to get a rich man into heaven than it is to get a Mercedes through a revolving door. The problem with rich people is that, like me, they think they can divide their lives into compartments, doing just what is necessary to be 'good', and leaving the rest of life unquestioned. This isn't the way it works. God wants you to be totally engaged by his love for the world, so that all the dark corners of your life are transformed by it, just as Professor Forker invited me to be passionately overwhelmed by the whole of Shakespeare.

✝ *God of my salvation, take all of me.*

Monday August 12   Luke 9.23–27

LETTING GO   What does it profit you to gain the world but lose your soul? In a cartoon, a minister asks a wealthy parishioner this very question. Without missing a beat, the parishioner answers with scrupulous accuracy: 'Twenty-three billion, four hundred and seventy-six million, five hundred and thirty-four thousand, seven hundred and twenty-four dollars and seventy-three cents.' 'Let me put it another way,' the minister says... The hard facts of our market-dominated life can overwhelm us. But Jesus says the real hard facts are just the opposite.

> **For those who want to save their life will lose it, and those who lose their life for my sake will save it.** (verse 24)

We must learn to find our joy in giving, not taking. We must learn to be vulnerable. We must learn to die. Some won't. Some of those standing right there with Jesus would not risk dying before they could see the Son of Man coming in all his glory (*verse 27*). Some reading this will be just as reluctant to let go. But Jesus says that such vulnerability needs to be part of ordinary, everyday life.

✝ *Liberating Lord, help me to let go of what possesses me.*

Tuesday August 13   Luke 9:57–62

BREAKING AWAY   A few weeks ago I was sitting in the office of a regional director for Social Services. He was explaining to me that they had not been prepared for the increased demand last summer for residential care, both for children and elderly people. The increased demand, he said, had to do with family breakdown. I winced. Twelve years ago I answered a call to serve the United Reformed Church here in Britain, as a 'missionary' from the United States, leaving my mother at home alone. She is now 84, and increasingly frail. Will Social Services in her small town in Indiana be taking on her support in my absence? Jesus says, 'Don't look back.' It is hard not to, but Jesus is very, very clear about this.

'No one who puts a hand to the plough and looks back is fit for the kingdom of God.' (verse 62)

The churches more often emphasise what we like to call 'family values', focusing on our domestic responsibilities; they need to do this, given the prevalence of family disruption these days. But Jesus pushes us in the opposite direction, to leave the nest, to become independent adults, to discover our own creativity in responding to God's love. The transition is not easy to make. There is a sense in which following God's calling (which is, in the end, to be truly who we most deeply are) is like being a rebellious and rather irreverent teenager. Sometimes it just has to be that rough. But unless there are some people with the courage to break away from the cosy inwardness of family life, who will care for those who, inevitably, find themselves among the scraps of family breakdown? The Good Shepherd calls us to look after lost sheep. And it's not easy.

† *Lord, give me courage when I am perplexed.*

Wednesday August 14   **Mark 9:42–50**

ALL TOGETHER

'If your hand causes you to stumble, cut it off; it is better for you to enter life maimed than to have two hands and to go to hell, to the unquenchable fire.' (verse 43)

In some countries they actually do chop off the offending hands of thieves, and I imagine there are places where they pluck out the offending eyes of the inquisitive. I do not think Jesus is asking us to follow these instructions literally, any more than I think he is speaking of a literal 'hell' here, though many have taken this literally, too. The extreme language here carries the strength of Jesus' challenge to what it means to be 'whole'. If we think wholeness is merely a matter of having all our bits in good order, then we are woefully mistaken. While our contemporary ideas of healing and wholeness have more to do with the kind of personal wellbeing that can be developed at the health club, the biblical understanding of wholeness is being connected to other people and to God. Life is life together. Those bonds with one another give us our very identity as human beings; violating them leaves us more broken than if we were missing hands, feet, eyes. Some may think, as Jean-Paul Sartre said in *No Exit*, that hell is other people. For Jesus, hell is to be without them.

✝ *God my Father, following your Son I know that I am most whole when I am most broken.*

Thursday August 15   Matthew 10:34–39

PEACE AT LAST   When I was growing up there was a brand of tinned milk that was advertised as having come from 'contented cows'. Whether that made for better milk or not, it always seemed to me a perfect image of the Christian life: Sunday afternoon was always the laziest of afternoons. We were not to mow the lawn or wash the car or polish the floor on Sundays – just sit around reading comic books, or maybe play a slow game of baseball with the neighbouring kids. It was ever so peaceful, having been saved by grace. Somehow mother was always exempt from this forced indolence. She always provided roast chicken for Sunday dinner. But this is not the picture of Christian life given by Jesus. He is not bringing peace, he says.

> **'Whoever does not take up the cross and follow me is not worthy of me. Those who find their life will lose it, and those who lose their life for my sake will find it.'**
>
> **(verses 38–39)**

Jesus teaches us to be uncomfortable with a world where mothers don't get a Sabbath rest, to cite only one small example of an unjust world. Jesus teaches us to be uncomfortable with the way things are until the only place we can rest with any integrity is the cross – whatever that will be for us. To take up one's cross is to risk the pain of rejection in solidarity with all outcasts – those abandoned both by neighbour and by God. To take up one's cross is, perhaps paradoxically, to live in community sustained by God's love alone. If the biblical view of life is life together and the biblical view of death is total estrangement, then the cross is that strange place where life and death meet. This place may not be what you call peace. But it's what God calls peace.

† *Lord, may I be restless until I find my rest in you.*

Friday August 16   Mark 3.28–30

YES, YOU *CAN* BE FORGIVEN   When we look at the Bible's uncomfortable words, we need to differentiate between words that are uncomfortable because they are hard to follow and words that are uncomfortable because they are hard to understand. Certainly, when we read that Jesus says,

> **'Whoever blasphemes against the Holy Spirit can never have forgiveness'**   (verse 29)

we have double discomfort. Is there something that can never, ever be forgiven, even by the one who embodies for us the unqualified forgiveness of God? That is not a comfortable thought. But what is this unforgivable sin? I can't, comfortably, give a straightforward answer. Some say the unforgivable sin is to be a backslider, an apostate, to be one who questions previous convictions. Others say the unforgivable sin is to say that people can't change, that the broken can't be healed, that sinners can't be forgiven. The two interpretations seem to move in opposite directions. I prefer the latter. If I say I can't change, then that has pretty much destroyed any possibility of forgiveness, hasn't it? – no matter how much God wants to forgive me.

† *Forgive my trespasses, as I forgive those who have trespassed against me.*

Saturday August 17   Matthew 5:38–48

A FUNNY VALENTINE   Jesus teaches us to love our enemies.

> **'If you love those who love you, what reward do you have? Do not even the tax collectors do the same?'**   (verse 46)

When you think that the Mafia does better than anyone else in confining their love to insiders, some of the discomfort of this teaching begins to disappear. But only some of it, because most of us do not naturally love our enemies. Otherwise, they wouldn't be enemies, would they? There is nothing wrong with having enemies. It is natural not only to disagree with people but to bitterly oppose them. It is natural to want to resist those who force you into ways that you consider unethical, demeaning, or treacherous. But love, in the Bible, is something that can be commanded. It is an obligation to respect the humanity and dignity of the other person, even if there is violent disagreement. The great twentieth-century martyrs Gandhi, Martin Luther King, Jr, and Oscar Romero have shown us how to convert our enemies not by force but by turning the other cheek – by non-violent resistance. Loving one's enemies is a challenging, tough business. Are you ready for a real challenge? Or would you prefer something easier, something even the tax collectors can achieve?

† *Lord, as you have loved me even when I have set myself against you as an enemy, so may I love those from whom I am most estranged.*

For group discussion and personal thought

● Share experiences of overcoming pain or disorientation in a variety of situations, such as learning a language, resolving marital tensions, learning to be an attentive listener, becoming an accomplished ballroom dancer, etc. How do such experiences relate to the challenges of these difficult sayings?

● Think of some specific, practical things you can do to experience the gracious discomfort we meet in this week's texts.

FROM GLORY TO GLORY 1
The glory of God the Almighty

Notes by Estela Lamas

based on the New Revised Standard Version

Estela Lamas was born in Mozambique at a Swiss Presbyterian Mission. At present, she lives in a town in northern Portugal. She is a literature professor involved in teacher training. Her involvement in the church, particularly with women's issues, led her to make a comparative study of the problems of Portuguese women living in a rural area and those of African women living in a big European city – Lisbon. Based on this study, she is now preparing a PhD thesis on 'Pastoral Work with Women'.

Day by day, step by step, we go from glory to glory and deep inside us our faith in God grows and gets stronger and stronger. In our daily life, we experience the wonders of God's creation, the magnitude of his love, the mighty power of his protection. We experience the same feelings through this week's readings. They offer us the opportunity to share others' experience of God's glory. We discover God's omnipotence and omnipresence. He is the one who is. He is for ever. He is YHWH. He is the Almighty.

Text for the week: Isaiah 42:10–12

Sunday August 18   Exodus 3:1–6

THE LORD APPEARS TO US   God appears to us in many different ways, even if we are not expecting him. That's what happened to Moses when he was keeping the flock of his father-in-law, Jethro, in Horeb, the mountain of God. He was not aware of God's constant presence in his life, but when God manifested himself, then Moses was curious and wanted to find out more. However, he went to look at something ephemeral and discovered instead the timeless existence of God.

> Moses said, 'I must turn aside and look at this great sight, and see why the bush is not burned up' ... [The LORD] said further, 'I am the God of your father, the God of Abraham, the God of Isaac, and the God of Jacob.' And Moses hid his face, for he was afraid to look at God.   (verses 3 and 6)

Often, we keep busy with worldly affairs, forgetting to be linked to God. We forget that we live in God's world and that he watches us all the time. We forget that God is and was before we were and that he will be after we no longer exist. Unexpectedly, the ever-present God appears in our daily lives and, astonished by the wonder of his presence, we concern ourselves with unimportant details, explanations, evidence. Like Moses, we only trust in our senses; we want to make sure of what is going on. However, God is beyond our limited experience. We are insignificant; we are very small; we have no power. When we are called to be face to face with God we feel ashamed and are afraid to look at him.

† *Dear God, we pray that we may always be linked to you, in constant communion with you. Fill our lives with your wonders and allow us the gift of believing without wanting and needing physical proof of your presence in our lives.*

Monday August 19   Psalm 19:1–4a

GOD'S GLORY is present all around us, all over the world. Wherever we look, his works are displayed in front of our eyes. The psalmist not only sees them but he hears the sounds they produce, glorifying God. It is like an echo constantly coming and going.

> **The heavens are telling the glory of God;**
>   **and the firmament proclaims his handiwork.**   **(verse 1)**

Today, we are always running, in a hurry, stressed. We look at things every day but do not see them. Africa, my homeland, fascinates me! In the wilderness we discover the beauty of every single creature; we listen to the most tiny and insignificant sounds. We feel the wind blowing on our skin, the water splashing. Let us be aware, let us be ready to look and see, to hear and listen, to feel the smoothness of the wind and the velvet water touching our skin. Let us stop and take time to look and see what is around us. Let us stop and take time to hear the sounds that nature produces – and to worship their creator.

† *Bless you, O Lord, for your glory is for ever and ever!*
Bless you, O Lord, for your mighty power and for your endless love!
Bless you, O Lord, for the wonders you have created!
I praise your glorious name, O Lord, for you have created the heavens and the earth and the seas.

Tuesday August 20   Exodus 33:17–23

CHRISTIAN EXPECTANCY We Christians often lie still, waiting for God to interfere in our lives, waiting for

God's action. However, there is no activity in our own daily life. We do not move towards God, or look for him – we just sit and wait! In today's passage, the Lord addresses Moses because Moses had looked for him and asked for a revelation. And the Lord was pleased that Moses had looked for him; he not only knew Moses by name, but he wanted to show him his works.

> The LORD said to Moses, 'I will do the very thing that you have asked; for you have found favour in my sight, and I know you by name ... I will make all my goodness pass before you, and will proclaim before you the name, "The LORD"; and I will be gracious to whom I will be gracious, and will show mercy on whom I will show mercy.'
>
> **(verses 17 and 19)**

As a professor, I deal with many students each day. I find it easy to learn the names of the students who talk to me and come to me with their questions and doubts. However, I have a hard time learning the names of those who keep silent and sit quietly in their places. Teachers are often told that they favour this or that student simply because he or she comes and talks to them. This is true. Do we do the same to God? Have we, like children, found favour in his sight? Have we taken the trouble to address the Lord and let him know our weakness and our doubts?

† *God, make us grateful for having been called to life and chosen by you!*
God, give us the courage to move towards you and address you!
God, give us the courage to allow you to enter into our daily lives!
May we be able to proclaim your name and respond to your choice without questioning your will!
May we open ourselves so that your will may be done in our lives!
May we fulfil your will, God, so that the world may know you and be saved!

Wednesday August 21   **1 Chronicles 29:10–13**

WITNESSING TO GOD'S GLORY   is the true destiny of every human being. When the people of Israel stopped to contemplate the Lord's works, they simply recognised his great glory. That is why they decided to build the temple in his honour and brought offerings to pay for it, as their witness to God.

> Yours, O LORD, are the greatness, the power, the glory, the victory, and the majesty; for all that is in the heavens and on the earth is yours; yours is the kingdom, O LORD, and you are

exalted as head above all.   (verse 11)

Throughout history, people have gone into the world to witness to God's glory. We too are called to witness to God's glory. If we stop running for a moment in our daily life, as the people of Israel did, we will discover the right way to exalt our Lord. The spread of the Christian community depends on us.

† *Blessed are you, O Lord, Almighty God! Although I am humble and small, you have revealed yourself to me, O Lord. Exalted are you, O Lord, Almighty God!*

Thursday August 22   2 Chronicles 7:1–3

REJOICE IN GOD'S ETERNAL LOVE   Once again the people of Israel were full of joy and at the same time full of astonishment. God appeared to Solomon and to them. They had the opportunity to watch and experience once again the steadfastness of God's love. They rejoiced and were grateful for the strength and endurance of God's love.

They bowed down on the pavement with their faces to the ground, and worshipped and gave thanks to the LORD, saying,
   'For he is good,
      for his steadfast love endures for ever.'   (verse 3b)

Sometimes it is hard to believe that God will answer our request and, because our faith is limited, we experience failure. However, if we keep on asking – in Jesus' name – we shall surely get an answer and rejoice in our heavenly Father.

† *We worship you, O God, for you are powerful!*
We worship you, O God, for you are a loving father who never abandons us, who is always near us, who loves us deeply and abundantly beyond all limits.
O Lord, come and abide among us!
Lord, help us to grow in thankfulness!
Lord, fill our hearts with the joy of being loved by you!

Friday August 23   Isaiah 42:8–13

WAYS OF PRAISE   God says that our life should be a hymn of praise, a constant song spreading from one end of the earth to the other.

Sing to the LORD a new song,
   his praise from the end of the earth!   (verse 10a)

Once again, we are invited to find a new way to praise the Lord. Let us learn from our brothers and sisters from other cultures, from other countries; let us learn their way of praising the Lord and share our worship with them.

† *Give us grace, Lord, never to get away from you!*
Give us grace, Lord, never to forget your wonders!
Give us grace, Lord, to praise you with all our heart, with all our strength, with all our creativity!
May your spirit fill our hearts and our lives!

Saturday August 24   Psalm 90:1–12

GOD'S GIFT: ETERNAL LIFE   What a magnificent Father and Mother we have in God! What a wonderful love, a boundless love, strong enough to sacrifice the life of a sinless son! If God is a God of integrity, always true to himself, we human beings must also be true to that loving God who gives us eternal life.

For all our days pass away under your wrath;
    our years come to an end like a sigh ...
So teach us to count our days
    that we may gain a wise heart.   **(verses 9 and 12)**

Love forces us to love! God's action – his creation of the heavens, the earth, the sea and every creature that lives – 'forces' us freely to answer him and the only answer we can give is to be aware of God's daily offering. If we count the blessings we receive, day by day, we will certainly become wiser and wiser. Becoming wiser means becoming more conscious of our dependence on God's love. Becoming wiser means becoming more aware of and thankful for God's love. We join the psalmist in his prayer: 'teach us to count our days that we may gain a wise heart'. Humbly we ask God to fill our hearts with wisdom and faith.

† *We praise you for all your wonders.*
We praise you for every day of our lives.
We praise you for the blessings received day after day.

For group discussion and personal thought

● Have you met a person or a community that praises God in a way different to your own? If so, try using this way in your own praise.

● Make a list of the blessings you have received during this week, and praise God for them.

● Usually, when we talk about wisdom, we refer to the head and intellectual knowledge. What do we mean by having a wise heart?

FROM GLORY TO GLORY 2
The glory of God, the Creator and Rescuer

Notes by Peter Cotterell

based on the New International Version

Many people recognise that God's glory is seen powerfully in his creation. During this week we shall also look for God's glory in his concern for the poor and broken ones, and in his future plan for the whole of his creation.

Text for the week: Psalm 95:2–3

Sunday August 25   **Psalm 95:1–7a**

I WILL SING A NEW SONG   When I was a child I could not sing in tune to save my life. I tried to join the school choir but was very quickly weeded out. When I was sixteen years of age I became a Christian and made a joyful (but not very tuneful) noise to the Lord in worship.

> **Come, let us sing for joy to the LORD;**
> > **let us shout aloud to the Rock of our salvation ...**
> **Come, let us bow down in worship,**
> > **let us kneel before the LORD our Maker;**
> **for he is our God**
> > **and we are the people of his pasture,**
> > **the flock under his care.**   **(verses 1 and 6–7)**

Ten years later, during my second year at Theological College, I was touched deeply by the Spirit of God and experienced his glory in a new and wonderful way. When I woke the next morning I found that I could sing in tune for the first time in my life. How or why God did this I do not know, but it seems that whenever renewal comes it is always accompanied by a new outpouring of creative energy, particularly in songs. Come, let us sing a new song to the Lord...

✝ *Lord, I thank you for all who have served and glorified you through an outpouring of creativity.*

Monday August 26   **Psalm 8:1–9**

WHEN I CONSIDER THE HEAVENS   Tasmania, where I live, is one of the most beautiful places on earth. The air is clean, the winds are fresh and the night sky is wonderfully clear and free of the big city lights. This allows us to see the stars more distinctly than in many other parts of Australia or the world. The Milky Way stretches as a glorious band across the night sky, the moon passes through its phases, and when Halley's Comet passed over the earth a year or two ago, we were able to watch it with the aid of only a pair of binoculars. It is easy to appreciate the psalmist's wonder:

> **When I consider your heavens,**
> **the work of your fingers,**
> **the moon and the stars,**
> **which you have set in place,**
> **what is man that you are mindful of him?**　　**(verses 3–4a)**

Dominating our southern sky, we see the star formation known as the Southern Cross, a reminder to us that we are immensely valuable to our God. The cross, the symbol of our redemption, is blazoned across the sky. God loves his creation so much that he gave his own son for the salvation of the whole world.

✝ *O Lord, our Lord, how majestic is your name in all the earth!*

Tuesday August 27　　　　　　　　　　　　　**Psalm 138:1–8**

HIGH AND LIFTED UP　　Gazing at the night sky can lead us to imagine God as being 'out there, somewhere', seated upon a glorious throne, high above all the earth's trouble and pain. Although the scriptures do portray God as 'high and lifted up' they never imply that our God is somehow removed from the reality of our world.

> **Though the LORD is on high, he looks upon the lowly,**
> **but the proud he knows from afar.**
> **Though I walk in the midst of trouble,**
> **you preserve my life.**　　　　　　　　　　**(verses 6–7a)**

God is intimately concerned for the poor and the widow, the orphan and the stranger. God reverses the fortunes and the values of this world: the first shall be last and the last shall be first. His glory is seen in majesty and splendour, in divine throne rooms and radiant light. But his glory is also seen in a humble act of kindness, the care shown to the leper, the embrace of the untouchable, the lifting up of the downtrodden. His glory is seen in an act of reconciliation and the quiet word of forgiveness. His glory is seen in striving for peace, standing for justice and caring for the whole of creation.

† *Help us to recognise and praise your glory, O Lord, in its many forms and disguises.*

Wednesday August 28   Isaiah 51:1–6

'THE FIGURE IS IN THE ROCK'   Michelangelo is considered one of the world's greatest sculptors. From childhood he knew he had a gift for art. He described his way of working with the blocks of marble as simply cutting away the rock to reveal the figure trapped within. Even a damaged block of marble could produce a masterpiece, like Michelangelo's magnificent statue of David, in the hands of this genius.

Look to the rock from which you were cut
and to the quarry from which you were hewn.

(verse 1b)

When he was young Michelangelo worshipped both God and beauty. His first Pietà (a Pietà is a statue of Mary the Mother of Jesus holding her dead son) was carved when he was just 21 years old; it is a stunning piece of work. It is so well balanced that it appears almost weightless; a testimony to the beauty he worshipped.

But my salvation will last for ever,
my righteousness will never fail.   **(verse 6c)**

Forty, fifty and sixty years later he carved three more Pietàs. For Michelangelo the beauty he had worshipped in his youth gave way to deeper faith. These later Pietàs reflect that shift. They are more angular, filled with greater tension and grief. It is as though he had learned that it is faith, not beauty, that will last for ever.

† *Lord, you are the Master who has carved us from the rock and you shape our lives. May we grow in faith and learn to worship you, our Creator, more deeply.*

Thursday August 29   Jeremiah 17:7–8, 12–14

THE SEASONS OF GOD'S PURPOSE   In Australia we often have long, hot, dry summers. It is common for restrictions to be placed on the use of water. The gardens can only be watered during certain hours, and then only with a hand-held hosepipe. Only those plants which have deep roots will survive. Jeremiah understood the importance of deep roots in drought conditions and he compared such trees to people of faith.

'But blessed is the man who trusts in the LORD,
      whose confidence is in him.
He will be like a tree planted by the water
      that sends out its roots by the stream.
It does not fear when heat comes;
      its leaves are always green.
It has no worries in a year of drought
      and never fails to bear fruit.'   **(verses 7–8)**

Our root system will be tested in the times of drought, when trouble comes and we cry, 'Where are you, O God?' At such times we need to continue to walk by faith, knowing that, though the heavens seem shut even against our prayers, deep in the soil of God's grace the spring of living water still flows. As we hold fast in faith, the fruitfulness of God's purpose for our lives will appear in his time.

† *Thank you, Lord, for the blessing of your seasons in our lives, the times of drought and the times of harvest.*

Friday August 30   **Exodus 3:7–12**

I HAVE SEEN THEIR MISERY   One of the most difficult, and sometimes rewarding, aspects of ministry is to share with people at their most difficult moments. I have shared with families in times of suicide, accidental death, prolonged cancer, times of deepest sorrow and grief.

The LORD said, 'I have indeed seen the misery of my people in Egypt. I have heard them crying out because of their slave drivers, and I am concerned about their suffering.'   **(verse 7)**

It is sometimes hard to believe, yet comforting to know, that God is concerned with suffering. On one occasion, a family who did not have a close connection with our church asked me to come and be with them during the steady progression of an inoperable cancer. It was a privilege to enter into their inmost hearts. It was also a time of wonderful growth in faith of the one who had the cancer.

'When you have brought the people out of Egypt, you will worship God on this mountain.'   **(verse 12b)**

The funeral service was a confident affirmation of God's presence with us in suffering and the assurance that Christ has conquered death for us all. It was a celebration of life in the midst of death.

† *Lord, the glory of Christ is seen in his cross as much as his resurrection. Help us to celebrate life in the midst of death.*

Saturday August 31　　　　　　　　　　　Isaiah 65:17–25

NEW HEAVENS AND A NEW EARTH　Whenever I get out in my garden (which is not often) to weed and generally tidy up the rampant growth since last time, I witness a startling transformation. Everything seems new! Isaiah looked forward to a glorious day when the whole of creation would be transformed. The former weed-infested days of suffering and oppression, pain and injustice, would give way to a new day.

'Behold, I will create new heavens and a new earth ...
Never again will there be in it an infant who lives but a
　few days,
　or an old man who does not live out his years; ...
They will build houses and dwell in them;
　they will plant vineyards and eat their fruit.
No longer will they build houses and others live in them,
　or plant and others eat ...
The wolf and the lamb will feed together,
　and the lion will eat straw like the ox.
　　　　　　　　　　(verses 17a, 20a, 21–22a and 25a)

This new day is testimony to the glory of God: the creation has a future and God is directing it towards that future. In the meantime we are called to co-operate with God in the transformation of his world. Our concern for the environment, for issues of justice, as well as for the salvation of individuals, bears witness to the glory of our God, who is the Lord of all creation.

† *Praise be to God, who holds the future in the palm of his hands.*

For group discussion and personal thought

● Reflect on your life experiences and on the creation around you.
● Where do you see evidence of God's glory?
● How can you co-operate with God in bringing in the new heavens and new earth?

FROM GLORY TO GLORY 3
The glory revealed

Notes by Joan Stott

based on the New International Version and the New Revised Standard Version

Joan Stott is a lay person in the Uniting Church in Australia and has served in a variety of leadership roles. She has also been an Officer in the World Federation of Methodist and Uniting Church Women for many years, including being World Secretary.

The word 'reveal' means to make known, to be visible, seen, exposed, experienced and exhibited. In Old Testament times God revealed himself through symbols of his divine presence, when the holy places were filled with smoke, as a voice from the mountain, or in a cloud. Now God has become a human being, a reality in our world. He came and 'dwelled' with us, pitching his 'tabernacle' amongst us for all time. The reality of God is revealed through the presence of his Son in the world, the unique 'One', the 'Only', filled with the love and glory of the Eternal God.

Text for the week: John 1:14

Sunday September 1 John 1:1–14

PERFECT LOVE REVEALED The word 'perfect' is often used lightly in common speech. It is used for 'perfect' scores in sport, or 'perfect' designs in industry and fashion. This perfection may be judged by a set of numbers, the ideas of judges in a competition, or the understanding of an observer. This perfection is always measured against something or someone else.

> **The Word became flesh and lived for a while among us. We have seen his glory, the glory of the one and only [Son], who came from the Father, full of grace and truth.**
>
> **(verse 14, NIV)**

The writer of this text was a person whose eyes of the heart, mind and understanding were opened and who really 'saw' the glory of the Lord, present in Jesus Christ. Through this recognition within that community, a new relationship was established between the community of people who knew and believed, and God, the initiator of these actions. In Jesus Christ, the man, they recognised the glory of God revealed in the form of perfect love for humanity. They discovered that God's love and glory are intertwined and undivided. This is the great wonder and mystery of our faith in Christ Jesus.

✝ *May the love of God continue to be revealed in and through our lives. Amen*

Monday September 2 John 12:23–30

PERFECT OBEDIENCE REVEALED There are 'obedience schools' for dogs where they are taught to obey commands through repeated actions and rewards. Children learn to be obedient to their parents by encouragement and training, by example and, sometimes, by rewards.

'Now my soul is troubled. And what should I say – "Father, save me from this hour"? No, it is for this reason that I have come to this hour. Father, glorify your name.'

(verses 27–28a, NRSV)

The personal agony of Jesus is revealed in his struggle to obey God's will perfectly. Jesus' obedience was not a matter of learning by making mistakes or through rewards; it was a personal choice he alone made. God's voice was heard again, after centuries of apparent silence, at Jesus' baptism, his Transfiguration, and now in his personal struggle for perfect obedience to God's will for the salvation of the world. God's message of hope and assurance to Jesus was: 'I have glorified it and I will glorify it again' (*verse 28b*). Jesus' perfect understanding of God's love and glory empowered him to give his all in the certain hope that, in the end, love would triumph over death. The Cross of Christ was to be the sign for ever of the obedient 'One', the 'Only', giving his all for the world, for ever.

✝ *Praise to you, Lord Jesus, for your perfect obedience; may we learn from your example. Amen*

Tuesday September 3 Luke 9:28–36

GOD'S FULFILMENT REVEALED

As he was praying, the appearance of his face changed, and his clothes became as bright as a flash of lightning. Two men, Moses and Elijah, appeared in glorious splendour, talking with Jesus. They spoke about his departure, which he was about to bring to fulfilment at Jerusalem.

(verses 29–31, NIV)

At the Mountain of Transfiguration the past and present also became the future. The past was symbolised by the presence of Moses, the great Law giver, and Elijah, the Prophet. The present was the reality of their situation, when Jesus was about to set out on his journey to Jerusalem and to the climax of his mission and ministry. The 'conversation' between the people of the past and the present was about Jesus' departure, his own personal 'exodus'. The 'coming' of Jesus at his baptism was to be fulfilled by his 'exodus' as the new Moses who, by his crucifixion, would establish the new reign of God in the world for ever, which is the future. Jesus' imminent death would be the fulfilment and exaltation of God's love for all humanity and the created world. God's voice from the cloud was the benediction and blessing on Jesus' life and death. God said: 'This is my Son … Listen to him!'

✝ *Lord Jesus Christ, may we listen for the voice of Jesus in all things. Amen*

Wednesday September 4   **2 Corinthians 4:1–6**

GOD REVEALED IN AND THROUGH JESUS The glory of God is often described in physical terms as a 'shining bright light' surrounding a person or place, or as a flame burning brightly. Mere words alone cannot reveal the mystery of the presence of God.

> **For it is the God who said, 'Let light shine out of darkness', who has shone in our hearts to give the light of the knowledge of the glory of God in the face of Jesus Christ.**
>
> **(verse 6, NRSV)**

When Paul attempted to describe the glory of God, he urged his readers to look at Jesus to see the glory of God revealed. He had seen for himself, on the road to Damascus, the glory of God in the Risen Christ. However, the real understanding and comprehension of the glory of God are not always achieved with physical eyesight but, rather, through the eyes of faith and within the heart and mind of the believer. The wonder and mystery of God in human form enable us, as human beings, to look at Jesus and to seek, through faith and prayer and study of God's Word, to understand how and why he lived and acted, and the priorities he chose to live by.

✝ *Risen Lord Jesus, reveal yourself to us when we humbly seek your will and way. Amen*

THE PIONEER OF SALVATION REVEALED   Australia has a relatively short history of European settlement, and the people who came to this land as pioneers over 200 years ago are honoured for their courage and bravery. The early settlers in this vast land encountered very different conditions and experiences. The landscape was harsh and the climate vastly different.

> **It was fitting that God, for whom and through whom all things exist, in bringing many children to glory, should make the pioneer of their salvation perfect through sufferings.**   **(verse 10, NRSV)**

Jesus was the great pioneer who would 'blaze the trail' back to God, so that others could follow that trail. The only way this pioneer could be effective was for him to know and identify with those who would follow him. Jesus, as a human being, was able to identify fully with the difficulties associated with being human. He experienced pain, sorrow, laughter, joy, friendship, fear, anger and loneliness. He understood the interdependency involved in being human. Jesus became the pioneer of salvation for all when he died on the cross and revealed the glory of God in that self-giving, so that those who believe are enabled to be daughters and sons of God in a new and living relationship.

✝ *Jesus, only Son of God, give us courage to reveal to others the hope of new relationships to be found with God. Amen*

THE NEW CREATION REVEALED   Jesus Christ is the head of all things, the 'One', the 'Only' through whom all things were and are created. He was from the beginning of creation, and will be at the end of creation, and all that is in between. Within his being all things are gathered together and balanced.

> **In him all things hold together. He is the head of the body, the church.**   **(parts of verses 17 and 18, NRSV)**

Following his exaltation and glory through his death and resurrection, he is now the head of the new creation, the Church, which is the visible expression of the will and purpose of Christ in the world. The Church, the 'Body of Christ', is where the great partnership of love is revealed. Love for Christ and love for humanity cannot be separated, the one cannot exist without the other. Through the Church, active in the world, Christ is revealed as the means by which those 'who were once far off have been brought near by the blood of Christ' (*Ephesians 2:13*). Jesus is the source and strength of the life in the 'new creation', he is the 'guiding spirit' of the Church. He is the One who holds all things together.

† *Lord Jesus, help us to reveal to others the great partnership of love – love for Christ and for humanity in our daily work and witness. Amen*

Saturday September 7   Ephesians 1:17–23

THE INHERITANCE REVEALED

So that ... you may know what is the hope to which [Jesus] has called you, what are the riches of his glorious inheritance among the saints.   (part of verse 18, NRSV)

'Knowing' is a personal conviction, accepting with certainty and understanding and an experience and memory of certain events. Knowing what is the identity, the purposes and role of the Church in the world, and the part that individual members play in these, is the challenge that faces every member within the universal Church. The resources that are available to members for this knowledge to grow and develop are found in the 'fellowship of believers', and in God's grace and mercy experienced through prayer and study of the scriptures. The riches of Christ's 'glorious inheritance' are experienced through the lives of the followers of Christ in the present and the past. Without their faith and witness we have little on which to build for the present, or for the future inheritance of the faithful. All this can only be achieved in and through the power of Christ at work in us through the Holy Spirit, who guides and leads the Church in its mission in the world.

† *Holy Spirit, bless and guide your Church in its mission in the world. Amen*

For group discussion and personal thought

● What does it mean in your situation to be a pioneer of the faith?
● What is the 'great partnership of love'? How can you participate in this partnership?
● How do you express your obedience to God?

FROM GLORY TO GLORY 4
Changed into his likeness

Notes by Kate Hughes

based on the New Revised Standard Version

So far in this theme we have been looking at different aspects of the glory of God; this week we begin to look at that glory in relation to ourselves. God does not keep his glory to himself. As we have seen, the glory of God is revealed in Jesus Christ, translated into human terms that we can understand and share in. In the words of St Athanasius, 'He was made man that we might be made God'.

Text for the week: 2 Corinthians 3:18

Sunday September 8   John 17:21b – 24

THE GLORY OF BEING ONE

> **The glory that you have given me I have given them, so that they may be one, as we are one.**   **(verse 22)**

Our God is the God of love, and love means sharing with the one who is loved. If we love, we want to give. We only share in God's glory because God himself chooses to share it with us. How do we share God's glory? Our glory is to become more and more like God as he reveals himself in Jesus. One of the characteristics of Jesus is his unity, his oneness, with his Father and the Holy Spirit. This should also be a characteristic of the followers of Jesus. We should be one with God, Father, Son and Holy Spirit, and we should be united to each other. We may not have reached this point yet, but are we aiming for it, working actively in the power of the Spirit to heal wounds, support the weak, share knowledge and hold others in prayer within the Body of Christ, the Church? Our oneness with each other will give us a share in God's glory and reveal it to his world.

✝ *O God, may our unity with you and with each other reveal your glory to the world.*

LIVES WORTHY OF THE LORD   Paul, in this lovely passage
of prayer for his converts in Colossae, asks that they may be

> **filled with the knowledge of God's will in all spiritual
> wisdom and understanding, so that you may lead lives
> worthy of the Lord, fully pleasing to him, as you bear fruit
> in every good work and as you grow in the knowledge of
> God.**   **(verses 9b – 10)**

Christianity has a bad reputation in some societies as a religion
which always says, 'You must not...'. 'Don't do this... Don't do
that...' People complain that it smothers life and makes people
narrow-minded. But in fact the opposite is (or should be) true.
We can only give glory to God when we are fully and
completely alive, and we only know what God's idea of
human life is like when we get to know him. Jesus shows us
what is possible for human beings who are completely in tune
with God, who always try to find out God's will and do it.
God's gift is life in all its abundance. As we know his plans for
our life, as we see what that life was like in Jesus, so our own life
grows more and more full and spills over in good works to
other people. St Irenaeus, a second-century martyr, wrote: 'The
glory of God is man fully alive; the life of man is the vision of
God'.

✝ *O Lord, help me to open my hands to receive your gift of life in all
its fullness, so that my life may glorify you.*

CLOTHED WITH THE NEW SELF   The clothes we wear tell
other people a lot about us: the way we dress can reveal how
much money we have, what sort of work we do, what age
group we belong to, which country we live in and what kind of
weather it has, and what kind of person we are. We can
deliberately give other people a false picture of who we are and
what we are like, by the way we dress. Clothes are also used in
a symbolic way, to show that someone has taken on a new role
or responsibilities: kings and priests wear special clothes,
members of the army or the Scout movement wear a uniform.

> **[You] have clothed yourselves with the new self, which is
> being renewed in knowledge according to the image of its
> creator.**   **(verse 10)**

As we change into the clothes which suit our new life as

followers of Christ, other people will recognise that we belong to him, that we have become new people, that we share his glory.

† *O Lord, fill my life, that I may be clothed from head to foot in the love and glory of God.*

Wednesday September 11   **1 Corinthians 15:42–49**

RAISED IN GLORY

Just as we have borne the image of the man of dust, we will also bear the image of the man of heaven.   (verse 49)

Christianity is all about change. The natural world is constantly changing: plants and animals grow and die, stars appear and disappear, the seasons and the weather change from moment to moment. God changes things. Above all, he changes human beings. He changes sinners into good people, hatred into forgiveness, enmity into love, fear into confidence, doubt into faith, anxiety into trust. And he has promised that he will change our weak and sinful humanity into his glory. At death, we enter into the full glory of his presence; how shall we endure it, unless some of that glory rubs off on us? This letter to the Christians at Corinth provides no details about *how* we shall change; it simply assures them that they – and we – will change. And we have to let God begin to change us now.

† *Lord, you know how much I need to change. Thank you that you are already at work in me, so that at the end I may be changed into your glory.*

Thursday September 12   **2 Corinthians 3:12–18**

THE IMAGE OF HIS GLORY

And all of us, with unveiled faces, seeing the glory of the Lord as though reflected in a mirror, are being transformed into the same image from one degree of glory to another.
(verse 18)

As Christians, we are called to be the Body of Christ. Jesus, the incarnate Son of God, has ascended to his Father; he no longer has a human physical presence on earth as the Jewish individual, Jesus of Nazareth. The Holy Spirit is constantly at work in the world, but, like the wind, he is invisible. No, if human beings in 2002 are to glimpse Jesus, meet with him and allow him to show them how much God loves them, then they must see him in his Church and in his followers. We, the members of the Church, are called to be the continuing physical presence of Jesus on earth. We, the followers of Christ, are called to reflect his glory like a mirror. People should be able to see us and catch a glimpse of God. What a calling! We cannot transform ourselves, but 'all of us ... are being transformed' by the love and power of God into true reflections of his glory.

† *Transform me, Lord, so that I may be your hands, your feet, your eyes, your voice, your love in the world, and help your Church to reflect your love and your glory.*

Friday September 13   2 Corinthians 4:16–18

GLORY BEYOND ALL MEASURE

Even though our outer nature is wasting away, our inner nature is being renewed day by day.   **(verse 16)**

Reflecting the glory of God has nothing to do with being young, strong, talented, successful, wealthy. I have seen the glory of God shining in a frail 80–year-old lady whose prayer kept her on the frontline of the battle with evil. I have seen the glory of God in a 40–year-old friend dying of cancer with laughter and serenity. I have seen the glory of God in a woman filled with peace and compassion for others after years of mental illness. Day by day, God renews his world and his people. Day by day, our outer physical bodies, and the mess we have made of our human natures through sin, waste away; they move towards death. But our true nature, the person God created us to be, can be renewed by his power day by day, until it comes to reflect the glory of its creator.

† *Lord, when our outer nature is wasting away through illness, old age, suffering, failure, poverty and sin, renew our inner nature day by day.*

Saturday September 14   Ephesians 3:16–21

FILLED WITH ALL THE FULLNESS OF GOD

That Christ may dwell in your hearts through faith, as you are being rooted and grounded in love.   **(verse 17)**

Growing into the glory of God is not something we can do for ourselves. Over and over again, our readings this week have spoken of '*being* renewed', '*being* transformed' '*being* rooted', and this verb means that something is done to us by somebody else. Only God can renew us and transform us; our part in the work is to let him, to allow him to change us, to co-operate with him. Why does God bother? Because he is God. Because the glory of God is to give: to give life to the world, to give love to his creation, to give his Son, to give his Holy Spirit, to give himself in a scrap of bread and a sip of wine. Because the glory of God is that he wants to share that glory with us, to share all that he is and has with his creation. Our glory is to be rooted and grounded in his love, planted in his love like a sturdy tree with strong roots, which cannot be shaken by cold, drought or rough weather.

† *O God, root me and ground me in your love, so that through faith I may grow to your glory.*

For group discussion and personal thought

- What does it mean for your congregation to be the Body of Christ to the people around you?
- Who has shown you the glory of God by their life or actions?

INTERNATIONAL BIBLE READING ASSOCIATION
1020 Bristol Road, Selly Oak, Birmingham, Great Britain B29 6LB

ORDER FORM – for 2003 books

Please send me the following books:

Name: _____

Address: _____

_____

_____ Postcode: _____

*To qualify for 2003 books at these special IBRA readers' prices, this order form must be used (photocopies not accepted). Your order will be dispatched when **all** books are available.*

Code	Title of Book	Quantity	Unit Price	Total
ZYW1006	Words for Today 2003		£6.50	
ZYL1007	Light for Our Path 2003		£6.50	
ZYF0897	Finding Our Way Together Book 1		£8.00	
ZYF0910	Finding Our Way Together Book 2		£8.00	
ZYF0938	Finding Our Way Together Book 3		£8.00	
ZYF0974	Finding Our Way Together Book 4		£8.00	
ZYF0897-SET	Finding Our Way Together series (4 BOOKS)		£25.00	
ZYS1009	Sharing God's Word 2003		£8.00	
ZYD0989	Discovering Christ *Advent & Christmas*		£8.00	
ZYD0994	Discovering Christ *Ascension & Pentecost*		£8.00	
ZYD0999	Discovering Christ *Lent & Easter*		£8.00	
ZYL0781	Living Prayers For Today		£15.50	
ZYM0902	More Living Prayers For Today		£15.50	

❑ I enclose a cheque (Payable to IBRA)

❑ Please charge my MASTERCARD / VISA / SWITCH

Card No: Issue No (Switch): ☐ ☐

☐☐☐☐☐☐☐☐☐☐☐☐☐☐☐☐

Expiry Date: _____

Signature: _____

Total cost of books	
UK postage included Overseas – add £3.00 airmail per book	
Donation to International Fund	
TOTAL DUE	

Payments in <u>Pounds Sterling</u>, please

The INTERNATIONAL BIBLE READING ASSOCIATION is a Registered Charity

International Bible Reading Association

Help us to continue our work of providing Bible study notes for use by Christians in the UK and throughout the world. The need is as great as it was when IBRA was founded in 1882 by Charles Waters as part of the work of the Sunday School Union.

Please leave a legacy to the International Bible Reading Association.

An easy-to-use leaflet has been prepared to help you provide a legacy. Please write to us at the address below and we will send you this leaflet – and answer any questions you might have about a legacy or other donations. Please help us to strengthen this and the next generation of Christians.

Thank you very much.

International Bible Reading Association
Dept 298, 1020 Bristol Road
Selly Oak
Birmingham B29 6LB
Great Britain
Tel. 0121 472 4242
Fax 0121 472 7575

Charity Number 211542

FROM GLORY TO GLORY 5
The glory to come

Notes by Supriyo Mukherjee

based on the New Revised Standard Version

Supriyo Mukherjee is an Anglican priest. He was ordained in the Church of North India in 1975. Since 1979 he has been living and working in England. At present he is the Diocesan Adviser for Community Relations and Inter-faith for the Diocese of Coventry, and a Team Vicar of Coventry East Team Ministry.

The first Christians were born out of the events of the first Easter morning, reinforced by repeated encounters with their risen Lord. In place of hopelessness they gathered courage and confidence, in place of gloom they found an abundance of happiness and optimism. They believed that death did not have the last word, that Jesus was victorious over death and that the same will happen to all who believe in Jesus. Christianity has continued to cherish this optimism – an optimism of hope beyond hopelessness, life beyond death and freedom beyond repression.

Text for the week: Romans 8:18–21

Sunday September 15   **Revelation 12:7–14**

GOD HAS THE LAST SAY The Book of Revelation was probably written in Asia Minor towards the end of the reign of the Roman Emperor Domitian (AD90–95) or soon after that. Domitian demanded divine worship of himself as emperor. Christians refused to worship him and they suffered persecution. In today's passage we try to understand the dilemma faced by the persecuted Christians: if Jesus has won the victory, then why is evil still at work?

> **Woe to the earth and the sea,**
> **for the devil has come down to you**
> **with great wrath.**   **(part of verse 12)**

However, a suffering Christian community believes that God is indeed victorious and the pain and suffering are just temporary measures, like passing clouds before sunshine. That is why, during apartheid in South Africa, Archbishop Desmond Tutu could say, 'This we believe: Goodness is stronger than evil, love is stronger than hate, light is stronger than darkness, life is stronger than death. Victory is ours through him who loved us.' The devil is angry precisely because 'he knows that his time is short!'

† *Lord, open our eyes to see your saving power at work.*

Monday September 16 Revelation 19:1–8

VISION AND HOPE   Christian hope is not a hollow hope. God indeed brings justice. Moreover, this hope is not just a futuristic hope which happens at the end of time. For early Christians, the visions in the Book of Revelation had materialised in this temporal world. The Roman persecution did end and the Church was vindicated. Time and again we see this happening in our human history. Hitler was defeated, slavery was abolished, colonialism has ended and apartheid has now become a memory of our painful past. We need to have visions, they give us courage and trust in our sovereign Lord.

'Hallelujah!
For the Lord our God
    the Almighty reigns.' (part of verse 6)

† *Almighty God, give us the vision of your glory. In our suffering give us the courage we need to fight against injustice and oppression. But when we are helpless, give us the assurance of your love that you always bring justice and peace.*

Tuesday September 17 Revelation 21:22–27

YOUR KINGDOM COME

The city has no need of sun or moon to shine on it, for the glory of God is its light, and its light is the Lamb. The nations will walk by its light, and the kings of the earth will bring their glory into it. (verses 23–24)

God is constantly at work in making things right. When people refer to 'the good old days', believing that the present world is getting worse, this is not a Christian attitude. God indeed listens to our prayer when we pray, 'Your kingdom come, your will be done, on earth as in heaven.' Jesus compared the kingdom of God to a tiny mustard seed which grew into a tree big enough for birds to nest in, and to yeast which leavens a large quantity of flour (*Luke 13:18–21*). So the world should be getting better, not worse. The Kingdom of God started at the coming of Jesus and gradually the world is being transformed. Of course, there is still evil in this world. But in the fullness of time, the world will at last be ruled absolutely by the King of kings and the Lord of lords.

† *Lord, grant us a positive world-view of your creation.*

Wednesday September 18   **Hebrews 12:18–29**

THE LAST JUDGEMENT   God will shake the earth and the heaven, like shaking wheat in a sieve to separate the good grain from the chaff (see *verse 27*). Jesus also talks about the last judgement as the removal of evil from good – weeds are burnt and wheat is harvested (*Matthew 13:30*), goats are separated from sheep (*Matthew 25:32–33*). At present, good and evil live side by side in our world, but at the last judgement evil will be destroyed. God's created world was good and at the end of time the creation will once again be good.

Therefore, since we are receiving a kingdom that cannot be shaken, let us give thanks, by which we offer to God an acceptable worship with reverence and awe.   (verse 28)

At the coming of the kingdom, God will restore the order of his creation. That is why we wait for the kingdom with thankful hearts, not with a longing desire for vengeance against our enemies.

† *O Lord, remove all evil from our hearts and from our society.*

Thursday September 19   **1 Corinthians 15:50–57**

THE FINAL GLORY   The concept of physical resurrection partly developed out of an Old Testament idea that we might not have a conscious existence after death. Sheol was a place where the dead could not remember or praise God, or even work, think or have knowledge or wisdom. So the dead could not praise God. But how could they be punished or rewarded unless they had bodies? However, Christian understanding of resurrection goes beyond the concept of final judgement.

'Death has been swallowed up in victory.'
'Where, O death, is your victory?
Where, O death, is your sting?'   **(verses 54b – 55)**

By raising our bodies, God gives us immortality. Our imperfect and temporal bodies turn into glorified bodies which will never age or suffer pain and deformities.

† *We pray for people who suffer pain, people who have mental or physical disabilities, people who have lost limbs because of human cruelty and war. Comfort and heal them according to your will.*

Friday September 20   Isaiah 40:3–5, 28–31

EQUALITY IN THE KINGDOM

Every valley shall be lifted up,
   and every mountain and hill be made low;
the uneven ground shall become level,
   and the rough places a plain.   (verse 4)

The Gospel writers quoted this passage at the coming of John the Baptist. John came to prepare the way for the Kingdom of God – for the work of Jesus of Nazareth. The world is full of inequalities: the high and the low, the rich and the poor, the loved and the unloved, the respected and the oppressed. Jesus came to establish equality and had compassion on the sick, the lepers, the outcasts and the sinners. We are the body of Christ and must continue the work of God's kingdom. Many Christians worship Jesus the King without doing any work for his kingdom. Others work only for the kingdom without acknowledging the king. We should do both.

† *Thank you, Father, for all who work for your kingdom. Give us the desire to work more for your kingdom.*

Saturday September 21   Romans 8:18–25

THE GLORY OF THE CHILDREN OF GOD

The creation itself will be set free from its bondage to decay and will obtain the freedom of the glory of the children of God.   (verse 21)

This is the ultimate glory to come! The whole creation will be made perfect. Yet the creation is still waiting with eager longing for the revealing of the children of God (*verse 19*) – why? Because in God's plan, his children have to bring this freedom to the creation. We know that human beings can bring harmony or disharmony to nature. If we act irresponsibly we cause disharmony to nature – for example, causing global warming or creating a hole in the ozone layer. However, responsible children of God bring harmony and healing to the whole creation. Jesus says, 'Blessed are the peacemakers, for they will be called children of God' (*Matthew 5:9*). Peace may start within our human society, but if we are not at peace with our environment, no lasting peace is possible. Famine, natural disasters and destruction of species will continue until we ourselves become the children of God, co-creators with our heavenly Father.

† *O Lord, make me an instrument of your peace.*

For group discussion and personal thought
- How optimistic are you about this world? Do you believe that God will ultimately bring his kingdom into our world?
- How often do you remember that piety alone does not make us Christians – we must also work for the Kingdom of God ?

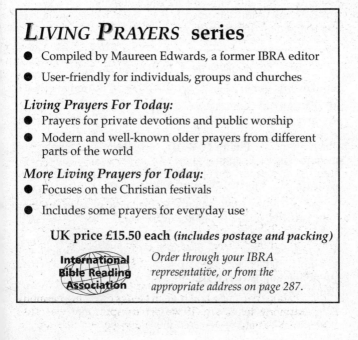

LIVING PRAYERS series

- Compiled by Maureen Edwards, a former IBRA editor
- User-friendly for individuals, groups and churches

Living Prayers For Today:
- Prayers for private devotions and public worship
- Modern and well-known older prayers from different parts of the world

More Living Prayers for Today:
- Focuses on the Christian festivals
- Includes some prayers for everyday use

UK price £15.50 each *(includes postage and packing)*

International Bible Reading Association

Order through your IBRA representative, or from the appropriate address on page 287.

PHILIPPIANS 1
The mind of Christ

Notes by Ann Hadley

based on the Revised English Bible

Ann Hadley spent many years in Africa, first in Zimbabwe and later in Zululand. She is now a priest in the Anglican Church and lives in the Diocese of Worcester.

Much of the advice Paul gives to the church at Philippi could be applied to any one of our local churches. He warns of disunity. When people are really zealous in their beliefs, they can cause friction with each other, resulting in fights and quarrels. Jealousy and selfish ambition can also wreck a church fellowship. Instead, we should dwell on the fact that we share the Holy Spirit, who binds us to God and each other. Encouragement and harmony are key words this week. We are called to lay aside any discords we may have and live in accordance with the example given us by Jesus.

Text for the week: Philippians 1:27

Sunday September 22   **Philippians 1:1–11**

BE ENCOURAGED Letter-writing to friends and family whom we are not able to meet very often is important. It is good to keep in touch and exchange news. Paul's letter to the Christians at Philippi is a wonderful example of encouragement. Even though he was in prison and could have been feeling sorry for himself, he writes to his friends expressing his high hopes and fondness for their little church:

> **And this is my prayer, that your love may grow ever richer in knowledge and insight of every kind.** **(verse 9)**

We may belong to a small, perhaps struggling, congregation. If so, we can take heart from this letter of Paul's. Encouragement is a great enabler and brings out the best in people, whereas grumbling and criticism seek to destroy any initiative, stifling growth and wellbeing.

† *Lord, lead me to be an encourager of people. Bless our local congregation and give us a heart for the gospel.*

Monday September 23   **Philippians 1:12–18**

USING YOUR OPPORTUNITIES How many of us would recognise being in prison as an opportunity? That is what Paul did. He says:

> **My friends, I want you to understand that the progress of the gospel has actually been helped by what has happened to me.**   **(verse 12)**

Instead of moaning about the situation, he thinks positively, saying that it is all in the cause of Christ. There are many opportunities to talk about his faith to the prison guards, as well as other people who come and go in the prison. Paul gives fresh heart to those who are suffering and courage and confidence to carry on in difficult circumstances. However, he also warns that some believers preach in a partisan spirit and from personal ambition. They need to consider their motives. But what really matters is that Christ is proclaimed whenever the opportunity is appropriate.

✝ *In times of difficulty and despair, renew in us the spirit of hope, that we may use the opportunities you give us to encourage others.*

Tuesday September 24   **Philippians 1:19–26**

DO YOU HAVE A CHOICE TO MAKE? Paul, too, had to make choices. From this reading we have an insight into his mind:

> **If I am to go on living in the body there is fruitful work for me to do. Which then am I to choose? I cannot tell.**
>   **(verse 22)**

The issues before Paul are life or death choices. He is torn in two directions. On the one hand he longs to go and live with Christ; on the other he is convinced that it is better to remain and help the church to go forward in Christian living. Paul urges the Philippians to stand firm with a united spirit, persevering with a single mind for the faith of the gospel.

✝ *Whatever choices we have to make in life, whether personal or as a community, we are reminded to pray for each other in our decision-making, that the Spirit of Jesus Christ may be given us for support. Lord, give us wisdom to make the right choices.*

Wednesday September 25   **Philippians 1:27–30**

IS YOUR CONDUCT WORTHY? Paul continues on the topic of unity and witness, stressing the importance of working together as a team. There is a saying, 'United we stand, divided we fall' and this is Paul's theme in today's reading:

> **Whatever happens, let your conduct be worthy of the gospel of Christ, so that whether or not I come and see you for myself I may hear that you are standing firm, united in spirit and in mind, side by side in the struggle to advance the gospel faith.** (verse 27)

It is worth thinking about this word 'conduct'. Is the way I live out my life pleasing to God? Am I standing firm and resisting temptation to stray from my Christian calling? Paul warns that there will be opponents. People will suffer. There will be conflict and struggle. Is our conduct worthy of the name of Christian, especially during the tough times?

✝ *Lord, break down the barriers which separate us from one another and from you. Teach Christians to love one another and lead us united in your cause of peace.*

Thursday September 26   **Philippians 2:1–4**

DO I NEED TO CHANGE MY ATTITUDE?

> **Fill up my cup of happiness by thinking and feeling alike, with the same love for one another and a common attitude of mind.** (verse 2)

As we have discovered, the one danger which threatened the Philippian church was disunity, and this of course is still a problem within our local churches today. People are apt to hold strong opinions, want their own way, and ultimately quarrel. There is a real sense in which Christians can destroy each other with their wrangling. This then brings the church into disrepute. It is against this danger that Paul wishes to safeguard his friends. He names three causes of disunity:

● Selfish ambition – that is, advancing my own purposes at the expense of others.
● Desire for personal prestige – vanity, as Paul calls it in verse 3. It is a great temptation to be admired and respected and to have the best seat!
● Self-interest – putting self first, pushing others out of the way and putting them down. Let us learn to see things from the other person's point of view.

The fact that we are in Christ should keep us together in unity. We are to love one another, even those we do not like! Our relationship with others is surely an indication of the quality of our relationship with Jesus. Disunity breaks up the very structure of life and holds back the work of the gospel.

† *Lord, begin with me and be the example for my attitudes. Where there is hatred let me bring your love. Make me a channel of your peace.*

Friday September 27 Philippians 2:5–11

TAKE HEART

Take to heart among yourselves what you find in Christ Jesus.   **(verse 5)**

Once again Paul encourages the congregation at Philippi to take heart; verse 5 can also be translated as 'Have the same mind among yourselves as you have in Christ Jesus'. Let the mind of Christ permeate your relationships with each other. There follows a description of Jesus' way of life, the great characteristics of which are humility, obedience and self-renunciation. He did not come to seek power but to serve; not to have his own way but to follow God's way. Selfishness and self-seeking destroy our likeness to Christ and our fellowship with each other. Our first priority is to seek to live within the will of God and rejoice in our worship of him. It is then that we experience a new way of living.

† *Love so amazing, so divine, demands my life, my soul, my all. Lamb of God, I come, I come.*

Saturday September 28 Philippians 2:12–18

SHINE LIKE STARS Encouragement is again evident and Paul's enthusiasm for the gospel rings out loud and clear – rejoice, he says, and shine like stars; far better than grumbling and arguing! There follows an appeal to Christians to live diligent and consecrated lives, above reproach and daily offering themselves in the service of Christ. Oh that we could catch a vision of such missionary endeavour! Christians who are honest and loving in a world which has become corrupt and greedy will stand out like lights in the darkness. The passage concludes with two vivid pictures. Paul was fond of picture language, no doubt taken from his own experiences. Verse 16 uses an example from athletics – perhaps the Olympic Games – about running a race. Paul's prayer is that he may not be like an athlete whose training and effort have been in vain. For him the greatest prize in life was to know and to love Jesus Christ and to share that joy with others, even if it meant great sacrifice.

Show yourselves innocent and above reproach, faultless children of God in a crooked and depraved generation, in which you shine like stars in a dark world.   (verse 15)

† *Lord, fill us with your Spirit so that we may be renewed in faith and inspired in hope and love; and shine like stars as we spread the gospel of your kingdom in a dark world.*

For group discussion and personal thought

● Can you identify any cause of disunity within your church fellowship which needs to be talked through?
● Is there any reason to review your own attitude or conduct towards any individual or church fellowship?
● Do you feel that your congregation is generally encouraging and offers a warm welcome to newcomers?

PHILIPPIANS 2
The life of Christ

Notes by Carol Mouat

based on the Christian Community Bible (Catholic Pastoral Edition)

This letter that Paul sent from prison to the community in Philippi is personal and full of tenderness. In it he gives news and advice and gives thanks. His advice is centred on being of one mind in Christ.

Text for the week: Philippians 4.1

Sunday September 29   **Philippians 2:19–3:1a**

GOD'S MESSENGERS   We are entrusted by God to convey his message to people in a variety of different ways. Paul announces two visitors to the Christians at Philippi, Timothy and Epaphroditus. Timothy was Paul's assistant and was involved in a number of missions to the various communities of Asia Minor. Both these men were committed Christians who left their families and faced many risks in order to follow Paul.

> **He risked his life to serve me on your behalf.**   (verse 30)

We are sometimes called by the Lord to serve him in the most unexpected ways. Perhaps we are called to minister to AIDs patients, listen to the lonely and depressed, visit the sick, or spend time with a friend or family member who needs our help and encouragement. Are we ready to leave behind our own affairs and interests and perhaps even risk our lives for others?

† *Jesus, you risked your life for all humankind. Help us to give without counting the cost, and be prepared to respond generously to your call at all times.*

Monday September 30   **Philippians 3:1b – 11**

LAW VERSUS LOVE   No one was better qualified than Paul to write about his own experience of being obedient to the laws and customs of the Old Testament. He saw firsthand the pagan feasts and sacrifices, but was proud of belonging to God's people, of being circumcised and instructed in God's promises to his race. He was a model of a strict Pharisee. He was faithful to the religion of his ancestors, and he believed that it was necessary to persecute and even kill those who preached a new doctrine. Once Paul discovered the true meaning of the law of love, he could experience the power of God's divine grace. The death and resurrection of Christ became a reality for Paul:

> **May I know him and experience the power of his resurrection and share in his sufferings and become like him in his death.** (verse 10)

We cannot journey in this life without experiencing the cross as well as the resurrection. The trouble is that most of us only want to experience the joys of life. When we are faced with trials, can we look at Christ carrying his cross, and unite our pain with his?

✝ *Jesus, you carried your cross and died because of love for each one of us; help me when I feel discouraged to carry my cross without complaining.*

Tuesday October 1   **Philippians 3:12–14**

WHAT IS THE PRIZE?   Paul uses the metaphor of a race: he runs to achieve his goal, keeping

> **my eyes on the prize to which God has called us from above in Christ Jesus.** (verse 14)

The prize is simple, and yet winning it is a life-time task: it is continually living and being in the presence of the Lord. The race is not a competition, it is a race in which we all take part and, like Paul, we strive to know our Saviour, to relate to him more intimately and experience a deepening of his presence within ourselves.

✝ *May I never forget the power of your presence in me, Lord.*

Wednesday October 2   **Philippians 3:15–4:1**

WHERE DO OUR TREASURES LIE?   Do we stock up with earthly treasures? It is so easy to become self-satisfied and live our lives as if everything depended on ourselves. We can pride ourselves on certain gifts that we possess, our achievements, and even our goodness. If we think that we are perfect, it is only because God has made us perfect. Let us never forget that we continue to strive for perfection in this life, and we shall only reach this perfection when we finally meet Christ face to face.

None of us can claim to have this treasure of perfection. Paul warns us that we are heading for ruin if we base our treasures on selfishness and greed:

For many live as enemies of the cross of Christ, I have said it to you many times, and now I repeat it with tears: they are heading for ruin; their belly is their god and they feel proud of what should be their shame. They only think of earthly things. (verses 17–19)

Our true treasures lie in the way of the cross, in following Christ in both his death and resurrection. As long as we search or try to store up earthly treasures for ourselves we shall continually be disappointed.

† *Lord, teach me to focus on you and not on myself.*

Thursday October 3 Philippians 4:2–9

CHEERFUL HEART Paul exhorts his listeners in the church at Philippi to have joyful hearts:

Rejoice in the Lord always, I say it again: rejoice. (verse 4)

When we are at peace with ourselves and united in the Lord, we shall be at peace with others. As Paul states:

May everyone experience your gentle and understanding heart. (verse 5)

If we are closely united with the Lord, all those with whom we come into daily contact will experience our gentleness, warmth and understanding heart. We shall remain open in order to allow the Lord to speak and act through us, and others will recognise his presence in us. His radiance will shine through us, and our cheerful heart can build up the many in our society who are crying out for love and understanding.

† *I rejoice in you always, Lord.*

Friday October 4 Philippians 4:10–14

GRATITUDE Gratitude is something that we can so easily take for granted in our daily lives. How many of us give a symbolic expression of gratitude to those who have performed well? Do we go out of our way to let people know how grateful we are? For example, we may attend church services regularly and can sometimes be critical of a sermon, yet how often do we praise the minister or priest? Paul expresses his gratitude to the people of Philippi, and above all he exclaims his gratitude to God:

I can do all things in him who strengthens me. (verse 13)

This is a very powerful statement, and it has meaning for ourselves. We can become puffed up with pride because of our wonderful achievements, and forget that all we have is a gift from God. We are reminded to give thanks and praise to him – he is entitled to all the glory.

✝ *Lord Jesus, we praise and thank you for the gifts you give us.*

Saturday October 5   **Philippians 4:15–23**

GOD WILL PROVIDE YOU WITH ALL YOU NEED Paul's words of encouragement and support to the church at Philippi are an example of true leadership. His words of gratitude assure the people that God himself will provide them with everything that they need. God is never outdone in generosity, for whenever we give without counting the cost, he very often gives back in abundance. Often what we receive in return is not what we expect, but if we are open, we will recognise God's generosity, and acknowledge that his gifts are exactly what we need. The gifts which we give can be compared with the offerings that Paul speaks about:

fragrant offerings pleasing to God. (part of verse 18)

We need to be generous with our giving, whether we give our time, availability or material goods. Sometimes we are tempted to hoard possessions, but this is being selfish. It is good to give away what we do not need and put our trust in God, because he will always provide us with what we really need.

✝ *Help me, Lord, to be unselfish in my giving.*

For group discussion and personal thought

● How can we, as the Church, affirm others?

LIFE TOGETHER 1
Planting and pruning

Notes by Paul Duffett

based on the New International Version

The picture of a vine occurs several times in this week's readings. The vine belongs to God. He planted it and tends it. It is a symbol of his people, whom he called out of slavery and 'planted' in their own land. But a vine is no good as a decoration. It is intended to be useful. For a vine, this means being pruned in order to be fruitful. In human terms, it means being taught and disciplined. The followers of Jesus need such lessons today, just as much as the people of the times when the words were written.

Text for the week: Psalm 80:7

Sunday October 6   **Matthew 21:33–46**

WALLS AND DOORS   Today's parable about a vineyard was spoken by Jesus in the temple in Jerusalem. He has come to the headquarters of his nation's political and religious institutions. Now he gives those in charge their marching orders. They had two alternatives: either to change and join Jesus, or to stick to their ways and get rid of him. They were the 'tenants' who wanted to kill the owner's son, and they knew it. There was no turning back.

> **'Therefore I tell you that the kingdom of God will be taken away from you and given to a people who will produce its fruit.'**   **(verse 43)**

Christians are called to be that 'people'. I heard a Baptist Superintendent preaching at the installation of a local elder. He said, 'Sometimes, congregations act as though they pray for their leaders like this: "Lord, you keep him humble and we'll keep him poor". 'But remember,' he said to the elder, 'Although you are their servant, you are not their doormat! You are to obey Jesus and seek his kingdom above everything else.' Our churches have walls to help us grow in identity and faith, but the doors are all-important. We go out of them to bear fruit for God and in through them come as many people as possible to be welcomed and shown love. For the religious leaders of Jesus' day, the temple door was closed, but for him it was wide open so that people could meet with God.

† *Lord, work in us your own work of grace, so that we can bear fruit of love and joy and peace for you.*

Monday October 7   Isaiah 5:1–17

SINS OF SOCIETY Jesus may have based yesterday's parable on today's reading. The meaning is much the same, except that for Isaiah it is not so much the leaders and priests who are accused by God. It is the whole of society, especially the rich, the abusers of pleasure and the criminals, which is at fault. How often in history has human behaviour become corporate corruption! Isaiah spells it out:

> **Woe to you who add house to house**
>   **and join field to field**
> **till no space is left**
>   **and you live alone in the land ...**
> **Woe to those who rise early in the morning**
>   **to run after their drinks ...**
> **They have harps and lyres at their banquets ...**
> **but they have no regard for the deeds of the LORD.**
>   **(verse 8 and parts of verses 11 and 12)**

You could say that this describes most cities in most countries today! Human nature is basically self-centred and self-seeking. If we refuse to acknowledge that there are laws which are God's will for a harmonious society, then we should not be surprised if we end up in chaos:

> **Therefore my people will go into exile**
>   **for lack of understanding.**   **(verse 13a)**

Being aware of the problems and finding ways to solve them are human responsibilities. We may feel we can do little, but doing that little is what matters.

† *Father, what we know not, teach us; what we have not, give us; and what we are not, make us, for your kingdom's sake.*

Tuesday October 8   Philippians 3:4b – 14

PROFIT AND LOSS There was an obituary for a bishop in the newspaper recently. He was quoted as saying that his 'job' was fantastic. It included autonomy, travel, pastoral care, a roof over his head, and 'you name it, it's got it'. Undoubtedly he also had exhausting duties and even exhausting situations and people, but if you have love in your heart for someone, especially for someone who loves you, no task is too great or difficult and can become a pleasure. Paul's experience was like that. He knew what his work had cost him, how painful it had been at times, but still his enthusiasm and joy were unlimited. God always had more in store for him, and what Paul had once thought important – education and status – now seemed like rubbish compared with what he had found through Christ:

I want to know Christ and the power of his resurrection and the fellowship of sharing in his sufferings, becoming like him in his death, and so, somehow, to attain to the resurrection from the dead ... I press on towards the goal to win the prize for which God has called me heavenwards in Christ Jesus. (verses 10–11 and 14)

That is how love works: it is mutual and never runs out; it is a well of life in all its fullness.

✝ *Lord Jesus, may our worship and service be both a duty and a joy, day by day.*

Wednesday October 9   Psalm 19:7–14

GOLD COMES FROM A FURNACE   The person who wrote this psalm was deeply spiritual. He was probably male, and he had read God's law – the commands, the precepts (perhaps in Proverbs) and the ordinances for the celebration of religious festivals in the temple and at home. He found that putting this law into practice made his life stable and worthwhile. God had planted and the psalmist was reaping.

The ordinances of the LORD ...
are more precious than gold ...
they are sweeter than honey ...
By them is your servant warned;
    in keeping them there is great reward.
                             (parts of verses 9–11)

But the author is also aware of the spiritual battle which goes on within. There are faults that worry his conscience. Some of these are hidden from his mind (but not from God); others are the deliberate result of the weakness of human nature. How can the two sides in the battle be integrated? God gives the psalmist insight: thinking well can lead to speaking well (*verse 14*). However, this kind of thinking is not about superficial ideas – it is *meditation,* being still in God's presence and asking him to let his Spirit come to us through his word and sink down into the depth of our being and consciousness. In this way our living can become an offering of love to God.

† *Father God, you are the source of our wellbeing. Draw us into your love so that our lives may wholly reflect your eternal being.*

Thursday October 10   **Genesis 2:4b – 15**

REMEMBER YOU ARE DUST AND TO DUST YOU WILL RETURN The words of today's title are used in some churches in a service for Ash Wednesday, the beginning of Lent. The minister says them as he or she makes the sign of the cross in ash on the foreheads of the worshippers. The words remind us to be humble: our physical bodies consist mostly of water and flesh that will one day be dirt. The words are based on today's reading and stress that we are not separate from the rest of creation, but part of it. Animals, plants, trees, rocks – they are all made from the same basic ingredients as we are.

The LORD God formed the man from the dust of the ground and breathed into his nostrils the breath of life, and the man became a living being.   (verse 7)

And then the man is put into the Garden of Eden. This is an ordinary garden, but it is also special because it contains the tree of 'Life' and the tree of 'The Knowledge of Good and Evil'. Eden too is part of creation, with the rivers of the Middle East flowing through it. Human beings belong to the rest of creation, but they are also set apart from it, placed in an environment that has a spiritual dimension. We are related to both – and both belong to God.

† *Father God, help us to see you in all you have made, humbly grateful for life in all its aspects and serving you in all we do.*

Friday October 11   **Exodus 20:1–20**

LAWS FOR LIVING TOGETHER The Jews who had been slaves in Egypt knew very well what repressive laws were like. But now they are free. Do they need any laws to limit their freedom? God knows human nature: we need laws to shape our freedom, so that we can live securely and use our freedom responsibly. The breakdown of law and order is disastrous for any group of people. God's laws are designed to inspire reverence and respect for him and the respect for other people – both our family and our neighbours – which is essential for living in harmony. Jesus made this need for law fundamental to his teaching, summarising the law into the two great commandments: 'Love God with your whole being and your neighbour as yourself' (see *Mark 12:30–31*).

Moses said to the people, 'Do not be afraid. God has come to test you, so that the fear of God will be with you to keep you from sinning.'
                                                                (verse 20)

Of course, the Ten Commandments are meant to lead us to the grace of God so that we obey out of love and not awesome 'fear'. We need God's help all the time. Without God's law, however, we might never know his love, which is always there for us. Sadly, within many communities there is complete ignorance of God's laws and when human nature is left to rule itself, there can be terrible results. Interpreted in the light of Christ and with the guidance of the Holy Spirit, God's laws remain the true basis for good community life.

† *Lord our God, help us to apply your laws to our daily living and to the laws that we make in order to live together.*

Saturday October 12   **Psalm 80:7–15**

THE COMMUNITY PRAYS   Local and national communities go through bad times as well as good. Christian communities need to pray for faithfulness to God when the going gets tough. We rely on his help:

Restore us, O God Almighty;
  make your face shine upon us,
  that we may be saved.   **(verse 7)**

But God seems to be the problem, rather than the solution; he allows his vine to be damaged:

Why have you broken down its walls
  so that all who pass by pick its grapes?
Boars from the forest ravage it.   **(verses 12–13a)**

The writer of this psalm attributes these disasters to the absence of God; he wants God to return to his people and magically make everything right again (*verse 14*). But has God ever gone away? Or has he been involved all the time, and simply allowed human beings to do their own will until they learn to do his? It is doing God's will that leads to peace, serving him within the difficulties and disasters of life. At least the psalmist is praying and looking to God for help in his bewilderment, so perhaps the community learnt from this experience of pruning.

✝ *Lord Jesus, light of our lives, give us the grace to be faithful in all circumstances, turning to you in all our needs.*

For group discussion and personal thought
- What elements do you think make up a good community?
- Is there anything more that you could do to make your community (family, neighbourhood, church) better?

LIFE TOGETHER 2
God's party

Notes by Kate Hughes

based on the New Revised Standard Version

An image which runs through both the Old and New Testaments is that of the Kingdom of God, the Kingdom of Heaven, as a feast, a celebration, a party. A good party has two characteristics: it is enjoyable, and it involves other people. You cannot have a party on your own, and people should enjoy each other. This is the week of prayer for world peace: peace will never come until the peoples of the world learn to come together and enjoy each other – to join in the party which God, the perfect host, has prepared for us.

Text for the week: Psalm 23:5

Sunday October 13   **Matthew 22:1–14**

ACCEPTING THE INVITATION

The kingdom of heaven may be compared to a king who gave a wedding banquet for his son.   **(verse 2)**

Having a party usually means sending out invitations. Most hosts do not welcome gatecrashers, those who come to a party without an invitation. And it helps the catering if the guests reply to the invitation and say whether or not they are coming. The king in this parable had already sent out his invitations. Now it was time for the guests to gather. But the king ran into trouble: his invited guests did not want to come. So eventually, after killing the original guests, he invites other people. But one of those is not dressed correctly and gets thrown out. Compared with the version of this parable in Luke's gospel (*Luke 14:16–24*), the story here is rather confusing, but some points are clear: the party is a splendid royal wedding feast, people are invited, but it is the king who lays down the rules. We shall be invited to the party, but our eventual presence is not automatic; it depends on our co-operation with God, the party-giver.

† *Lord, I hope to get an invitation to your party, and I look forward to enjoying it, but please help me to fit in with your requirements.*

Monday October 14   **Isaiah 25:1–9**

NO MORE TEARS

> **This is the LORD for whom we have waited;**
> **let us be glad and rejoice in his salvation.** (verse 9b)

A party usually implies food and drink, and these are indeed part of the picture here (*verse 6*). The rich food and good wine would be an attractive picture of the future for farmers, traders and craftsmen whose livelihoods were precarious due to bad weather, disease, wars and other disasters. But God's party is so much more than just a good meal. He will ensure that everyone enjoys themselves, by destroying the darkness that hangs over the world like a shroud and swallowing up death (*verse 7*), wiping away tears and getting rid of disgrace (*verse 8*). This is God's salvation, and it is worth waiting for.

✝ *O Lord, I look forward to your day, when all pain and suffering will be swept away by your love and power.*

Tuesday October 15   **Philippians 4:1–9**

THE GOD OF PEACE WILL BE WITH YOU

> **Finally, beloved, whatever is true, whatever is honourable,**
> **whatever is just, whatever is pure, whatever is pleasing,**
> **whatever is commendable, if there is any excellence and if**
> **there is anything worthy of praise, think about these**
> **things.** (verse 8)

Many of the pictures of a future heavenly banquet, with good food and wine, which we find in the Old Testament were written during times when the Israelites were experiencing great difficulties: occupation by enemies, threats of invasion, exile. The promise of something wonderful in the future helped them to keep going in the difficult present. But if we want to have an invitation to this future party, we need to be in contact with the host, God, now. Today's reading tells us how to keep in touch with God: by fixing our minds and our energies on what is true, honourable, just, pure, pleasing, commendable, excellent and worthy of praise. These things come from God and bring us into contact with him; they give us a foretaste now of what the kingdom is like.

✝ *Help me to focus on the things which keep me in contact with you and give me a foretaste of your kingdom.*

Wednesday October 16   Psalm 106:1–6, 19–23

REJECTING THE GLORY OF GOD This psalm recalls the central event of Israelite history, the exodus from Egypt. On their journey from Egypt to the Promised Land of Canaan, God made a covenant with his people: they would be his people and he would be their God. However, the Israelites repeatedly focused on only one side of this covenant, God's promise to take care of them. They forgot their side of the bargain, that they would obey God. They wanted the rights and privileges of being God's chosen people, but not the duties and responsibilities.

> They exchanged the glory of God
>   for the image of an ox that eats grass.   **(verse 20)**

To see the glory of God, to share in it and reveal it to others is not a right. God is faithful, his love is steadfast, a share in his glory is always offered to us – but we have to accept it. We are free to reject it, or lose it through carelessness or laziness. We have to do our part, so that we stay in a right relationship with God, a relationship, as the opening verses of this psalm say, of justice and righteousness, which will lead to prosperity and gladness.

✝ *Lord, you constantly give me glimpses of your glory; help me not to lose sight of it through rejection or carelessness.*

Thursday October 17   Jeremiah 33:1–11

A PRAISE AND A GLORY Today's reading is full of wonderful words: mirth, gladness, sing, thank offerings, restoration, rebuilding, cleanse, forgive, recovery, healing, prosperity, security. What a glorious future we have to look forward to! A wedding banquet again, because a bridegroom and bride are mentioned (*verse 11*), a time of happiness and delight, of rejoicing together in the purified Jerusalem of the future:

> And this city shall be to me a name of joy, a praise and a
>   glory before all the nations of the earth.   **(verse 9)**

The writer of Revelation saw the final coming of God as the arrival of a purified and glorified Jerusalem, the city of God becoming God's dwelling-place on earth (*Revelation 21*). We might use a different picture to try and describe what it will be like, but any picture must include the sheer joy described by Jeremiah.

† *Thank you, Lord, for the joy which you have prepared for us in your kingdom.*

Friday October 18   Exodus 32:1–14

DON'T GO TO THE WRONG PARTY   In today's reading Aaron and the Israelites decide to have their own party, complete with a new god, burnt offerings, sacrifices, food and drink. Aaron might say that 'Tomorrow shall be a festival to the LORD' (*verse 5*), but God didn't agree. Aaron's was the wrong party.

'I have seen this people, how stiff-necked they are.'

(verse 9)

God nearly gives up on his people and decides to start again with a nation founded only on Moses. But finally he agrees to give them another chance. To begin with, we may not think much of God's idea of a party; we may want it to include the satisfaction of seeing our enemies defeated and the worst sinners punished; or perhaps a guest list which includes only those people we think are worthy of an invitation. But gradually, as we get to know God better, we will discover that the party he is planning will be perfect and we do not need anything else. If we don't get to know him better, and don't discover how good his party will be, we may end up going to the wrong party – the party that God will not attend.

† *No eye has seen, nor ear heard, nor the human heart conceived, what God has prepared for those who love him (1 Corinthians 2:9).*

Saturday October 19   Psalm 23

GOD'S TABLE   I am rather shy at parties, especially if there are people present that I do not know very well. I usually try to cover up my shyness by making myself useful – helping in the kitchen or handing round the food. I find it quite difficult to think of a party given by God where I would simply be a guest, not one of the servants. Yet that is what God promises us in this psalm. We shall be his guests, honoured, welcomed, cared for. He will get the table ready, look after our needs, make sure we have food and drink – in other words, enfold us in his love. The Bible does not say very much about what heaven will be like (though the writer of the book of Revelation does his best); but the most important point it makes is that heaven is being surrounded by God's love, being welcomed by someone who is already familiar to us (although only seen dimly in a mirror), coming home. Heaven is God standing in a doorway, opening wide his arms and saying, 'Welcome to my party.'

> **You prepare a table before me**
> **in the presence of my enemies;**
> **you anoint my head with oil;**
> **my cup overflows.**
> **Surely goodness and mercy shall follow me**
> **all the days of my life,**
> **and I shall dwell in the house of the LORD**
> **my whole life long.** (verses 5–6)

✝ *O God, help me to long for and live for the welcome you are preparing for me and all your people at your heavenly party.*

For group discussion and personal thought

● The biblical writers used the picture of a renewed and purified Jerusalem to describe their future with God. What picture would you use to try and describe what our future in the Kingdom of God will be like?

AMOS 1
The challenge of justice
(Week of prayer for world peace)

Notes by Piotr Siejkowski

based on the New Revised Standard Version

Piotr Siejkowski was ordained as a Dominican priest in Krakow
in Poland and lectured on ancient Greek philosophy and early
Christian theology in the Dominican House of Studies in
Warsaw. In 1998 he was received into the Church of England
and continues his parish ministry in the Diocese of Coventry; he
also continues his academic research into Alexandrian theology
and Gnosticism in the second and third centuries.

This week's passages recall the names of some of the nations
and tribes almost 3,000 years ago and the political situation of
Israel and Judah, with its internal divisions and external
military danger from Assyria. Today's readers may be
surprised that we still need to remember and respect the
message of an ancient prophet, which comes to us from a totally
different culture and political situation. However, these ancient
events and towns and kings still carry the word of God. They
remind us of the need for justice and respect of God's law in our
world, our country and our hearts.

Text for the week: Amos 5:4

Sunday October 20   Amos 1:2–6, 11–13

THE LORD IS FULL OF WRATH!   The Almighty God, who
cares like a mother for her children, is now a God who is full of
wrath: he 'roars from Zion' (*verse 2*). The prophet points at
Damascus, the capital of Syria, and its kings, describing their
wrongdoings:

> **For three transgressions ...**
> **and for four, I will not revoke the punishment. (verse 3)**

The nations sinned repeatedly and committed 'crime after
crime', injustice after injustice. The faithful prophet echoes the
dramatic voice of God. The army of Damascus persecuted the
people of Gilead with great cruelty, and Hazael and Benhadad

(the kings of Syria) had blood on their hands. But both will be punished (*verse 5*); no one can escape the eye of the Lord:

I will break the gate bars of Damascus. (verse 5)

It is quite easy to be the prophet of a god – or rather an idol – and pay compliments to everyone, particularly to stronger neighbours or a powerful boss in the office. We justify such 'prophecy' by calling it 'wise compromise'. But tomorrow could be the day when we will be called to say publicly: 'Sir, you are oppressing other people!' And that could be the moment when we ourselves become persecuted, because 'Sir' is a very powerful man, my superior or even a whole institution or organisation. But still we are called, like the Lord, to proclaim the message with a roar from Zion (*verse 2*).

† *Lord, give me your strength to be faithful to your word.*

Monday October 21 Amos 2:5–8

DOES EVERYONE HAVE THEIR PRICE? When Amos proclaimed these words condemning slavery, had he watched the news on TV about child slavery, the prostitution of very young girls or the hard work of children in a factory? What a silly question! But how could he describe the modern scandal of using poor, defenceless young people to indulge sick desires or increase industrial profits? The answer is that the world may have changed its ways of sending information, but it is still the same world which has little respect for those who are poor. The sickness of using people as a tool, as an instrument to achieve my ambitious goal, is still the same:

because they sell the righteous for silver,
and the needy for a pair of sandals. (verse 6b)

It really does not matter if I use others for just five minutes or for five years, for noble religious purposes or simply because I have authority over them. Nobody is my possession – not my husband or my daughter, or even the person who works for me. All those people are my sisters and brothers, and I am brother to all of them. An idealistic, romantic view? No, it is Jesus' message – the Good News. Every human being has Jesus' face, but we need to have good eyes to see this miracle.

† *Lord, open my eyes to see my neighbours who need my help, consolation, bread and water.*

Tuesday October 22 Amos 2:10–13

ISRAEL ON TRIAL FOR ITS SHORT MEMORY   The wrath of the Lord now turns against his own beloved nation! Until now, Amos has been accusing other nations of sin against God's law. But now the finger of accusation points at Israel itself. We can imagine Amos surrounded by his fellow-countrymen, looking through a window at the foreign tribes and proclaiming the Lord's condemnation from on high. Suddenly this window, with its nice view on others, becomes a scary mirror that reflects the same kind of sins. We can see our own faces in it. What is worse, the Israelites were well aware of the Lord's commandments and his disapproval of any injustice. Israel had a unique relationship with God and had also received a unique lesson about God's kindness. They were saved by his mercy, but they have completely forgotten it.

> **Also I brought you up out of the land of Egypt,**
> **and led you forty years in the wilderness.**   **(verse 10)**

Amos points this out. It may not be easy to be a prophet to other nations, but how much more difficult it is to be a prophet in your own country! Amos, and in our day Bonhoeffer, Archbishop Romero and many others, show us how to fulfil this vocation to the end, even if this end means – to the end of my life on earth.

✝ *Save me, Lord, from hypocrisy and help me to remember all the miracles you have done in my life.*

Wednesday October 23 Amos 3:1–8

WE ARE BELOVED, SO – WE CAN SIN!   Amos uses a series of brief pictures to express the same basic logic of his and God's message: events are the result of cause and effect. The nation of Israel had been chosen to be a unique messenger of the divine plan of salvation for all people! But their blindness of heart obscured that simple logic and they committed the same sins as the pagans, even while they were proud to be the chosen people.

> **You only have I known**
> **of all the families of the earth;**
> **therefore I will punish you**
> **for all your iniquities.**   **(verse 2)**

'To whom much has been given, much will be required' (*Luke 12:48*). Our dignity as Christians is at the same time the highest challenge to our way of life, because other people are scandalised by our weakness or sin: 'Look at them, they call themselves disciples of Christ and see what they did in Northern Ireland, Bosnia, Kosovo...' The list of our sins as Christians is long. We cannot be proud of our relationship with God and carry on living as if we have never heard his message!

† *Teach me just one thing today, O Lord: how to be responsible in my dignity as your child.*

Thursday October 24 (United Nations Day)   Amos 4:1–5

AMOS, COULD YOU PLEASE BE MORE POLITE? At this point, all translators of the book of Amos struggle with the prophet's language, which is simply rude! Obviously, Amos is furious at some Samaritan women who oppress the poor and needy.

> **Hear this word, you cows of Bashan.**   **(verse 1)**

This language teaches us a very important lesson: where there is human suffering, injustice, pain and oppression, there is no room for a diplomatic, sophisticated, clean theology of justification. Christ's reaction to the Pharisees and other teachers of the Law is much the same. In some circumstances, silence, words of prayer, blessing, pastoral letters, or pious sermons are not enough. God's people are to shout out: 'God's law is broken'. Thanks to God's Providence, in the history of the Church there have been many heralds who defended the gospel with zeal: John the Baptist, St Stephen, Justin Martyr, Martin Luther, Savanarola – the list of those who were foul-mouthed is quite long.

† *Holy Spirit, show us how to use the power of words to bring your kingdom to all our brothers and sisters. Today we especially pray for the UN agencies, that they may help to create better lives for all people.*

Friday October 25   Amos 5:4–8

SEEK ME ... DO NOT SEEK BETHEL! My own private picture of the Lord is rather like the children's game of 'hide and seek'. One of the children closes her eyes and counts up to 100. When she has finished counting she starts looking for the other players, and when she finds them, behind doors or trees, she must touch the hiding place and say the name of the one found. The Lord is sometimes like a little child playing 'hide and seek' with us, but after counting we stop looking for his presence. Instead, we are quite happy to find and play with something else: Bethel, Gilgal or Beersheba (*verses 4–5*) or computers, TV and many other things. And still the Lord is waiting in his hiding place to fling his arms around our neck and show us how much he misses us.

For thus says the LORD to the house of Israel:
Seek me and live. (verse 4)

Did Amos have the same experience of playing with the Almighty who is sometimes a little child?

† *Strengthen us, Lord, to seek you all our life and never stop looking for you, because you love us.*

Saturday October 26 Amos 5:10–15

AT THE CITY GATE The city gate played a very important social and political role in ancient Israel. Every town or even village had its 'meeting place' which was the city gate. There the people of the town came together to discuss important political and social issues. It was the ancient parliament building and law court, the place where disputes were settled and practical decisions were made. Amos calls for fair judgements in this special place, for justice to be proclaimed and respected at the city gate...

For I know how many are your transgressions,
and how great are your sins –
you who afflict the righteous, who take a bribe,
and push aside the needy in the gate. (verse 12)

Somewhere deep in our hearts we discuss, judge and think of many issues and many people. What is important is that we should always invite God to join us in this place. Only with him are we able to show mercy to others; only in the light of his presence can we forgive and practise justice. We desperately need the Lord when we enter into this place in our hearts.

† *Merciful Lord, teach us to be merciful and just, today, tomorrow and any time when we gather at the city gate.*

For group discussion and personal thought

● When have you experienced God's mercy or providence in your life?

- Have you ever experienced being 'a prophet in your own country'? Why is it important to be accepted as a prophet within your own Christian community or church?
- Are you still looking for God in your life? Does baptism guarantee that you have found God or does it mean that God has found you and is now waiting for your mature confirmation of that first step?

AMOS 2
The cost of true discipleship

Notes by Joy Pegg

based on the New International Version

This week we look at some of the hard and challenging words of Amos. There are two parts of our pilgrimage that we constantly need to keep in tension – the unremitting wonder of God's love and grace towards us, and the joyful, yet often costly, response to that love in our daily walk with him. The readings this week concentrate on the latter.

Text for the week: Amos 5:24

Sunday October 27   **Amos 5:18–24**

JUSTICE AND RIGHTEOUSNESS   This is a great theme that runs right through the Old Testament in particular. It is the cry of God's heart, and an expression of it. Our attendance at times of celebration and worship are not enough unless it is undergirded by a life that reflects these values.

> **Away with the noise of your songs!**
>   **I will not listen to the music of your harps.**
> **But let justice roll on like a river,**
>   **righteousness like a never-failing stream.**
>
> **(verses 23–24)**

Righteousness and justice must be part of those 'streams of living water' that Jesus promised would flow from us out to others. As we seek to allow the Holy Spirit to change us and make us more like Jesus, so we will increasingly be able to worship God 'in spirit and in truth' and then our praise will be acceptable. We cannot simply live as we please, sing our worship songs and attach the words 'in the name of Jesus' to all our prayer requests. Instead, our lives have to be a true expression of his and reflect the values of justice and righteousness in our homes, and wherever we are involved in our community. This in turn will affect the way we pray.

✝ *Lord, help me to be brave and creative in finding ways of bringing justice and righteousness to my community and the wider world.*

COMPLACENCY   Amos is here addressing both the northern and southern kingdoms. When we consider the dangers of complacency, we must recognise that they apply to each one of us. Although this passage particularly applies to leaders to whom people come (*verse 1*), all of us are examples to someone else, and as such we must take heed.

> **You put off the evil day ...**
>> **and lounge on your couches ...**
>> **and improvise on musical instruments ...**
> **You drink wine by the bowlful**
>> **and use the finest lotions,**
> **but you do not grieve over the ruin of Joseph.**
>> **(parts of verses 3–5, and verse 6)**

The luxuries enjoyed by these men blinded them to the imminent danger – the state of their kingdoms and the coming day of the Lord (see *5:18*: the day would not at all be what they expected). Does this remind you of the Lord's warning in Matthew 7:21–23 that some would hear the words, 'I never knew you. Away from me, you evildoers!'? Do we care about those around us or is it more comfortable to 'lie on beds inlaid with ivory' (*verse 4a*) and 'strum away on [our] harps' (*verse 5a*) at the expense of those in need?

† *Shake us awake, O Lord, that we may turn to you in repentance, and to our neighbour in love and compassion.*

Tuesday October 29   **Amos 7:8–9**

A PLUMB-LINE

> **This is what he showed me: the Lord was standing by a wall that had been built true to plumb, with a plumb-line in his hand. And the LORD asked me, 'What do you see, Amos?'**
> **'A plumb-line,' I replied.**
> **Then the Lord said, 'Look, I am setting a plumb-line among my people Israel.'**   **(part of verses 7 and 8)**

I was wandering around the Anglican cathedral in Coventry one day when I was stopped in my tracks by a beautiful symbolic sculpture of the city, made in various metals; hanging over it was a large plumb-line. It was one of those special 'God moments' when the Spirit deeply challenges and speaks to you. I have a postcard of this sculpture in my study. But unless I am prepared to look hard at the plumb-line over my own life, the life of my own church and the life of the Church itself, no postcard will be effective. I bought it to remind me to come to the great Architect. He has laid the only foundation, Jesus (see *1 Corinthians 3:11*), but am I building with poor materials, 'wood, hay and straw' (*1 Corinthians 3:12*) or am I building something that is true and straight?

† *Lord, show me those areas where my life is out of true and show me how to correct them.*

Wednesday October 30   Amos 7:14–16

THE UNEXPECTED Amos had a settled and reasonably prosperous life. Various tasks needed his attention throughout the year, as well as the daily work of being a shepherd and caring for a crop. It was not particularly hard work and there was a predictability about it. A good, honest, hard-working life, that did not bother anyone else and gained him a certain amount of respect and standing in his community. But how things can change if we are prepared to be obedient, as Amos was.

> **'I was neither a prophet nor a prophet's son, but I was a shepherd, and I also took care of sycamore-fig trees. But the LORD took me from tending the flock and said to me, "Go, prophesy to my people Israel."'**
>
> **(part of verse 14, and verse 15)**

Now Amos was going to do something that he had not prepared for, and to become very unpopular as well. This was certainly not part of his plan for his life but he was very aware that the Lord had intervened. Only you know for sure what the Lord has called you to do with your life. Do not let any Amaziah (see *verses 12 and 13*) turn you away from following the Lord's directions.

† *Dear Lord, I pray that I may be willing for you to change my plans today, or at any time.*

Thursday October 31   Amos 8:4–7

BEING MISERLY Because we don't 'trample the needy' or 'do away with the poor' (*verse 4*), we may feel that these strong words of Amos do not really apply to us. For instance, you may never have said

'When will the New Moon be over
   that we may sell grain,
and the Sabbath be ended
   that we may market wheat?'   (verse 5a)

Or you may never have been caught

   skimping the measure,
      boosting the price
   and cheating with dishonest scales.   (verse 5b)

Or, even worse,

   buying the poor with silver
   and the needy for a pair of sandals.   (part of verse 6)

But does having time off on Sunday ever seem a nuisance,
when we have so much work still to do? And does the profit
motive ever come before our delight in and worship of God?
Are we scrupulous in our dealings with others or could we be
more generous in our outlook? There are many ways that the
love of money and position can destroy our walk with God. But
the Lord looks on the heart, and sees all that we do (*verse 7*).

† *Abundant God, let me love you and others with a generous heart.*

Friday November 1   **Amos 8:8–12**

FAMINE Although there are many strong warnings in the
Bible concerning judgement, the worst thing that can happen is
that the word of God is not heard and not proclaimed. We may
continue to attend church services, but the continual repetition
of familiar words can blunt their meaning until we hardly
notice what we have heard, for it has gone over our heads and
not touched our hearts. If the leaders have turned from God,
then we may seek everywhere and not find that word which
would encourage, restore and change us.

'The days are coming,' declares the Sovereign LORD,
   'when I will send a famine through the land –
not a famine of food or a thirst for water,
   but a famine of hearing the words of the LORD.'
Men will stagger from sea to sea
   and wander from north to east,
searching for the word of the LORD,
   but they will not find it.'   (verses 11–12)

However, in Amos's day the one place that the people from
northern Israel would not go was south to Jerusalem, where the

word of God was coming from (see, for example, *Amos 1:2*). Consciously or unconsciously, we too can choose to create our own famine by avoiding those places or situations where we might be exposed to the word of God. And just as certainly, we will 'faint because of thirst' (*verse 13*).

† *Lord, hearing your word is not always a comfortable experience; please give me the courage not to starve myself of your word through fear.*

Saturday November 2   Amos 9.13–15

RESTORATION   Just as there is a cost to true discipleship, so there are rewards. Not always immediately, and sometimes after necessary repentance, but always there is restoration after destruction. With justice, there is mercy and grace. I used the word 'rewards', but that is not strictly accurate, because we do not earn these rewards. But this is what redemption is all about: the restoration of all that sin has marred. When God planned the earth and everything in it, it was 'very good', and that is how he intends it should be.

I will bring back my exiled people Israel;
they will rebuild the ruined cities and live in them.
They will plant vineyards and drink their wine;
they will make gardens and eat their fruit.   (verse 14)

This restoration appears to be a two-way thing. The Lord brings us back but we have to do the actual rebuilding. What 'ruin' in your life is the Lord giving you the opportunity to rebuild? Today, what looked like a 'space' in my diary had got filled up again, but the phone has just gone and I have the day off work tomorrow. I have been given back my time, but it will be up to me to use it for restoration and true re-creation – or to fill it up with something else.

† *Thank you, Lord, for times of restoration. May we recognise them and use them wisely.*

For group discussion and personal thought

● What ways can you think of that would express justice and righteousness in your community?
● What unexpected ways has the Lord led you into?

MISSION 1
Gathering in

Notes by Marian Holmes

based on the New International Version

Marian lived in a Christian Community for 13 years, travelling extensively in the USA and England as a worship leader, and teaching at worship conferences. She is a trained musician and is currently Head of Music and Religious Studies at a school in Surrey, England.

When Jesus returned to his Father, he left us with a commission: to make disciples of all nations. We are to be witnesses to his love and his peace. But we can only do this if we experience his love and peace in our lives. This week, we shall be thinking about different aspects of our calling, and how we can prepare ourselves for the task.

Text for the week: Isaiah 49:6

Sunday November 3   **Genesis 28:10–17**

BLESSED BY GOD   Jacob knew God had blessed him, giving him a mission to become a nation revered by others. He would often have heard about God's prophecy given to Rebecca before he was born. Yet it is possible that Jacob had doubts: after all, he had tricked his brother out of both his birthright and the special blessing reserved for the eldest son. Was God *really* pleased with him? Had he gone about it the right way? God confirms his blessing to Jacob in the dream of the ladder from earth to heaven and angels ascending and descending.

> **'I am the LORD ... Your descendants will be like the dust of the earth, and you will spread out to the west and to the east, to the north and to the south. All peoples on earth will be blessed through you.'**   (part of verse 13 and verse 14)

Doubts are a necessary part of faith. How do we handle them? Do we let them freeze us into inactivity, or do we, like Jacob, rest with God and wait? We can be sure that, if God's call is real, he will confirm it. Then, like Jacob, we will bow down and worship as we recognise that the living God has been with us.

† *Lord, help us in the mission that you have given us. Reassure us when we doubt you, and help us to trust that you are with us.*

Monday November 4   Micah 4:1–4

PREPARING FOR PEACE   Micah, like all God's prophets, had a job on his hands. Proclaiming God's judgement to a nation of evildoers was never easy. But in today's reading Micah prepares the people of Judah for peace, when all people will come together to Jerusalem to worship God.

> **Many nations will come and say,**
> **'Come, let us go up to the mountain of the LORD,**
>   **to the house of the God of Jacob.**
> **He will teach us his ways,**
>   **so that we may walk in his paths.'**   **(verse 2)**

How do we prepare for peace? Although most of us want a world without war, peace is not as easy as it seems. Our mission to share God's peace begins at the place within each of us where our emotions and conflicts rage. We cannot be peacemakers in the world until we allow God's peace to grow within us. Like achieving world peace, this will take a lifetime and will often be difficult. But God's love will reveal our resistance to him, our denial of truths about ourselves, where we find it difficult to face him. As we allow his love to penetrate these dark places, he will replace conflict with peace. Then we will really have a message to share with the world!

† *Lord, help me to accept my weakness. Help me when I cannot find peace within me. Fill me with your peace, that I may be able to share it with others.*

Tuesday November 5   Isaiah 49:5–6

PRECIOUS AND HONOURED!   Our mission is a big one! We are to be lights to the world, bringing salvation to all people. I don't know about you, but I'm not sure how to do that. Today's reading helps us a little. God's call to us gives us a sense of our littleness, as well as our greatness in his sight. We often focus on the former but forget the latter: God could achieve his purposes easily without us, but he chooses not to.

> **I am honoured in the eyes of the LORD ...**
> **he says:**

'It is too small a thing for you to be my servant ...
I will also make you a light for the Gentiles,
    that you may bring my salvation to the ends of the
    earth.'   (parts of verses 5 and 6)

How he must trust me, to give to me the most vital part of his work. How he must believe in me: knowing that I will fail him, he still wants to rely on me to be his ambassador on earth. We may feel unworthy sinners, but you and I are also honoured servants of the Most High God. Let us not forget it!

✝ *Lord, help me never to forget that, even though I am a sinner, I am precious in your sight, and that you have chosen me to take your message to the world.*

Wednesday November 6   **Zechariah 8:20–23**

EVANGELISM BY ATTRACTION?   God chose the people of Israel as his own because of the faith of Abraham. Surrounding nations recognised this, and often revered the Lord as they saw what he did for his people. Today's reading is one of many prophecies telling that God's salvation is for all. The coming of the Messiah *is* good news for all, but like the Israelites, we must live in such a way that others can see and believe it.

In those days ten men from all languages and nations will take firm hold of one Jew ... and say, 'Let us go with you, because we have heard that God is with you.'   **(verse 23)**

Statistics say that we remember a much higher percentage of what we see than what we read or hear. How do people see Jesus in the way I live? People will see me fail, but if they also see me forgiven, they will see Jesus. They will see me in conflict, but if they also see reconciliation, they will see Jesus. People are curious to see if Jesus makes a difference to our lives. We know he does. Let's make sure they do too!

✝ *Lord, help me to live my life in a way that honours you, so that people may come to believe your word through me.*

Thursday November 7   **Isaiah 55:1–5**

GOD'S FREE GIFT COSTS EVERYTHING!   The good news we are taking to the world is salvation: sins forgiven, God with us, and eternal life in Christ. Good news indeed, but even better: it's *free*!

'Come, all you who are thirsty,
    come to the waters;
and you who have no money,
    come buy and eat!
Come buy wine and milk
    without money and without cost.' (verse 1)

However, there is irony in this invitation. While we cannot pay money for God's gift, it will nevertheless, cost us everything we have. The life of faith requires commitment to God and the offering of our life to him, just as Jesus gave his life for us. Following Jesus requires us to be changed. This demands a willingness to open to him areas of our life we would rather keep closed: the pain, the sins we are ashamed of. If we are serious about our faith, we must be prepared to give everything. Just as Jesus told of the soldier who sat down and counted the cost before going to war, so we must be sure to warn people who are outside God's salvation that to follow him will cost them everything. The good news is that it's worth every penny!

✝ *Lord, your love cost you everything. Help me to be willing to give all I have to follow you, that others may see you and believe.*

Friday November 8   Jeremiah 3:15 –18

FOLLOWING THE PRINCE OF PEACE   Following the days when there was bitter war between the northern kingdom of Israel and the southern kingdom of Judah, the holy places were desecrated, and the precious Ark of the Covenant was captured, Jeremiah dares to proclaim peace.

'In those days the house of Judah will join the house of Israel, and together they will come ... to the land I gave your forefathers as an inheritance.' (verse 18)

I wonder what the people thought about peace. Did they want it, or did they desire revenge? When we are wronged, our first response is often not a desire for reconciliation and forgiveness, but retaliation, a natural human reaction. And yet, God calls us continually to preach peace to the nations, and therefore peace to ourselves. How easy it is to go our own way and ignore God's call. Yet if we are being true to our mission to make disciples of all nations, God requires obedience, even in the face of our humanity. All around us today we see how difficult it is to transform war into peace. Let us stand out as followers of the Prince of Peace.

† *Lord, forgive me when I want revenge more than reconciliation. You came to me as Prince of Peace: heal me, and help me take your peace to others.*

Saturday November 9　　　　　　　　　　Isaiah 66:18–23

A NEW HEAVEN AND A NEW EARTH!　I cannot imagine what it must be like to live in exile. My home and family are very important to me, and to be deprived of them would be extremely difficult. Yet that is what God's people endured. And they longed to return. So they must have been strengthened by this beautiful message of hope and the promise of God's help in restoring their lives.

> **'They will bring all your brothers, from all the nations, to my holy mountain in Jerusalem as an offering to the LORD ... As the new heavens and the new earth that I make will endure before me,' declares the Lord, 'so will your name and descendants endure.'**　**(part of verse 20 and verse 22)**

Many people live as exiles from the word of God, because they have never heard the good news of God's salvation. As Christians, we have the message of hope and restoration. God has given us the task of bringing people back to him. How will we respond? Let us not forget our mission: to make disciples of all nations. Let us also not forget that we are honoured servants of God. It is up to us to prepare ourselves and then to respond.

† *Lord, you have made me a light in this world. Help me to be faithful to you and to that calling. May your name be blessed through me today.*

For group discussion and personal thought

- Within the larger picture of the Great Commission, what is your particular calling? How has God confirmed it?
- It is easy to believe that we are sinners, but God has said that we are honoured in his eyes *(Isaiah 49:5)*. Do you believe this?
- What aspects of Jesus do people see when they meet you? What would you like them to see?

MISSION 2
Going out

Notes by Iain Roy

based on the Good News Bible

The Church's existence into a third millennium is closely linked to its continuing purpose: to share the good news of God's love with the world in word and in action. It is a task which sets fresh challenges for each succeeding generation of believers. It requires different forms of expression in different cultures.

Text for the week: Luke 10:8–9

Sunday November 10   **Jonah 3:1–10**

THE MESSAGE   Jonah was a reluctant evangelist. When he finally did respond to God's call, the message he proclaimed to the people of Nineveh was doom-laden and uncompromising and apparently offered no hope of salvation.

> [Jonah] proclaimed, 'In forty days Nineveh will be destroyed!' The people of Nineveh believed God's message. So they decided that everyone should fast, and all the people, from the greatest to the least, put on sackcloth to show that they had repented.   (verses 4b – 5)

By contrast the Christian message is a hopeful message, firmly based on God's love and compassion for humanity. But it too looks for repentance, that self-awareness of our faults and sins which allows God to enter our lives and create them afresh. In a world where there is an increasing culture of blaming others for the things which go wrong in our own lives and in the life of the world, this is not the easiest message to proclaim. But the gospel calls each of us to recognise our share in the world's sin as well as our place in God's love and purposes.

† *Lord, help us to confess not only our own sins but our share in the world's sin, and give us the humility to forgive others as we ourselves are forgiven by you.*

Monday November 11   **Luke 10:1–9**

A LARGE TASK   The enormity of the task which faced the first Christian evangelists is captured in this passage.

The Lord chose another seventy-two men and sent them out two by two, to go ahead of him to every town and place where he himself was about to go. He said to them, 'There is a large harvest, but few workers to gather it in.'

(verses 1–2a)

In New Testament times there was a whole world to be won for Christ, a fact which made the task for these men both daunting and exciting. Today the existence of the world-wide Church should in theory make the task easier for us. But equal measures of hostility and indifference greet the Church's message in many parts of the world, and this makes the task equally daunting for us. Like Jonah, we too can so easily become reluctant evangelists. We need the courage of conviction of those first Christians and their awareness that it is Christ himself who calls us to be his witnesses.

† *Lord Jesus, give us the courage to go on witnessing in the world to your love for us and all humanity even when we face open hostility or sheer indifference.*

Tuesday November 12   John 20:19–23

MESSAGE AND MESSENGER In preparing for the task of Christian mission it is crucial to realise not only the importance of the message but also the importance of the messenger. In this resurrection appearance Christ shows both.

Jesus said to them again, 'Peace be with you. As the Father sent me, so I send you.' Then he breathed on them and said, 'Receive the Holy Spirit. If you forgive people's sins, they are forgiven; if you do not forgive them, they are not forgiven.'

(verses 21–23)

Jesus was conscious that, as God's word had become real in his life, so it must also become real in the life of those who followed him. Nothing less could or can make it possible for the world to take in the good news. This is the work of his Spirit – to give reality to God's love in our lives. God's forgiveness can have no meaning for others unless we show in everything we say and do that we ourselves are ready to forgive them for his sake.

† *Lord Jesus, help us not to pay lip service to your truth and love, but to make both of them the ruling influences in our lives.*

Wednesday November 13   Acts 5:12–21

NO EXCUSES   Sometimes, when we read accounts like this in the book of Acts, it is hardly surprising that New Testament times seem so much more exciting than today!

> **More and more people were added to the group ... And crowds of people came in from the towns around Jerusalem, bringing those who were ill or who had evil spirits in them; and they were all healed.**
>
> **(verses 14a and 16)**

This can lead to self-questioning: what do we lack which they had? The answer is: nothing. It is the same Christ who loves us who loved them; the same Christ who calls us to witness who called them; the same Holy Spirit who equips us who equipped them; and the same kind of world of need which calls for our service as it called for theirs. It is still possible for the Church today to do great things for Christ but not if we turn the past into a golden time and doubt whether the same God is with us now.

† *Lord Jesus Christ, the same yesterday, today, and for ever, keep us from making the excuse that the times today are more difficult for us than they were for your servants of old. Help us, like them, to witness, casting ourselves on the limitless resources of your love.*

Thursday November 14   Luke 24:44–53

SLOW WORK   Opening minds to truth is a slow task. Christ spent his whole ministry trying to open the minds of his disciples to the truth of God's love, yet so often they were blind and deaf to it and could not see or hear.

> **Then he opened their minds to understand the Scriptures, and said to them, '... the Messiah must suffer and must rise from death three days later, and in his name the message about repentance and the forgiveness of sins must be preached to all nations, beginning in Jerusalem. You are witnesses of these things.'**   **(verses 45–48)**

Even now, in the last moments of his earthly ministry, Christ was seeking to enlighten them, and he promised that the process of learning would not end there. His Spirit would continue the task even when he was physically no longer with them. This is the work of the Holy Spirit: enlightenment, opening the hearts and minds of both believers and unbelievers again and again to the truth of God's love. As we struggle with our own difficulties and problems, as well as those which beset our world, this must be our hope, that God will give us his insight both to cope and to overcome.

† *Holy Spirit, give us the strength we seek, the courage we need, and the insight we lack so that we may cope with the world we face every day and the problems we need to overcome.*

Friday November 15   **John 1:35–42**

OUR ASPIRATIONS   What are you looking for? It is a searching question, a question which we are asked by life as well as by God, a question that we ask ourselves as well.

> **Jesus turned, saw them following him, and asked, 'What are you looking for?' They answered, 'Where do you live, Rabbi?' ... 'Come and see,' he answered.**
> **(verse 38 and part of verse 39)**

What are we looking for in life? Success in our job? Security and peace? Happy family life, good relationships with others? A life free from worry and pain? Whatever we want, our faith will not guarantee any of these things for us. Faith gives no immunity from the hazards of life and living. What faith does offer through the presence of Christ and his love in our lives is one who will share all things with us, a companion and a friend. What Peter and Andrew found is what we can find too – that the one who asks the question is also the answer, not only to the question but to our deepest needs.

† *Remind us, O Lord, that you are with us in all things, seeking to bring meaning out of meaninglessness, hope out of hopelessness, and love out of all that is unloving.*

Saturday November 16   **Acts 16:1–10**

TURNING POINTS   The book of Acts is a record of mission. In all mission there are turning points. For Timothy it was when Paul asked him to share his work and his travels. For Paul it was when God showed him that the mission was even wider and even more demanding.

> **That night Paul had a vision in which he saw a Macedonian standing and begging him, 'Come over to Macedonia and help us!' As soon as Paul had this vision, we got ready to leave for Macedonia, because we decided**

**that God had called us to preach the Good News to the
people there.** (verses 9–10)

The task was more daunting, but the opportunity was so much
greater. This is often the case in Christian mission – the larger
and more difficult the task, the greater the rewards if we are
successful. What strikes me about this passage is that, although
the vision is Paul's, the task is everyone's. 'We got ready.' 'We
decided.' 'God called us.' The task of mission and evangelism is
not and must not be the task of the few. It is and must be the
task of all who believe. As with so much else in the life of the
Church, this is a joint task. At the heart of mission must be
fellowship.

† *Christ, help us to play our due part in the spreading of the Good
News of your love, and help us never to do alone what we can do so
much better with others.*

For group discussion and personal thought

- Why are we as individuals sometimes reluctant to discuss
  our Christian faith with others?
- Identify some of the needs in your community and discuss
  with others how the Church might try to answer them.
- What do you really want from life and how does Christ's
  teaching help you to set your personal priorities in daily
  living ?

MISSION 3
Proclaiming the Good News

Notes by Anthea Dove

based on the Jerusalem Bible

Anthea Dove is a great-grandmother, a retired teacher, retreat-giver and writer. She is a Roman Catholic with a strong commitment to justice and peace and ecumenism. Anthea has lived in India and France and several parts of England, but has now settled with her husband in a cottage near the sea on the north-east coast of England.

Today our world is badly in need of the Good News. Some of us have become coarsened, blinded and indifferent through our greed and consumerism, our lust for power and wealth; others are crushed and overwhelmed by violence, hunger, sickness or the loss of their homeland. Whatever our condition, we need to hear and believe the Good News, the story of Jesus who is still alive and caring for each one of us.

Text for the week: Luke 7:22

Sunday November 17   Luke 7:18–23

WHAT KIND OF PERSON IS JESUS?   People were puzzled by Jesus. Even John the Baptist does not seem to have been certain that he was the Messiah, the one the Jewish people were expecting to come as their Saviour. So John sent messengers to ask Jesus who he was. He answered:

> 'Go back and tell John what you have seen and heard: the blind see again, the lame walk, lepers are cleansed, and the deaf hear, the dead are raised to life, the Good News is proclaimed to the poor and happy is the man who does not lose faith in me.'   **(verses 22–23)**

Jesus is saying, 'If you want to know me, look at what I do, at how I live.' One way he proclaimed the Good News was to show his love for others by healing, serving and comforting them. We can try to live as he did, showing people what it means to be a Christian by the way we love and serve our neighbour. Missionaries are men and women of great courage who travel the world to spread the Good News of Jesus, and wise teachers and preachers proclaim him with their words. But each of us, even if we feel we are very ordinary, can be a powerful carrier of his message simply by the way we live.

✝ *Lord God, help me to look at the way I live, so that I can understand how I can best proclaim your Good News.*

Monday November 18   Acts 8:4–12

THE TRUE HEALER In Samaria, people thought a man called Simon was great because he was able to work magic. Then Philip, the disciple of Jesus, came along and performed such wonderful miracles of healing that Simon himself was astonished. The difference between the two men was that Philip preached to the people and taught them about the life and message of Jesus.

> **But when they believed Philip's preaching of the Good News about the kingdom of God and the name of Jesus Christ, they were baptised, both men and women, and even Simon himself became a believer.**   **(verses 12–13a)**

Unless we happen to be missionaries or ministers, we are not often called upon to preach. But people may sometimes ask us why we live as we do, holding different values from many of the people around us, and that is an opportunity to tell them about our faith. Sometimes people who are not Christians, perhaps not even religious in any way, lead compassionate and unselfish lives and are an example to everyone. This is often true of aid workers and nurses working with people with AIDS. It happens because God's Spirit is free to work wherever he chooses, and his love sometimes shines from unexpected people.

✝ *Lord Jesus, you excluded no one. Help us to welcome everyone we encounter with the same warmth and respect that we would give to you.*

Tuesday November 19   Acts 13:26–33a

JESUS IS HERE AND NOW The scriptures are a strange mixture of wonderful stories, beautiful poetry and history. The prophets of the Old Testament foretold what would happen and what would be revealed to us in the gospels, which describe the life, death and resurrection of Jesus. Because the gospels tell a story, and because Jesus lived as a human person on earth long ago, we sometimes forget that he is still alive, that he is with us here and now. St Paul, speaking to the people of Antioch, said,

> **'We have come here to tell you the Good News. It was to our ancestors that God made the promise but it is to us, their children, that he has fulfilled it, by raising Jesus from the dead.'** (verses 32–33a)

Paul, too, lived a very long time ago, but his words are as true for us today as they were for his listeners and readers. Jesus is our Saviour, and he has promised to be with us until the end of time.

† *Lord Jesus, I thank you with all my heart for dying on the cross and rising to new life for us. I thank you for your presence with us in all the events of our lives, in the sorrows and the joys and the ordinariness of our days.*

Wednesday November 20 Acts 17:22–34

WE ARE ALL HIS CHILDREN St Paul spoke to the people of Athens, telling them about God and explaining that he is not an idol or anything made by human skill, but the Creator of the whole world and Father of every person. He told them to repent and taught them about the resurrection and the last judgement. Paul said,

> **'In fact he is not far from any of us, since it is in him that we live, and move, and exist, as indeed some of your own writers have said:**
> **"We are all his children".'** (verses 27b – 28)

We sometimes forget this great truth – that we are all God's children – in our attitude to those who are not like us. Often we are prejudiced against people of other races, other faiths, different sexual orientation or social background. We fail to be truly concerned for the fate of the people in faraway lands and we are not always willing to work for justice on behalf of those members of God's family who are the victims of hunger and violence.

† *Father, remove the blinkers from our eyes. Help us to love our sisters and brothers, not in word only, but by action, whoever and wherever they may be.*

Thursday November 21 1 Corinthians 1:18–25

FOOLS FOR CHRIST In this letter to the Corinthians, Paul is writing to give them instruction and encouragement. Like many of us today in our different countries, they live in the midst of people who do not know Jesus. We are mocked and laughed at and called fools because we are Christians. Paul writes:

> **While the Jews demand miracles and the Greeks look for wisdom, here are we preaching a crucified Christ; to the Jews an obstacle that they cannot get over, to the pagans madness, but to those who have been called, whether they are Jews or Greeks, a Christ who is the power and the wisdom of God.** (verses 22–24)

Because the crucifixion and the resurrection brought us salvation, the cross is the holy symbol of every Christian. Sometimes when we wear a cross, people will ask us what it means, giving us an opportunity to tell them about Jesus. The crucified Christ is our Saviour, and because he is the power and wisdom of God, we do not need to be afraid when people call us foolish.

✝ *Dear Lord Jesus, help me not to be discouraged by the scorn and criticism of those who find my belief in you foolish and absurd. Give me the wisdom to accept such taunting with a good heart.*

Friday November 22   Colossians 1:24–29

CHRIST IS FOR EVERYONE Writing to the Colossians, St Paul says, 'It makes me happy to suffer for you' and 'I struggle wearily on'. Few people can have worked so hard and under such difficult and dangerous conditions to proclaim the Good News as Paul. So it is no wonder that he sometimes complains a little! He writes,

> **I became the servant of the Church when God made me responsible for delivering God's message to you, the message which was a mystery hidden for generations and centuries and has now been revealed to his saints. It was God's purpose to reveal it to them and to show all the rich glory of this mystery to pagans.** (verses 25 –27a)

For most of us, life as a Christian today is much easier than it was for Paul, yet we are still called to spread God's message wherever we can. It may be that we can encourage those who doubt, enlighten those who have never even heard of Jesus, or by our way of life convince non-believers of the truth of our faith.

† *Dear Lord, you know that without you we can do nothing. Give us a cheerful trust in your loving power.*

Saturday November 23   1 Thessalonians 2:1–8

ENTRUSTED WITH THE GOOD NEWS Proclaiming the Good News often means simply talking about Jesus to another person, someone who doesn't know him. It might not even involve speaking; it could be that someone is attracted to know Jesus through the behaviour of a believer. But however that may be, what matters most is the *way* we approach someone. We cannot expect to bludgeon anyone into accepting our beliefs. In his first letter to the Thessalonians, Paul describes how he went about converting them:

> **We were unassuming. Like a mother feeding and looking after her own children, we felt so devoted and protective towards you, and had come to love you so much, that we were eager to hand over to you not only the Good News but our whole lives as well.** (verses 7b – 8)

This is a beautiful description of how our relationship with others might be, a relationship of total giving, serving and loving.

† *Lord Jesus, when I approach people to tell them about you, help me to come to them in a spirit of gentleness and sensitivity.*

For group discussion and personal thought

- What, for you, is the most important message of the Good News?
- How do you think you most effectively proclaim the Good News?
- Are you sometimes embarrassed when asked to explain your faith, or are you more likely to push your convictions onto an unwilling hearer?

MISSION 4
Hearing the Good News

Notes by Chris Duffett

based on the New International Version

In his letter to the Romans, Paul presents a very obvious lesson on evangelism: if people have not heard how can they believe? (See *Romans 10:14*.) In other words, for people to respond to the good news they have to hear it in the first place! Therefore, it is our responsibility, as the people of God, to convey the good news for others to hear in a way that they can understand. How we deal with this responsibility will result in the life or death of Christianity. However, this task must be done with great wisdom. In order to be relevant to our hearers, we need to relate to their culture – but if we are absorbed by that culture's values, we shall have nothing worth communicating. This week's readings teach and encourage us to communicate and engage with our communities in such a way that they can understand the good news.

Text for the week: Acts 16:14

Sunday November 24   Mark 2:13–17

GOOD NEWS RECEIVED, GOOD NEWS SHARED
Matthew's response to the call of Jesus underlines my own lack of commitment to the commands of Jesus. For a moment, imagine that you are a tax collector, doing your daily work in the heat of the day by the Sea of Galilee in Capernaum. Then, all of a sudden, breaking the daily routine, a travelling preacher from Nazareth says two words to you: 'Follow me.' What do you do? Would you respond as dramatically as Matthew? Would you be worried about losing your job, or about leaving the money unattended in the street? Today's reading inspires us to be more like Matthew, to get up and do what Jesus commands.

> **As he walked along, he saw Levi son of Alphaeus sitting at the tax collector's booth. 'Follow me,' Jesus told him, and Levi got up and followed him.** (verse 14)

Matthew's immediate reaction to Jesus' call led him to tell others about the Messiah. The evening after his encounter with Jesus, Matthew threw a party for all his friends, with Jesus

258

being the guest of honour. Sinners, tax collectors and the like enjoyed the company of Jesus. Matthew did not selfishly keep the good news to himself; he felt compelled to share it with his community. Today, take time to look at the people around you. Who does Jesus want you to share him with? Who could you invite into your home for a meal?

† *Help me to hear your call, to respond to what you command, to follow you and to share you. Amen*

Monday November 25   Acts 26:12–18

STORY TELLING We all love a good story; in today's reading Paul tells his story to King Agrippa. It is indeed mesmerising; his conversion experience on the road to Damascus is compelling, involving bright lights and the audible voice of Jesus.

> 'About noon, O King, as I was on the road, I saw a light from heaven, brighter than the sun, blazing around me and my companions. We all fell to the ground, and I heard a voice saying to me in Aramaic, "Saul, Saul, why do you persecute me? It is hard for you to kick against the goads."'
> (verse 13)

I have met many Christians who use Paul's story as a standard for what should happen when we become a Christian! Often, however, these Christians don't share their own story with others. If their conversion is not as dramatic as Paul's, they don't feel that they have much of a story to tell. But each Christian's story of coming to faith is powerful. We all have a story to share, one that Jesus wants us to tell. As Christians we are the greatest miracle ever: that a holy and righteous God could love us so much that he gave his only son and that through his son we are saved by grace – what a story we have to tell!

† *Lord Jesus, help me to share my story with others. Thank you so much for all that you have done in my life. Thank you that you have given me a story to tell. Thank you that I am able to share the most powerful news ever heard on this earth – that I, a sinner, am saved by grace!*

Tuesday November 26   Acts 16:11–15

WE DO NOT WALK ALONE At the end of the Gospel of Mark, Jesus commissioned his disciples to go and preach the good news to all creation. After Jesus' ascension, we read that 'the disciples went out and preached everywhere, and the Lord worked with them' (*Mark 16:20a*). In today's story we have a classic example of Jesus working with one of his followers.

> **One of those listening was a woman named Lydia, a dealer in purple cloth from the city of Thyatira, who was a worshipper of God. The Lord opened her heart to respond to Paul's message.** (verse 14)

In many places in Acts we can read the 'sermon outline' of Paul's message (for example, in *Acts 17:16–34*). What Paul said by the river in Philippi is not recorded, perhaps because it was not very different from his usual teaching. Instead, the emphasis is placed on the work of Jesus. Lydia, one of the wealthy businesswomen of Philippi, responded to Paul's message because the Lord opened her heart. So many of the great preachers of the past have only been 'great' because the Lord worked with them. For example, Charles Spurgeon, known as the 'prince of preachers', used the basement below his church as a place where many Christians could pray while he preached – he called it the powerhouse. We don't need powerhouses to persuade Jesus to work with us in our daily lives; if we simply acknowledge that he is with us, he will open people's hearts. Recently, I met a young man sitting on a bench; almost before I began to talk to him about Jesus, he said, 'I'm pleased I've met you as I've been wanting to find out how I can know Jesus!' The Lord had opened his heart for me to share the gospel. There are many people like that young man around us and Jesus will work with us to share the good news with them.

✝ *I do not walk alone. I walk with the King of kings. I walk with Emmanuel, God with me.*

Wednesday November 27   Acts 16:25–34

A PERFECT PARTNERSHIP! Today's story teaches us that telling others about the gospel needs a healthy balance of prayer and praise. Paul and Silas saw the power of praising the living God, which resulted in the Church growing dramatically by the addition of a whole household.

> **About midnight Paul and Silas were praying and singing hymns to God, and the other prisoners were listening to them. Suddenly there was such a violent earthquake that**

the foundations of the prison were shaken ... [The jailer] asked, 'Sirs, what must I do to be saved?' They replied, 'Believe in the Lord Jesus, and you will be saved – you and your household.' Then they spoke the word of the Lord to him and to all the others in his house.

(verses 25–26a and 30–32)

Praising God causes the spiritual atmosphere around us to change. There have been times in Chester when an open-air evangelistic event has produced great fruit simply because we spent time publicly praising God. In today's story the prisoners were not the only ones to hear Paul and Silas singing and praising. God also heard their praise and drew near to them – and when God turns up dramatic things happen! As you try to help others to hear the Good News, let them hear you praise God. Psalm 113 tells us that 'the name of the LORD is to be praised' from the rising of the sun to its going down (*verse 3*). This means that wherever we are, at work, at school or at home, we can praise the Lord!

† *Praise the LORD!*
Praise the LORD from the heavens;
Praise Him in the heights!
Praise Him, all His angels;
Praise Him, all His hosts!
Praise Him, sun and moon;
Praise Him, all you stars of light!　　　　*(Psalm 148:1–3, NKJV)*

Thursday November 28　　　　　　　　**Ephesians 1:3–14**

AN OPPORTUNITY TO HEAR AND RESPOND　　In all my different projects in Chester, from running youth clubs to spending time with people on the streets, the underlying goal is to give everyone an opportunity to hear and understand the gospel. It is estimated that in one minute, 90 people throughout the world die without having the opportunity to respond to the good news. What will these people say when they meet God? I imagine many will simply say, 'But I didn't know, no one told me about Jesus.' At the beginning of his letter to the church at Ephesus, Paul outlines what the title in the NIV calls 'Spiritual Blessings in Christ'. Amongst these blessings Paul includes a vital lesson in mission: people become Christians when they hear the gospel (*verse 13*).

And you also were included in Christ when you heard the word of truth, the gospel of your salvation. Having

believed, you were marked in him with a seal, the promised Holy Spirit, who is a deposit guaranteeing our inheritance until the redemption of those who are God's possession – to the praise of his glory. (verses 13–14)

It is easy for me to say, 'Tell others the gospel'. Sometimes it is hard and there seems to be no opportunity. But I have learnt that simply making ourselves available to God results in meeting people who want to hear. God fixes up divine appointments for us. If you are willing to be used by God to share the gospel today, make this simple prayer with me:

† *Lord Jesus, I want to be used by you. I ask for divine appointments today, that you will bring to me people with whom I can share the gospel. Help me to be available, to be willing to share you. In Jesus' name, Amen*

Friday November 29 1 Peter 2:4–9

WHO ARE YOU? It is vital to remind ourselves who we are in Christ. Why? Because as Christians our very faith is compared to a battle and fight (*1 Timothy 6:12*) and Peter also tells us that the devil prowls around us like a lion looking for someone to kill and eat (*1 Peter 5:8*). Whether we are aware of it or not, this daily battle makes it easy for us to forget the promises we have as Christians, and to feel useless and without purpose. Peter encourages us to look beyond our circumstances and feelings to our true identity:

But you are a chosen people, a royal priesthood, a holy nation, a people belonging to God, that you may declare the praises of him who called you out of darkness into his wonderful light. (verse 9)

Spend a little time meditating on this verse. Do you ever feel distant in your relationship with God? He calls you chosen. Do you ever feel unworthy of knowing the King of kings? He calls you royal. Do you ever feel dirty or unclean? He calls you holy. Do you ever feel that you don't belong? He says that you belong to him. Do you ever feel in the dark? He says that he has called you out of darkness into light. Knowing the riches we have in Jesus, we can 'declare his praises' so that he overflows to others around us.

† *Lord Jesus Christ, thank you that I am clothed in pure white garments instead of filthy rags. You dwell within me and have made me a new creation. Enable me to know more what it means to*

be in Christ. Reveal to me who I am in you, so that I may praise you more and more for the glorious work that you have done in my life. Amen

Saturday November 30   **1 Thessalonians 1:2–10**

WE MAY BE THE ONLY GOSPEL PEOPLE WILL READ

You became a model to all the believers in Macedonia and Achaia. The Lord's message rang out from you not only in Macedonia and Achaia – your faith in God has become known everywhere.   (verses 7–8a)

It has been said that one in a hundred people will read the Bible; the other ninety-nine will read Christians. When I first started working as an evangelist, I spent much of my time giving away piles of literature. I thought that giving away tracts was the only way to share the gospel! I soon learnt that my very life needed to tell others what the gospel was all about. Paul shows us that the chief way in which people will hear the good news is through how we live our lives. If we do not live the gospel we have nothing to tell others. Let us take encouragement from the Thessalonian church whose lifestyle became a model to all the believers in Macedonia and Achaia. I marvel at Paul's description of this church; he simply tells us that 'the Lord's message rang out' from them. May this be true for you too!

† *May my life cause a noise! May people hear the gospel through how I live and not only through what I say. May my life ring out with Jesus. May people see the gospel through what I am, for the praise and glory of my Father.*

For group discussion and personal thought

- Have there been times when you have seen Jesus work in someone's life as Paul saw with Lydia?
- In what ways can people hear the gospel without you using words?

ADVENT: THE COMING KINGDOM: READINGS IN MARK'S GOSPEL 1
Watch and wait

Notes by Helen Van Koevering

based on the New Revised Standard Version

Helen Van Koevering was involved in mission work in rural Zimbabwe and Mozambique for 12 years, and is presently secretary to MANNA, a charity which supports the work of the Anglican churches in Mozambique and Angola. She lives in an Urban Priority Area in South Wales, working with women in a Local Ecumenical Parish. She is married with three children.

Advent is the season when we prepare for the coming of the Messiah in Bethlehem. This week's readings focus on the parables of Jesus which show us the need to watch and wait for the Messiah, and which also point us to the coming kingdom of God which Jesus Christ brought in.

Text for the week: Mark 4:11a

Sunday December 1   Mark 13:32–37

KEEP AWAKE!   Being prepared is a hallmark of a Christian's life. In today's passage we are told of the event for which we are to be prepared: the second coming of Christ. How strange these words must have sounded to the disciples! They had learnt so much from being with and listening to Jesus, they understood him to be the Messiah (*Mark 8:29*), but they had not yet experienced his death, resurrection and ascension. Here Jesus discloses part of the mystery of his humanity and divinity in his one person. Although Jesus prophesies his return, he does not know the time (only the Father knows that) and he speaks, through a parable, as man and not as God. Mystery surrounds our understanding of the life and work of the trinitarian God, and being awake to the revelation of mystery is part of the beauty of the season of Advent.

Beware, keep alert; for you do not know when the time will come ... And what I say to you I say to all: Keep awake.

(verses 33 and 37)

The waiting period is not known, but we are to be wakeful – not leaving our duties of prayer and work, but persevering faithfully in order to be prepared for anything.

✝ *Lord, may this Advent be a time when we prepare our lives and hearts for the mystery of the birth of Jesus. Awaken in me a desire to be prepared for your coming. Amen*

Monday December 2   Mark 4:1–9
LISTEN!

He began to teach them many things in parables, and in his teaching he said to them ... 'Other seed fell into good soil and brought forth grain, growing up and increasing and yielding thirty and sixty and a hundredfold.' And he said, 'Let anyone with ears to hear listen!'   **(verses 2 and 8–9)**

Parables illustrate truth in the spiritual realm by a story in the earthly realm, and are meant to provoke serious thought and application of truth in our lives. The sower and the seeds is one of the best known parables, teaching us that our participation in the kingdom of God begins where we are. To listen and hear the stories of Jesus is to imagine ourselves as part of those stories. To be the good soil for the seed is to desire God so much that who we are and how we live our lives will be transformed by God's presence and life. Spiritual growth comes through God and with God, and listening is vital to our work of preparation for God.

✝ *God, you are all I desire, all I need. I want to be all that you desire of me. Amen*

Tuesday December 3   Mark 4:10–12

SURRENDER!   How can we prepare ourselves to be good soil for God's seed? By surrendering to the secret. Our capacity to receive revelation through listening to God, and to imagine ourselves as part of the stories and parables that Jesus told, depends on the previous surrender and obedience of our wills.

'To you has been given the secret of the kingdom of God, but for those outside, everything comes in parables; in order that

"they may indeed look, but not perceive,
and may indeed listen, but not understand;
so that they may not turn again and be forgiven."'

(verses 11–12)

For those who have begun to follow Jesus, who have understood something of the mystery of God's love towards us, the parables reveal open secrets. On gaining insight into a secret of the meaning of the kingdom of God, we are given space and inner freedom to choose the life offered by Christ. Repentance and reconciliation with God prepare the soil of our lives to receive God's life.

† *Lord Jesus, thank you for including me in your story and in your love. Forgive those times when I have forgotten you and failed you, when I have turned from you and the work of your kingdom. I choose your life today. Amen*

Wednesday December 4 Mark 11:12–14

BE FRUITFUL! Today's reading is a powerful parable of deeds, as full of spiritual meaning as any of Christ's parables of words.

When he came to [the fig tree], he found nothing but leaves, for it was not the season for figs. He said to it, 'May no one ever eat fruit from you again.' And his disciples heard it.

(verses 13b – 14)

At first sight, this perhaps seems an unjust judgement of the fig tree. How can the sweetness of figs be available out of season? Fig trees in this area of the world bear an early crop of green immature fruit before the leaves. Jesus, feeling hungry and seeing the leafy tree, had a right to suppose that there would be fruit. Christ's judgement of the barren tree is a parable for all the branches of his visible Church. Preparation for Christ's kingdom means reflecting on the activity of God in our lives. The visible and communal religious life to which we are drawn and the working of truth, love and holiness in our inner lives are the work of God. Hurtful sin, destructive lies and painful memories are obstacles which prevent God's life and love bearing fruit in our lives.

† *Lord, may my love and trust in you increase during this time of Advent, so that I may become ever more open to the guidance of your Holy Spirit and bear fruit for you when you come. Amen*

Thursday December 5 Mark 14:32–42

SUBMIT! From the raw humanity of Jesus' life, the open secrets of the life of God are revealed to us.

> **'Abba, Father, for you all things are possible; remove this cup from me; yet, not what I want, but what you want.' He came and found them sleeping ... 'Keep awake and pray that you may not come into the time of trial; the spirit indeed is willing, but the flesh is weak.'**
>
> **(verses 36, 37a and 38)**

Submitting to God is not easy or painless. The disciples were asked to stay awake, but their need for sleep got the better of them. Watching and waiting is hard work and against our natural impulses and needs. This passage shows us again that Jesus had a real human will, distinct from God yet submitted to God. And he reveals the secret of submission in a new way of praying. Jesus did not submit to a dominating, tyrannical oppressor, but to Abba. The desire of the Son is to do the will of his loving, trusted and ever-present parent, his Father. The submission of Jesus to God's will is an expression of his love for God the Father and for the world he created. The submission of the Son in Gethsemane won the saving victory of the cross for the world.

† *Father, we praise you for sending your Son to this world, to share our humanity and yet also to show us the way to fullness of life with you. Thank you for revealing these mysteries to us, and help us to be obedient to your will as our loving parent. Amen*

Friday December 6 Mark 8:11–13

SEE!

> **The Pharisees came and began to argue with him, asking him for a sign from heaven, to test him. And he sighed deeply in his spirit and said, 'Why does this generation ask for a sign? Truly I tell you, no sign will be given to this generation.' And he left them.** **(verses 11–13a)**

There are none so blind as those who refuse to see! The Pharisees' arguments caused deep grief to Jesus. Their hardened unbelief was at the root of their confrontations and questions, so that whatever Jesus did, they would never interpret it as a 'sign from heaven'. What they should have seen, and what we see with the eyes of faith, is that the life and person of Jesus Christ, the Messiah, are themselves a sign of heaven – God with us, for us, alongside us in our tears and joys. He is a sign of how we can be with the help of God's Spirit – loving God and letting God love others through us.

† *Thank you, Lord, that you are always with us and that signs of heaven are all around those with the eyes to see. Open our eyes, Lord, to the work of your Spirit, your love and your life. Amen*

Saturday December 7   Mark 4:26–29

BE INVOLVED!   Another parable of growing seeds draws together many of the thoughts we have explored this week.

> **'The kingdom of God is as if someone would scatter seed on the ground, and would sleep and rise night and day, and the seed would sprout and grow, he does not know how.'**   **(verses 26–27)**

The seed planted in well-prepared, good soil will mature until it can be harvested. This is the mysterious and loving work of God's grace in our hearts and lives. Our work is to be faithful, stay awake, and be prepared for the Messiah. By watching and waiting, we will learn to recognise the signs of God's activity and presence, the kingdom of God. By submitting to that presence, we shall become involved in God's embrace of this world, the heart of the mission of God and his Church.

† *Lord, I want to be involved! I want to see the fruit of your activity in the lives around me. Change me, so that I may be part of your mission of love and peace in this world. May your kingdom come and your will be done, for your glory. Amen*

For group discussion and personal thought

● Is there some part of your life that you do not allow God to touch and embrace?
● In what new and specific way can you prepare for the birth of the Messiah this year?

ADVENT: THE COMING KINGDOM: READINGS IN MARK'S GOSPEL 2
The Baptist

Notes by Helen Van Koevering

based on the New Revised Standard Version

The life and ministry of John the Baptist can teach us a great deal about the cups of suffering and the crowns of grace and glory which are part of preparation for the coming Messiah, the coming kingdom.

Text for the week: Mark 1:3b

Sunday December 8   Mark 1:1–8

FORGIVENESS AS PREPARATION

'See, I am sending my messenger ahead of you,
     who will prepare your way;
the voice of one crying out in the wilderness:
     "Prepare the way of the Lord,
     make his paths straight,"'
John the baptiser appeared in the wilderness, proclaiming
a baptism of repentance for the forgiveness of sins.

(verses 2b – 4)

The New Testament regards baptism as a clear preparation for the ongoing life with Christ. John's ministry shows that baptism is a fundamental step of preparation because repentance and forgiveness of sins are at its heart. The Church calls baptism a sacrament, a visible sign of the mystery of God's grace – our humble desire for change and confession brings God's response of forgiveness and new life. A powerful step of preparation during this Advent season would be to remember our baptism – the promises that were made and received, the life that was laid down and taken up, the hopes and the responsibilities begun on that day of preparation.

† *Lord, I thank and praise you for the sacrament of baptism. I remember my own baptism today and those who were involved in bringing me to it, as well as those who have been part of my journey ever since. Amen*

PREPARED BY GOD

> And just as he was coming up out of the water, he saw the heavens torn apart and the Spirit descending like a dove on him. And a voice came from heaven, 'You are my Son, the Beloved; with you I am well pleased.'   **(verses 10–11)**

The awesome work of the Trinity is seen at the baptism of Jesus. Jesus' acceptance of his mission in the world is marked by his baptism with water by John. The presence of the Holy Spirit – the 'Go-Between God' – presents us with a beautiful picture of the love, hope and peace of God empowering the Son for his mission. The wonderful love existing within the Trinity is heard in the words of God the Father, fully approving of Jesus' mission to humanity. Those words of love and the presence of the Spirit encourage us in preparing our lives for mission; they show us that in Christ the kingdom of God has been brought near to us. Yet, more than this, we are accepted with the Beloved. 'He destined us for adoption as his children through Jesus Christ, according to the good pleasure of his will, to the praise of his glorious grace that he freely bestowed on us in the Beloved' (*Ephesians 1:5–6*). The love and full acceptance of the God of heaven and earth is with us, by his Spirit and through his Son – we are God's children.

† *Lord, I thank and praise you for your preparatory work of grace and love in my life. Belief in your Son and obedience to your word bring acceptance by the living God – this is so amazing, so wonderful. Thank you, my Father and my God. Amen*

Tuesday December 10   Mark 10:35–45

PREPARED TO SERVE

> 'Are you able to drink the cup that I drink, or be baptised with the baptism that I am baptised with? ... For the Son of Man came not to be served but to serve, and to give his life a ransom for many.'   **(verses 38b and 45)**

The cup and the baptism of Jesus are for us as well. What does that mean? If the life of Jesus is our example, then our lives must be marked by serving others, not ourselves. God has prepared us for this, so that humility is the only way to serve in his strength, on a path and in a future that are known only to him. We may perhaps think of serving God as leading a prayer group, organising events for the church, increasing our attendance at church, offering ourselves as missionaries overseas, but in these verses Jesus provides us with a model of service which is simply serving others. Imagine a world where everyone's primary motivation was to lessen sorrow and increase the joy of others, rather than to pursue our own self-esteem and reward! Imagine the effect if just the followers of Jesus lived in such a way!

† *God, may your kingdom come and your will be done by my service to you and to others. Amen*

Wednesday December 11   Mark 6:14–29
PREPARED TO SUFFER

[Herodias] requested, 'I want you to give me at once the head of John the Baptist on a platter' ... Immediately the king sent a soldier of the guard with orders to bring John's head.   **(verses 25b and 27a)**

Even though John the Baptist was known to be a righteous and holy man, he suffered a cruel and unjust end. The lives of many saints of God have not been noted for 'earthly' rewards and crowns of acclaim, riches and comfort; in many parts of the world the Church has grown with the blood of martyrs. As we read yesterday, followers of Jesus are called to lives of service, but there is no promise of either any earthly reward or freedom from suffering. The only promise we have is that the God who prepares and enables us for his service is the God who is with us always (*Matthew 28:20b*). Are we prepared for such service?

† *Thank you, Lord, for the promise that you will always be with me, through all the tears and joys of life. You are my shield, my rock and my comfort. Amen*

Thursday December 12   Mark 8:31–33
INWARD PREPARATION

Peter took him aside and began to rebuke him. But turning and looking at his disciples, he rebuked Peter and said, 'Get behind me, Satan! For you are setting your mind not on divine things but on human things.'   **(verses 32 and 33)**

I once heard it said that we can be 'so heavenly minded that we are of no earthly use'. This means that our understanding of God and our Christian faith must be integrated into the realities of our daily lives; it must be contextualised if our lives are to be truly changed by the knowledge and love of God. Jesus' mission was to announce the good news of the Kingdom of God for the lives of the poor, the needy and the oppressed, and not just 'pie in the sky when we die'. But there is a tension in this too. In our passage today, Jesus rebukes Peter for not considering God's perspective of eternity, and for judging a situation entirely from a human perspective. When we set our minds on divine things we inwardly prepare ourselves to hear and obey God's will, to be involved in the service of God and others, and to look for God wherever he may be found.

† *Lord, help me to recognise you in the world and the people around me, in the good and the bad times, and so learn to know and do your will. Amen*

Friday December 13   Mark 15:21–32
PREPARED BY THE CROSS

'Let the Messiah, the King of Israel, come down from the cross now, so that we may see and believe.' (part of verse 32)

Condemned, ridiculed, taunted and tortured, Jesus responded with silence and infinite love to those who had no understanding of his mission. With his mind on the eternal kingdom of God and the love of the Father for the world, Jesus died in such a way as a fulfilment of prophecy and as an atonement for our sins. The people of Israel misunderstood, and wanted a powerful king to lead them in a revolt against their oppressors, but that was not the kingdom of which Jesus spoke. It is right, in this period of Advent, this time of preparation for the Messiah, that we should set aside some time to meditate on the cross of Christ. Christ, through his suffering and death, has prepared us for the new life of the kingdom of God. Our understanding of the work of the cross should make us more prepared to be living sacrifices to him who lived and died for us (*Romans 12:1*).

† *Father God, help me towards a fresh understanding of the cross of Christ today. Amen*

Saturday December 14   Mark 12:38–40
BEWARE

'Beware of the scribes, who like to walk around in long robes, and to be greeted with respect in the marketplaces,

and to have the best seats in the synagogues and places of honour at banquets! ... They will receive the greater condemnation.' (verses 38 and 40b)

The Kingdom of God is not about appearances and status, but about hearts and minds inclined towards God. Lives belonging to Christ will reflect the fruits of the Spirit of God in their daily and religious lives: love, joy, peace, patience, kindness, generosity, faithfulness, gentleness and self-control (*Galatians 5:22–23*). We have been prepared for participation in God's kingdom, bringing glory to him; let us beware of any influences that might draw us away from that.

† *Lord, thank you for the many women and men in your Church who provide such wonderful examples and role models of lives belonging to God. Amen*

For group discussion and personal thought

- If you have children or godchildren that have been baptised, how can you be involved in preparing them for the birth of the Messiah this year?
- What does it mean for you to be an adult child of God?
- Does a desire to serve mark your life as a Christian?

ADVENT: THE COMING KINGDOM: READINGS IN MARK'S GOSPEL 3

The Holy Family

Notes by Helen Van Koevering

based on the New Revised Standard Version

New relationships come into being when we become followers of Jesus. As children of God, we now belong to a family which goes beyond blood kinship, and this week we shall explore some of the implications of membership of this family of God.

Text for the week: Mark 3:35

Sunday December 15   **Mark 3:31–35**

NEW RELATIONSHIPS

> 'Who are my mother and my brothers?' And looking at those who sat around him, he said, 'Here are my mother and my brothers! Whoever does the will of God is my brother and sister and mother.'   **(verses 33–35)**

For the sake of the kingdom, Mary had to let go of her son, just as Jesus had to leave his family. Many converts to Christianity have done the same; so have missionaries and others who have followed God's call. But we cannot let go of or leave the family of God. From today's passage we learn that our family now extends to all those who 'do the will of God'. New relationships and new ways of seeing and treating one another exist in the kingdom of God. Loving God means belonging to his family and allowing his love to expand our hearts to include every member of his family, however small, insignificant and marginalised.

† *Our Father, thank you for sending your Son and for including me in your family. I praise you for that mystery of your grace. Amen*

Monday December 16   **Mark 2:13–17**

CALLED

> As he was walking along, he saw Levi son of Alphaeus sitting at the tax booth, and he said to him, 'Follow me.' And he got up and followed him ... 'Those who are well

have no need of a physician, but those who are sick; I have come to call not the righteous but sinners.'

(verses 14 and 17)

How do we become included in God's family? It is not just by listening to the teaching of Jesus, like the crowd around Jesus in this passage, nor by following a set of rules, like the religious leaders of the day who excluded people like Levi. Inclusion in God's family comes by responding to the call of Jesus to follow him. Jesus called sinners, those who need the new life Jesus made possible. He continues to call, continues to take the first step in our inclusion into God's family. And the response called for is always 'Follow me'.

✝ *I want to follow you, O my God, all the days of my life. Amen*

Tuesday December 17   **Mark 1:16–20**

FOLLOWERS

'Follow me and I will make you fish for people.' (verse 17)

I have known several people who saw their gifts and skills in a new light when they became followers of Christ. Musicians and singers have brought their gifts to lead worship in church; nurses, doctors and teachers have taken their skills to the mission field; secretaries and accountants have helped in the administration of all sorts of Christian organisations; knitters and cake makers have raised funds for missions. Jesus called Simon, Andrew, James and John the fishermen to follow him and to see their lives in a new light – not as fishers of fish, but as fishers of people. Every follower of Jesus has gifts and skills which can be transformed in the service of God's kingdom. It is humbling that Jesus calls people not for who they are, where they come from, what they have or what they can do, but simply for who he is able to make them.

✝ *Lord, we praise you that lives are transformed in your hands, to the glory of your name. Amen*

Wednesday December 18   **Mark 7:24–30**

FAITHFUL

[A woman] begged him to cast the demon out of her daughter. He said to her, 'Let the children be fed first, for it is not fair to take the children's food and throw it to the

dogs.' But she answered him, 'Sir, even the dogs under the table eat the children's crumbs.' Then he said to her, 'For saying that, you may go – the demon has left your daughter.' (verses 26b – 29)

Jesus initiates the relationship with the disciples. Jesus' mission was first to the people of Israel, but his work on the cross was to reconcile the whole world to God. His interaction with this foreign, pagan, unnamed woman foreshadows God's inclusive embrace of all who have faith in the Son. This woman faithfully searched out Jesus and humbly persisted in her plea for mercy and healing for her daughter. Jesus responds to her words of faith. Faith allows us to respond to Jesus, to do the will of God and to be included as a child of God.

† *Lord, we bring before you all those who are crossing cultural boundaries, overseas as well as in their own countries, for the sake of the kingdom of God. Encourage their faith and be with them in their work for your glory. Amen*

Thursday December 19   **Mark 8:34 – 9:1**

SACRIFICE

'If any want to become my followers, let them deny themselves and take up their cross and follow me. For those who want to save their life will lose it, and those who lose their life for my sake, and for the sake of the gospel, will save it.' (verses 34b – 35)

Lives lived sacrificially are at the heart of discipleship. We can see the great value of a life dedicated to God, and the pointlessness of a life that denies the presence and teachings of Christ. Jesus tells us that such a life is regarded as lost. It is clear that faithfulness and obedience have a high rating as characteristics of members of the family of God. To live sacrificially for the sake of Jesus and the gospel is to follow Christ in a more profound way – the way of the cross. Sacrificial living recognises that only God can meet our deepest desires. Denying our own desires and supposed needs may feel painful, but our greatest consolation as followers of Christ will come when we choose what is life-giving – loving the Lord our God and our neighbours as ourselves.

† *Like the branches of a tree, I know that my life depends on your life-giving light. Lord, help me to make decisions today, and each day, in the light of your love, peace and grace. Amen*

Friday December 20   **Mark 6:1–6a**

PERSISTENT

> 'Prophets are not without honour, except in their home-
> town, and among their own kin, and in their own house.'
> And he could do no deed of power there, except that he laid
> his hands on a few sick people and cured them. And he
> was amazed at their unbelief.   **(verses 4–6)**

It is often harder to witness to our faith to those closest to us,
who have seen us grow up and know our failings and true
humanity. It was true for Jesus as well, but let us learn from his
example of persistence and faithfulness to the gospel. Obeying
God's call must take precedence over the expectations and
unbelief of our friends and families, and God's presence and
power are always with us, wherever we are, whoever we are
with. Being a Christian means being true to who we are called
to be and true to who we really are.

✝ *Lord, thank you for the encouragement and comfort of knowing
that you are always with me, always there for me. Amen*

Saturday December 21   **Mark 9:38–41**

TOLERANT

> 'No one who does a deed of power in my name will be able
> soon afterward to speak evil of me. Whoever is not against
> us is for us. For truly I tell you, whoever gives you a cup of
> water to drink because you bear the name of Christ will by
> no means lose the reward.'   **(verses 39b – 41)**

Living as the family of God means having a tolerant spirit. Our
denominational and party allegiances often lead us to judge
and condemn other Christians involved in works of goodness
and usefulness to the kingdom of God. Some of the blackest
times in the history of the Church have arisen from intolerance
and judgement. Jesus calls us to tolerance because he knows
that it is God who performs the good in others, and that God is
the judge of a person's heart. Anyone who recognises Christ,
even in a small way, should be encouraged to move closer to
Christ and to know their inclusion in the family of believers.

✝ *I thank you, Lord, that I am included in your family because of
your great love for me. Help me as I learn what it means to be part
of that family, that I may bring glory to you. Amen*

For group discussion and personal thought

- Do you have a gift or skill which could be used to benefit a mission or a church in some way?
- Expand your participation in God's family to include a Christian who lives far away, by praying for someone serving overseas, or Christians of an overseas church.

ADVENT: THE COMING KINGDOM: READINGS IN MARK'S GOSPEL 4
Christmas feasting

Notes by Helen Van Koevering

based on the New Revised Standard Version

Christmas marks the celebration of the birth of Jesus Christ, the Saviour of the world. Throughout the world, families and friends celebrate by getting together for feasting, as circumstances allow, and such special times are stored away as memories. Good and bad memories of past Christmases influence our preparations for this year's celebrations. Whatever memories we have and whatever our present circumstances, our readings this week will help us to focus on this Christmas as a time to feast our hearts on the story of God with us, and to approach this special time as pilgrims included in the Christmas story.

Text for the week: Mark 10:14–15

Sunday December 22   Mark 8:27–33

WHO AM I?

> 'Who do you say that I am?' Peter answered him, 'You are the Messiah.' ... Then he began to teach them that the Son of Man must undergo great suffering, and be rejected by the elders, the chief priests, and the scribes, and be killed, and after three days rise again.   **(verses 29 and 31)**

Let us remember who Christ is: the Messiah, the Anointed One. Old Testament prophets, priests and kings were set apart for their work by anointing. God's Son, the Anointed One, as Prophet, Priest and King, experienced the suffering of humanity all the way to his death on the cross in order to fulfil what other prophets, priests and kings could never do: bring in the Kingdom of God. Jesus, God's chosen Prophet, Priest and King, was humiliated and made a sacrifice for our sins in fulfilment of the Old Testament prophecies. As we focus on the baby in Bethlehem this week, remember the story of Jesus and the reason for the birth of the Messiah.

✝ *Lord, I am only just beginning to understand the beauty of your story, why you were born to die for us. You are the Messiah, God's Anointed One, and I praise you. Amen*

Monday December 23   Mark 10:13–16

A CHILD'S VIEW OF FEASTING

'Let the little children come to me; do not stop them; for it is to such as these that the kingdom of God belongs. Truly I tell you, whoever does not receive the kingdom of God as a little child will never enter it.' (verses 14b – 15)

Many people have lost a sense of joy and wonder in the celebrations and message of Christmas, because of their memories of past Christmases and the difficulties of their lives. Though the Christmas story may be well-known, we need to learn from children in order to reflect on the wonder and mystery of Emmanuel, God with us, God's gift bringing light and life to the world. When children feel welcomed, their innocence and healthy freshness enable them to respond eagerly to what is lovely, joyful and peaceful – the Kingdom of God. Let us direct our children to the beautiful mystery of Christmas and the Christian faith, and let them teach us how to be adult children, feasting again on the wonder of the story of the baby Jesus.

✝ *Lord, forgive us when we forget your great love for us, the love which sent your Son into the world to live and die so that we might have life, and life in all its fullness. Amen*

Tuesday December 24   Mark 14:12–31

THE FEAST OF REMEMBRANCE

The disciples set out and went to the city, and found everything as he had told them; and they prepared the Passover meal. (verse 16)

Jews have celebrated the Passover meal for centuries in obedience to the Lord's command, re-enacting that historic event of the freeing of the Israelites from slavery in Egypt. That freedom was brought about by the saving power of God, and it made them into a pilgrim people belonging together in a world of exclusion and hostility. Just as the celebration of the Passover brings that distant experience of salvation into the present for Jews, so does the Holy Communion for Christians. At the

Eucharist, our thanksgiving, we remember what Jesus did for us two thousand years ago by bringing in the kingdom of God, and we celebrate the reality of that life for us now. Remember and feast on the whole story of the coming of Christ re-enacted in the Eucharist. Celebrate the Messiah, the salvation and life that he brought with death, and let him be remembered in you today, on the eve of his birth.

✝ *Lord, may our remembrance of your life and death transform our hearts and minds, so that we may know your life-giving power today. Amen*

Wednesday December 25 (Christmas Day)   Mark 16:1–8
THE UNEXPECTED FEAST

'Do not be alarmed; you are looking for Jesus of Nazareth, who was crucified. He has been raised; he is not here. Look, there is the place they laid him. But go, tell his disciples and Peter that he is going ahead of you to Galilee; there you will see him, just as he told you.'   (verses 6–7)

In the midst of celebrating the birth of Christ, today's reading reminds us of that other great Christian feasting time of Easter, when we celebrate the resurrection of our Lord. The two events are connected by the work and purpose of God, and by a pilgrimage of faith. In both events, Jesus was not found where we might expect him to be: the King of kings and Lord of lords was born in a humble stable, and the crucified Son of Man was not in the tomb. Human understanding can misinterpret the biblical prophecy which pointed to these events, and watching and waiting (*Mark 13:37*) make the Advent season a pilgrimage to God. For those who have eyes to see and ears to hear, the life of God is often found in unexpected places, because he is the God of the unexpected. Remember to feast our hearts, minds and spirits on the unexpected gift and presence of Christ as we celebrate today.

✝ *Lord, we delight in your presence with us today and always, because of the great and unexpected gift of your love for us. Amen*

Thursday December 26   Mark 6:30–44
A FEAST OF THANKSGIVING

Taking the five loaves and the two fish, he looked up to heaven, and blessed and broke the loaves, and gave them

to his disciples to set before the people; and he divided the two fish among them all. And all ate and were filled.

(verses 41–42)

The disciples had been called away to a deserted place to rest for a while from their work. Yet people were still drawn to them and the teaching of Jesus. When the time came for the crowd to eat, Jesus turned this need into an opportunity to teach more about the kingdom of God. In his prayer for the five loaves and two fish to feed five thousand people, Jesus shows the power of the prayer of thankfulness. He is teaching a new way of praying to the Father, a way of praying characterised by thanksgiving. The Lamb of God shows us by his prayers that, although sacrifices to God will cease, our sacrifices of praise and thanksgiving will remain for ever. Thanksgiving is making the kingdom of God a reality. Now that the celebrations of the birth of Christ are over, the real work of building the kingdom of God begins, and sharing the feast of Christ with others begins with our thanksgivings.

† *Thank you, Lord, for all your gifts to us. Help us to share them with others with hearts full of thanks and praise to you. Amen*

Friday December 27   Mark 4:30–34

FEASTING AND GOD'S KINGDOM

'[The kingdom of God] is like a mustard seed, which, when sown upon the ground, is the smallest of all the seeds on earth; yet when it is sown it grows up and becomes the greatest of all shrubs, and puts forth large branches, so that the birds of the air can make nests in its shade.'

(verses 31–32)

Once again, Jesus uses a parable of a seed to teach a truth about the kingdom to those who will listen, understand and apply that truth to their life. The Christian Church began with God's gift of a tiny baby born in Bethlehem and the first disciples certainly did not seem a likely group to turn the world upside down. But the story of the Church's growth shows us that, like the tiny mustard seed sown in good soil, Christian pilgrims who feast on God's kingdom of love, peace and joy – the kingdom brought in by that baby's life – can in turn become a strong source of life and draw others to the same feast. In this way, the Church has grown, and continues to grow, spreading its branches throughout the world.

† *Lord, your kingdom is an upside-down kingdom when seen through the eyes of the world. Help me to understand more and more of the values of the kingdom so that I can be involved in the growth of your kingdom and your Church. Amen*

Saturday December 28   **Mark 12:41–44**

FEASTING AND THANKFULNESS

> **'Truly I tell you, this poor widow has put in more than all those who are contributing to the treasury. For all of them have contributed out of their abundance; but she out of her poverty has put in everything she had, all she had to live on.'**   **(verses 43–44)**

As we read yesterday, we belong to an upside-down kingdom. We feast on the values of this kingdom not simply to satisfy ourselves but also to share our abundant feasting with others for the sake of the kingdom. We who have received so much from God now have so much to give. Do we offer our lives to God as a generous dedication and sacrifice, or just as a part of our abundance that costs us nothing? The celebrations and feasting of Christmas have meaning when they reflect our pilgrimage of thankfulness for God's gifts of love, and encourage our participation in the coming of God's kingdom.

† *Lord, it is now, after the feasting and the celebration of Christmas, that the real work of your kingdom begins – bringing the good news of freedom and reconciliation to the poor. All that I am and all that I have, I give to you, for your glory. Amen*

For group discussion and personal thought

- In what concrete ways could you show your gratitude for all that you have received from God?
- A retreat or quiet time, for either several days or a part of a day, is a way of making a pilgrimage towards God. Think about arranging some kind of retreat for yourself as a rededication and refreshment of your Christian life.

ADVENT: THE COMING KINGDOM: READINGS IN MARK'S GOSPEL 5
Kingdom come

Notes by Helen Van Koevering

based on the New Revised Standard Version

During Advent we prepared for the coming of the Messiah; these next few days are a good time to prepare ourselves for the new year. The kingdom has now come near to us through the life of Jesus. It is important to reflect on what that means for us today, because it is now that our work with God for the sake of the kingdom begins.

Text for the week: Mark 13:31

Sunday December 29   Mark 13:28–31

SIGNS OF THE KINGDOM

> **'So also, when you see these things taking place, you know that he is near, at the very gates.'** (verse 29)

We have just celebrated the coming of Christ as the 'man of sorrows'. Mark 13 is full of warnings about the end of time and the second coming of Christ in all his glory and power. Jesus tells us that there will be many signs that this time is coming, and so it is important for Christians to be aware of current world events and to interpret these events with the heart and mind of faith. We are to look for signs of the coming Christ, as well as for signs of his kingdom. He has promised to be with us always, to strengthen and comfort us with the presence of the triune God. God has determined to be God with us. Whatever the signs of the times – the natural disasters, the devastation of humanity, the hopelessness and sadness – the eyes of faith will also recognise signs of the kingdom which will never pass away.

† *Lord, thank you that your hope, love and peace will always remain with those who have the wisdom of faith in Christ. Help us to interpret world events in the light of your life and love. Amen*